The Long, The Short and The Tall

Life with Rescue Dogs

Christine Brooks
Copyright ©2016

Note:

The stories I tell in this book are true and taken from my own experience and memory of events. I have however, changed some place and personal names and characteristics, in the interests of privacy, for the individuals concerned.

DEDICATION

This book is dedicated to the all the dogs of the world.

They give us their unconditional love, undying devotion and unswerving loyalty,

whether we deserve it or not.

Chapters

Homecoming	1
Four Years Previously	9
Fudge	17
Seamus	29
Tissues and Other Curiosities	39
Seamus and Fudge	55
Farewell Old Lady	59
Sophie	61
Shannon	91
Interlude – Paddy and Sadie	99
Shannon and Seamus	107
Minnie	111
Duncan	119
The Gang of Four	131
Bracken and More	163
Dog Days	173
New Times	179
Pendon Edge	181
Apple Tree Farm	201
Wayside Cottage	219
Egg-Citing Times	229
More Guests	263
The Final Journey	269
Friends and Loyalties	273
Era's End	275

Aftermath	283
Oliver	289
Leaving	297
Important Points to Remember	303
A Dog Came Home With Me Today	305
Two Legs, Three Legs, Four Legs	309
Scrumping For Lemons	311
And Finally	313

Homecoming

Driving slowly home, I glance at the dog sat next to me in the passenger seat. He seems quite calm now, but I have to admit that he is a whopper. Filling the passenger seat, he sits with his head bent low from the roof.

He is a Rottweiler crossed with perhaps German shepherd; black and tan with distinguished ginger eyebrows. He is a handsome lad but is also a hot contender for 'Hound of the Baskervilles look-alike of the Year'. He would easily win a part in the cheaper kind of horror movies and could handily be named 'Satan', 'Demon' or similar, but I am calling him 'Blackie'.

Blackie looks to be in good health. He is panting slightly, but I decide that he is a little warm rather than anxious. He is calm and soft eyed and not showing any particular signs of stress. That's not bad progress. Two hours ago, Blackie and I had not met.

I sigh. What am I going to tell the neighbours? I am about to arrive home with another dog. My own four dogs are waiting for me back at home. I returned them there an hour ago when our walk in the woods was cut short by meeting Blackie.

Two hours previously:

I park the car in my usual pull-in for this walk. From behind me there is general chaos and excitement. I feel slobbering and hot breath on the back of my neck, from four dogs of various shapes, sizes and denominations and there are assorted barkings and bayings as my 'Gang of Four' indicate their agreed wishes that the back of the car be opened *now*.

I pause for a few seconds to let traffic pass and then narrowly avoid a sprained wrist as, partially opening the car's rear door, it jerks upwards from my hand under canine pressure.

Four sundry, hairy shapes leap as one from the rear of the car and bounce joyously into the woods.

The Gang of Four are Seamus, Shannon, Minnie and Duncan. Seamus is 'Head Boy', and acknowledged leader of the pack. He is a greyhound/German shepherd cross; a lurcher, and he moves like a trained dancer. Shannon is 'Queen Bee' and is a large collie cross. She is white with black and tan markings and is one of the most beautiful dogs I have ever known. Minnie is a medium sized sheltie cross. She is fluffy, barrel shaped and endowed with legs three inches too short for her frame. Duncan is a three legged terrier. He ranks as the puppy of the pack and subordinate to all the others. He is however a true terrier and utterly indomitable. His three legged status in no way detracts from the fact that he moves like a greased piglet.

These woods are a favourite walk. We can do a simple circular walk around the woods, or from here, we can walk in any number of directions through glorious countryside overlooking the Ribble Valley, out to Whalley in one direction or to Pendle Hill in the other direction. There are sheep, horses and other livestock in the fields and farms in the area, but the Gang of Four are livestock trained. They all know that sheep are forbidden entertainments and that horses and cattle are too big to play with. Rabbits and squirrels are however, fair game, so our walks here are regular and popular.

Today I am doing the plain circular walk around the woods. The weather has been very wet, the fields are thigh deep in mud and so this circuit is a pleasant and relatively speaking, clean and dry option. One circuit of the woods, perhaps half a mile, is not enough to tire out the Gang, so I plan to do two or three circuits. The local squirrels should provide sufficient entertainment to run the Gang tired.

The route takes me through the centreline of the woods and back again around one edge. It is a lovely walk, being mainly beech woodland. After all the rain, it is a bright sunny day, the sunshine filtering down through the leaves and giving that gorgeous dappled light that can only be found in a beech wood, chequered yellow-green on last year's leaves. The air has that clean, just washed scent of Summer rain.

The return leg of the path takes me alongside a dry stone wall that is the boundary to a field of horses. I have a favourite; he spots me and, as always, comes galloping over. Horse and I have discovered together that he has a passion for Polo mints and now, whenever he sees me, he will trot up and down the other side of the wall demanding his mint allowance. Naturally the dogs join in, clamouring for their ration. This is the only time the Gang ever get sweets from me, but four dogs and a horse make a big hole in a packet of mints, so I have taken to buying them in wholesale boxes from the local cash and carry.

Horse, being satisfied that no more mints are forthcoming, accepts an ear scratch and then wanders off to resume his grazing. The Gang are distracted by a passing squirrel and dash off, demanding that the squirrel come down from its tree to play. The squirrel looks disdainfully down on them from on high, chittering insults. It sounds quite personal, but the Gang do not seem much chastised.

As I stroll along, continuing my walk, I become aware that all is not quite normal. I am being shadowed.

This does not concern me. Although a single woman, I have no qualms about walking out wherever I choose. My four dog, personal security option means that I am safer than most people on their own doorstep. I turn to face the shadow and call out. "Yes? can I help you?"

The shadow retreats into the undergrowth, and I realise that it is not tall enough to be human.

I wait a moment or so, noticing that now the Gang of Four, instead of racing round in random circles and hurling abuse at the squirrel, are instead dashing repeatedly up and down the track, gradually zeroing in on my 'shadow'.

And then I see it. In the shade of the bushes, keeping low and trying to hide is a dog. A very big dog. He is watching the Gang and following them. Not interested at all in me, it is my dogs he is following. I continue my walk, hoping to get a better view of him.

Oh-oh. No collar. Dumped?

These woods are a popular place for the kind of unprincipled morons who abandon animals in what they think are 'natural surroundings' ("There's rabbits and stuff there, so it's okay for him innit..."). Set between the villages and with handy parking, many an animal has been set loose here and left to fend for itself. I have two friends who came back from a walk in those woods with more dogs than they had set out with. Also abandoned in the area, just the animals I know of, have been several rabbits, a goat and once, I found a horse on the country lane just off these woods. So another dog dumped here is not news.

The dog finally breaks cover, introducing himself to the Gang. Seamus takes charge. This stranger is entirely too impressive to be allowed near Shannon. Minnie circles and yaps. Duncan three-leggedly, pogos backwards and forwards, a full set of teeth armed and ready for launch.

It is all show. The Gang are not warlike, just cautious. Having established that the stranger does not intend mayhem, they all calm down and exchange bum-sniffs.

The stranger is unsettled, but not by the Gang. He breaks away, dashing back up the track, looking for something. Returning, he dashes off again the other way up the track, still looking. After a couple of minutes of this, he returns to my Gang and stares at the ground, his sides heaving as he pants.

It is classic 'dumped' behaviour. A dog abandoned by its owners does not understand that they have simply left him. He will go over and over the same ground, convinced that 'Mum and Dad' must be there if only he can find them, not understanding the human impulse that leads to desertion. Have you ever heard of a case of a dog deserting its owner?

Why do people do this? I have no problem with someone who simply does not like dogs. It is fair enough; we are not all the same. If you don't like dogs, then don't have one. However, those who, on some whim, take on a dog or other animal, and then mistreat it, or get bored and dump it; with them I have issues. Why do it? At least pass the animal to the rescue societies.

The strange dog is standing at the edge of the clearing now, perhaps twenty feet away. Now that I have a good view of him, he looks scary as hell. He is huge; black and tan. He looks like the original hellhound.

So what next?

"Hello fella." I say. "What a good boy. Shall we be friends?" Just nonsense words, intended to placate. I take a step closer to the dog, but he reacts badly; instantly striking up a maddened bark, snarling manically at me, down on his haunches, ears back and eyes showing whites. This is no terrier yapping or even just a general doggy "Do I know you?" volley across the bows. This is full blown canine panic; fear aggression that makes for a really dangerous dog.

I back off and the barking subsides, but the dog is now staring at me, hard eyed and threatening. I am not invited to be a friend.

I pause for thought. There is no way that I can leave this dog here. Quite apart from my general high regard for dogs and all things canine, people walk in these woods with children. Leaving him here is an invitation for real tragedy. But what to do? This dog is big enough to fillet me if he chooses. I am undecided, hampered by having the Gang with me.

Even if I manage to calm the stranger to the point of co-operation, how do I get him home, when I already have to get my current Four with me?

Meg suddenly appears by my feet, waggy and enthusiastic. We are old friends. She is a small, vaguely spaniel shaped, little girl who also has a fondness for mints, and we meet regularly. Looking up, there is 'Meg's Mum'. I don't know her name. She has always been simply 'Meg's Mum', and like me, knows the names of all four of my dogs, but not mine.

Our words tumble out together. "Have you seen that dog?"

"Do you recognize that dog?"

"Scary isn't he." she says. "He's been in the woods for a least a couple of hours. There's no sign of any owners. I've looked in all the parking laybys and I didn't like to just leave him here."

"I don't have a spare lead, and I can't do anything with all my dogs here." I say. "If I take my lot back home, can you keep an eye on him until I get back?"

Meg's Mum nods. "Don't be longer than you have to."

"No more than fifteen minutes." I promise.

I dash back to the car, pile the Gang in the back and drive them home. They protest at this off-hand treatment but settle down as I toss a couple of handfuls of dried meat over the back lawn. That'll occupy them for a while, finding all the bits in the grass.

I grab a lead, a pair of leather gardening gloves and a dish of cooked sausages from the fridge, drive back to the woods and arrive to find Meg's Mum, Meg and the stranger all just where I left them.

"What are you planning?" she asks.

"Dunno, making it up as I go along really…"

As I step towards the dog, I keep hands in pockets and look slightly away from him. I am not tempted to offer the sausages. On reflection, he looks like the kind of dog that may be trained to refuse food from strangers. He growls, an impressive sound with a deep base rumble, like the threat of oncoming thunder.

There is an old tree stump, handily a step or so closer to him. Still looking away from him, I sit on the stump and start to talk rubbish at him. "Now then Blackie. What's it all about then? He's a handsome lad is Blackie. Shall we be friends? He's a good boy is Blackie, but it's all a bit scary eh?"

As I keep up the stream of nonsense, the dog visibly relaxes. I keep talking. "Now then Blackie. What a good boy Blackie is."

The dog wanders in my direction. He is not coming to me, but to Meg who is close by, but he now seems less concerned by my being there. Fortunately, Meg is only too willing to befriend this gigantic stranger. She wags and yaps welcome at him. As Blackie passes by, I let my hand trail over his back. He does not avoid my touch, instead circling around to make acquaintance with Meg. They exchange sniffs.

Each time he circles, Blackie gets a little closer to me and I let the touch of my hand last a little longer. He seems unconcerned by this and finally starts to pay attention to my continued babbling.

I see him visibly de stressing, his eyes softening and his panting beginning to abate. Dogs need people. Blackie is no exception.

"Blackie's a lovely lad isn't he. He's a good boy really. Blackie's too nice to be nasty. Blackie's just a bit scared isn't he…"

He now seems happy for me to rest my hand on his back, so carefully I reach a little higher over his shoulders and scratch his ear. Blackie's eyes soften completely, and he sits down next to me, allowing a full blown caress and a rub around his face and neck.

Pulling the lead out of my pocket, I show it to him and let him sniff it. Blackie is unconcerned, so I loop it over his neck and slowly stand up, still talking. He follows me like a lamb.

"I think we're okay now." I say to Meg's Mum. "I'll get him into the car and take him home."

"What are you going to do with him?"

I shrug. "God knows. I know the shelter's full. Right now it looks as though I have another dog."

She laughs "You won't be the first around here to come home with more dogs than you set off with. I'll put the word out; see if anyone knows anything about him, but I don't think he's from around here."

Blackie jumps into the car willingly, taking over the passenger seat like royalty, with just an air of "I think I left the crown and ermine robes in the other car."

And so, as I pull up at my tiny, perfect house, Whinshill Cottage, I have five dogs.

Four Years Previously

∽∼

I turn the key in the lock. It clicks open and I step inside. Freedom. I am single. I have come out of a divorce and I now have my very first 'own home', the first place I can really say is mine. I can do what I want, when I want, how I want. I am free.

My little house is 'small but perfectly formed'; a two up, two down stone terrace, Whinshill Cottage, built in 1670, with a tiny front garden and a postage stamp of a back garden, just big enough for my venerable Labrador cross, Fudge, to toddle around and have a bit of space.

For the same money in the area, I could have chosen a modern house with four bedrooms, integral garage and a thumping great garden. I have visited and viewed a number of these houses, asking myself each time, 'Can I see myself living here?', on a modern estate full of identical houses and surrounded by neighbours on all sides? Nope.

I have looked at cottages in the area; there is no shortage of lovely old places, but my extremely limited budget means that I must to choose my house very carefully indeed. I know that I will always have dogs, so some sort of outside space is essential. For the same reason I do not want to front directly onto a road.

I am not particularly materialistic and so do not have a lot of 'stuff', but what I do have is my vast collection of books. These have followed me around, all my adult life, growing and multiplying despite my regular attempts to thin them out, so I need space for some sort of library area.

I need a bedroom for myself, and another for when I have friends or family staying. I would give much to be able to have a house with a third bedroom that I could call my library and use as a study, but to do that, I would have to buy that modern house on an estate.

Three bedroomed cottages sell at a premium. As they say in the North *'You pays your money and you takes your choice.'*

I have viewed scores of cottages, and looked at hundreds in newspapers and on-line, trying to stretch my budget to that magic third bedroom. After a few months, I am reaching the conclusion that the house I want does not exist at a price I can afford; moreover, property prices are just starting to rocket. If I want to buy, I have to do it quickly. Finally, I go to view a little place I have found in an estate agent's window. It lacks that third room, but on the other hand it is close to a lot of lovely countryside; ideal for dogs. The living room looks quite large in the advert. Perhaps it could double as my study.

I am disappointed when I go to view. The property is perfect in every way except that it is just too small. I wish the owner goodbye and he sees me out to my car. Turning to take a last look at the cottage, I notice a blocked up window in the stonework of the roof area. It has not occurred to me to ask about loft space. Most of the cottages in the area have very shallow roofs and so the loft area is only ever suitable as storage space. But this one has a really steep roof pitch. It looks as though there is standing space up there. "Is there a loft access?" I ask the owner.

He looks startled "Er yes. But it's not very nice up there."

"Got a loft ladder? Can I see?"

The loft is huge. Granted it is dirty, the existing boards do not look too safe, and the spiders have nothing to do but eat and grow (memo to self: do UK spiders ever eat mice?), but that can all be dealt with.

Some old roof light windows simply need updating to turn it into a really beautiful room. Oddly, the window I have seen from outside is not visible on the inside. Someone has plastered over it.

I have found my new home, Whinshill Cottage, and I am already in love with it.

Three months later, I arrive with my worldly goods, consisting of my car, my book collection, my clothes, a wardrobe, a thumping great mortgage and my geriatric Labrador, Fudge.

Furniture has been an optional extra when budgeting. My entire aim has been to buy the house and it has taken every penny I have and that the bank would lend me.

I step into my new home. Fudge waddles in after me and wanders around randomly, sniffing at anything less than eighteen inches from the ground. The interior of the cottage gets a minute olfactory scrutiny and she then wanders out to the back garden to pass judgement, then pass water and declare it 'her' garden.

The house is echoingly empty. The only goods left behind by the previous owners are curtains and carpets. Those upstairs are aged but acceptable. However, the lounge carpet is baby pink and the lounge curtains are a series of elaborate flounces, twists and twirls in baby pink and baby blue. I am the owner of Barbie's sitting room. The carpets and curtains have got to go.

A knock at the door: it is my friend Mike, who volunteered to move my one piece of furniture; Wardrobe.

Wardrobe is not happy. A small single piece, originating in one of the cheaper furniture outlets, he did not want to move house and has taken his journey badly. Sulking in the bottom of Mike's van, he has thrown one of his doors off a hinge, a sure sign of bad mood in him. I know that I will have trouble with him when I want to hang up my clothes. He tends to shrug off his rails when he is moping.

"Shall we get it in?" says Mike. "Where do you want it?" Between us we shuffle Wardrobe out of the van and in through the front door. Fudge eyes this process with suspicion.

She knows Wardrobe from previous encounters and she does not like him. Wardrobe senses this and, breaking slightly from our grip, he flaps a door at her. Fudge withdraws to her basket.

Wardrobe is destined to live upstairs in my bedroom. Scraping across to the bottom of the stairs, we discover the flaw in the plan. My micro-cottage, built in the seventeenth century, has stairs never designed for any but the smallest of movables. The door at the bottom of the staircase is too narrow and the steps themselves make two right angles turns in the space of four feet. Wardrobe is not going to live upstairs without being dismantled.

I hear Wardrobe's sharp intake of dust at this suggestion. As Mike leaves, Wardrobe sags against the wall, clearly weak at the dowels. I reassure him that I will not dismantle him for the journey upstairs. Instead, he will live in the lounge. Wardrobe is disappointed. He has looked forward to his new, light and airy accommodation in the bedroom and shows his displeasure by throwing off a door entirely.

I tell him to behave, but make a note to buy a couple of pieces of 'two by one' to add some struts to his back. His strange angle of leaning does not suggest that he is yet willing to give lodging to my clothes.

I move in the remainder of my goods, mainly boxes of books. With no table or chairs, I pile up book boxes to produce a makeshift table while sitting on a box of collected works of 1950's classic science fiction. Wardrobe scowls at me as I do this, faintly pink in reflected carpet.

Fortunately, the kitchen is fully fitted, so there are no difficulties with making a meal. I enjoy cooking and hum to myself while I slice bread, tomatoes and mushrooms.

What with the move out by the previous occupants and my move in with my dusty cardboard boxes of books, the floor is not very clean.

Not worrying about this, in my usual practice, trimming rind off bacon and scraping burnt bits off toast, I simply slide the lot over the edge of the worktop, in the sure knowledge that Fudge is waiting below and the scraps will not actually touch the floor.

I push to the back of my mind the looming thought of my credit card bill. Having resisted buying almost anything at all, the one purchase I could not avoid is a washing machine.

Although now single, and with little washing of my own, having a dog means dog blankets, dog towels and the paraphernalia of outdoor life. I work full time and cannot cope without a washing machine.

A trawl of the local second-hand shops produced an array of dismal appliances, none of which look as though they would survive the month. There are some poor areas around here, and quality second-hand electrical goods get snapped up quickly. So I have bought a brand new washing machine and paid for it with plastic …. hmmm… I'll deal with that problem later….

Over the next few weeks, I address my furniture situation, and it is quite easily dealt with because I am on rather good terms with the supervisor at the local rubbish tip. He knows of my straitened furnitorial position and is keeping aside a few items for me. First there is a big basket chair, the kind where the top part is a complete bowl shape sitting on the base; a separate piece. It is a little worn in places but perfectly acceptable. The single large cushion is clean and fresh smelling. And it is not pink. Its jazzy, blue striped design is very appealing and I admire it as I place it under the window, clashing violently with the horrible pink carpet.

Making myself a cup of tea, I return to find Fudge in the chair, informing me that she likes it very much, thank you. It is warm, comfortable and up out of the drafts. And she can see out of the window too. Perfect! Fudge curls up into the cushion and goes to sleep.

Wardrobe is jealous of the new competition and throws his left hand door onto the carpet in a tantrum. Fudge regards him warily with one eye and then returns to her snooze.

A bedframe is my next acquisition from the tip, no mattress yet, but I am still looking. The bed is a relief. After several weeks of 'camping' in a sleeping bag on the floor, it is losing its novelty. The sleeping bag stands in lieu of a mattress and I buy some sheets and blankets from a charity shop. The bedding does not smell wonderful as I open the bag, so they go through a hot wash before making up the bed.

My friend at the tip next produces a rather elegant sideboard. It needs a little sanding down and re-staining, but it is a handsome and very practical piece. Suddenly I have drawers and cupboards. It amazes me, the perfectly good stuff that people throw away, the sideboard being a case in point. Its owner has gone to the trouble of taking it to the tip. Had he taken it instead to an antiques centre, he would probably have sold it for a couple of hundred quid. In fact, a buyer would probably have saved him the trouble of transporting it. The sideboard is a stylish piece and I love it with some beeswax before settling it into a corner of the lounge, its deep grained shine enhanced into lustre by the sunlight.

This is too much for Wardrobe. The constant assault on his sensibilities produces a panic attack and nervous collapse. He drops the central bar supporting my clothes, throws them out over the floor, then, with a crash, crumples into a heap. Fudge bolts out of the lounge. I find her later, crammed into the farthest corner of the understairs cupboard, a spot she normally only occupies during thunderstorms.

Rescuing my clothes from the corpse of Wardrobe and considering whether it worth giving mouth to mouth resuscitation, I decide against it. His foibles and personality defects are more than I feel prepared to deal with any more.

An autopsy reveals that the struts I screwed into position at his back have been rejected by his fabric and the screws are bent into right angles. Cold bloodedly, I dismember the corpse. There is some good shelving for the understairs cupboard here.

Second-hand shops are a huge resource. For a few pounds I buy a lovely oak drop leaf table, the drop leaf making the most of my limited space. Cleaned up and polished, it sits in my kitchen, warm and golden, smelling of wax and lemon juice. Then I buy a couple of stand-alone clothes rails. These will do me until I can afford a carpenter for built-in wardrobes upstairs.

A friend is helping to clear out a closed down Methodist chapel.

One of the pews comes home with me and finds a place out on my tiny terrace, overlooking the back garden. I sit with a cup of tea considering the possibilities offered by a small garden shed. The back garden is a sun-trap and I lean with my head back, to catch the rays on my face, eyes closed and listening to the sound of bees in the ivy.

It is wonderful. It is perfect. I have my home. *My Home.*

Fudge

～⚜～

I love being outdoors. Whinshill Cottage is in a village only a few miles from Pendle Hill, of Pendle Witches fame, and the walking here is to die for. In addition, there is the Ribble Valley twenty minutes away, the coast an hour to the West and the Yorkshire Dales a similar distance to the East. The Lake District is an hour and a half northwards.

My daily routine is: wake up early to the teas-made, my first extravagance' luxuriating in bed with my tea for half an hour before rising. A cat lick in the bathroom, brush my teeth, get dressed and out with Fudge.

I have only to walk twenty yards up the lane before I am off the road and away from such traffic as there is, and into the nearby fields on the footpaths. The footpaths here, run for miles in all directions. For my morning walk I usually only do perhaps a mile all round, enough to wake me up properly and allow Fudge to 'do the necessaries'.

Then to work. My current job is in a village only a couple of miles away and so I can pop home at lunchtime to let Fudge out, have a sandwich and a cup of coffee in the back garden.

Weather is immaterial. It is nice if it is sunny and warm, but it does not matter. If it is cold, I put on another sweater. If it is rainy I wear a waterproof. Fudge is less keen on the rain; if it is wet outside at lunchtime, she dashes out to the back lawn and then, moments later dashes back in, giving me a look of disgust en-route; a neat trick for someone whose face is entirely covered in fur.

After work I can have a real walk, wandering my way through the country lanes around my village if the weather is bad, but I much prefer to be up in the hills.

Packing Fudge into the car, we set off for Pendle Hill, a ten-minute drive.

Pendle Hill is one of the outstanding landmarks of Lancashire. For all those whose knowledge of Lancashire begins and ends with 'Coronation Street' and the paintings of Lowry, visit Pendle Hill and the Ribble Valley. This is real Lancashire and very few people are aware of these places, except for a few lurid stories of the Pendle Witch Trials of the 17th Century.

The Yorkshire Dales to the East are beautiful and everyone knows about them. The Lake District to the North is stunning and has a million visitors a year. But sandwiched between them is the Ribble Valley, and it is one on England's best kept secrets.

Centred on the River Ribble, the Ribble Valley homes miles of verdant rolling hills, ancient woodlands, beautiful villages and gorgeous inns and pubs. It is a walker's dream.

To the South East is the town of Clitheroe and beyond that, looming over Clitheroe, is Pendle Hill. It has become a regular haunt of mine over the past few years, and I look forward to having it so close. I will visit often.

But right now, I want to explore my immediate area. I have bought a map showing the local footpaths; the area is thick with them. The nearest starts only yards from my front door. I pop a lead on Fudge to get her over the road and then we are free to explore. There is a short track of a couple of hundred yards, uphill and a bit overgrown, going past a large house with a huge garden.

Solidly built gates separate me from the barking, nay, the baying of two or more very large sounding dogs. The owners of this house have no security worries. Judging by the sound, having burglars to this mansion would be just a cheap way of feeding the dogs.

Continuing on, at the top of the track there is a gate of the click-shut kind common in the area, and then the path leads up through pasture and fields into the great wide yonder.

There is a farm at the top of the hill and I wonder about that. Footpaths through farmyards can be problematic, depending on the personality of the farmer and the amount of trouble he may have had from inconsiderate ramblers.

As it turns out, I need not have worried. The farm is buzzing with people and horses. The farmer operates a livery stable and all her clients come with their dogs; spaniels and Labradors mainly but with a good dash of mixed mongrels and crossbreeds. There are dozens of them. Fudge is unimpressed by the canine confusion. She does not care for strange dogs and trundles through the farmyard grumbling and showing her teeth to any that venture too close. I check with one of the riders which way the footpath runs then continue on my way.

I discover that I can either turn off over fields through to a woodland at the top of the hill, or continue on to a narrow lane, only just wider than a car, taking me back on a wide loop to the village. This road, 'Back Lane', I am later told by one of the locals, is the oldest road in England.

I have no idea if this is true, but it could be. The lane runs high above a glaciated valley along the foothills to Pendle, and, if I were an ice age human, is probably just where I would have walked at the time if I wanted to travel directly East-West; not down in the valley where the current A59 runs, that would be full of ice, but here, on or just below the hill crests, following the best route to take me to or from the coast thirty miles away.

If I want to go further afield I can do so, following tracks, trails, paths and quiet lanes through to Sabden, Whalley and beyond. The area is stunning and at least once a day I walk up through these fields with Fudge.

I have lived at Whinshill Cottage for only a few days when, walking past the large house with the baying dogs, a voice "Hallooo..."s me. Looking around, not spotting the source of the voice at first, then I see him. A man is leaning out of an upstairs window of the large house. "Hello." he shouts. "Are you the new neighbour from the cottage?"

"I am that." I shout back. "I'm Chris. Nice to meet you."

"Are you in a hurry? Fancy some breakfast? A couple of boiled eggs and toast?"

It's nice to have friendly neighbours but this seems almost an invite too far. I hear the sound of large paws thumping over gravel, and the snarling and howling I heard before, starts up again. There is a thump, then another thump against the gate, which gives visibly, then rattles on its hinges under the force of considerable weight being hurled at it from the other side.

"Er, sounds lovely." I shout, trying to make myself heard over the racket. "But I do have my dog with me."

"Oh that's no problem. Your dog can make friends with ours. You're not nervous of dogs are you? Just hang on a jiff. I'll be right there."

He disappears from the windows and after a second I hear a female voice on the other side of the gate. "Down Elsa. Punch. Here! Come on you two. In. Now!" I make a mental note that the main 'Elsa' I knew of, was a lion.

The commotion subsides and the gate opens. A young woman is clipping leads onto two enormous dogs, Rhodesian ridgebacks. No wonder they could make so much noise. This is a dog that was bred to hunt lions.

"Hi, I'm Annie." she says, smiling. "I'll take Elsa round the back, she's a bit funny with strangers. You don't need to worry about Punch here though. He's a pussycat."

The man appears at the door, holding out his hand to shake. "Hi, I'm Jim. Come on in. It's nice to have a new neighbour." As I follow Jim into the house, the world's largest 'pussycat' trots in behind.

Fudge, wearing her 'Impress me if you can.' face, pads alongside me into the house, ignoring the dog beside her, at least twice her height at the shoulder, until she spots a huge bowl of food on the floor in the kitchen.

The bowl is bee lined and assaulted. Jim waves off my attempts to stop her. "We're having breakfast." he smiles. "Why shouldn't she?"

Jim has a pleasant, lyrically Scottish, accent. Annie sounds much more local, with an accent similar to my own; some variant on the theme of Northern English. They putter around the kitchen together, assembling breakfast. "Sit down." he says. "Make yourself at home." He waves me to the breakfast table and I take the nearest chair.

"Tea or coffee?" she asks.

"Tea please."

"Sugar?"

"No thanks."

"Milk or lemon?"

"Milk please. Just plain builder's tea is fine". Just gimme a cup of tea. I am a little edgy; conscious of breathing down my neck. Turning, Punch is sat just behind me, his face at eye level with mine. To be fair to Punch, for all his impressive appearance, his expression is amiable. However, I notice that he is watching carefully the food preparations, his eyes following eggs into a pan and bread into the toaster.

"Hmmm, Punch here, has he had his breakfast?"

"He has indeed." says Jim, nodding down at the bowl where Fudge is still gromphing away. "But he does like eggy toast." Now there's a surprise.

I am served two beautifully boiled eggs, perfectly done with set white and nice runny middles, and a rack of toast.

"Don't sit on ceremony." says Jim. "We don't. Dip your soldiers if you want to."

I enjoy a leisurely breakfast with my two new friends, three in fact. It is slightly unnerving sitting next to a dog who is looking down on my eggs, and Punch gets more of my eggy toast than is perhaps his due, but by the end of the meal he has sworn me undying loyalty.

Over the next few years, Punch is a regular visitor to my house. The first time he calls by, I think he has strayed and lost his bearings. Popping him on a lead, I take him back to Jim and Annie. However, he visits me again, a day or so later and I realise that he is just being friendly. I shout over the hedgerow separating us into John and Annie's garden, "Just letting you know. Punch is here."

Another of my canine neighbours calls by. This is Winston, a middle aged Labrador retriever from just over the road. He is on my doorstep, wagging his tail in a slow, regular rhythm and panting up at me with a hopeful expression. A lady I have not met before, comes running over, breathless and flustered. "Oh there he is. I'm so sorry. He jumps the wall. I just can't stop him." She gestures to a low, random stone wall over the road. It edges an exquisitely laid out garden which in its turn, houses an equally exquisite cottage. Unlike my own, no postage stamp cottage this, more post card. It is a substantial house, and is absolutely beautiful.

"No problem at all." I say. "Dogs are never turned away from my door." She relaxes. "It's a nasty corner though, for traffic."

She gulps and nods. "Have you noticed the signs coming up the hill? The first one says 'Thirty Miles an Hour Limit.' The second says 'Slow Down for Village.' and the third, a hundred yards further on, says 'No Speed Limit.' It's right before the corner. I'm Patricia by the way."

Fudge appears and shoves her nose into Patricia's hand with a swish of her coffee table sweeping tail, then turns and shows her teeth to Winston.

"He does like to wander. If he turns up again, just let me know. I'll come and get him."

"No need. I bring him over myself if I need to. It's not as though it's far to walk."

◈

The road is indeed an issue. If there is a downside to Whinshill Cottage, it is that it is built onto a corner, being one of a block of four terraced cottages and is, I learn, the oldest part of the block. My house was the original farmhouse in 1670. Since then, the three other properties have been added on, more or less one per century. I love old buildings like this; they grow like Topsy and the result is an unpredictable and fascinating building.

However, the road runs directly up a hill and takes a sharp right, with the four cottage terrace being built into that corner turn. It was not even actually a road until the 1950's I am told, but only a farm track leading to Willows Lane, which runs a little further up the hill. The road is called 'Straits Lane'.

One should always pay attention to old place names; they can tell you a lot. A couple of years after I first move in to the cottage, there is a winter storm. Rain deluges the area, a solid sheet of water, pelting down for hours.

The dry stone walls uphill from me, holding back the hillside from the road, are quickly overcome by sheer weight of water, collapsing to rubble in places.

As I stand watching the rain from an upper window, trees wash down Straits Lane, as it temporarily becomes a river. Whinshill Cottage itself, is not affected by this and the water washes by, but one unfortunate house, further down the hill, has recently had work done on the drive, with no proper kerb being replaced.

The rush of water diverts neatly off the lane, straight down the drive and into the house. By ill chance, the owners are away on holiday. Poor folks.

Water is not my issue with the road. Traffic is. Although this is a small country lane, there is always some idiot who thinks he is driving on the M6.

Just outside the cottage, across the road is a tiny green. Only perhaps twenty feet across, this micro-village-green has a bench looking right down the road through the village and across the fields of a neighbouring farm. I acquire the habit of sitting out on the bench with a coffee last thing at night with Fudge. One night, sipping my drink, Fudge sitting beside me, we are watching the world go by before we retire. The odd car comes by, driving up the hill, mostly turning off into the main village further down, but some continuing up, slowing down as they approach the right angled bend they must make as they pass us.

One car, its headlights dazzling, zooms up the hill, by-passing the village turn-off, and still speeding as it nears the green. "Slow down." I am thinking. "Too fast. You're going too fast."

The car continues to speed. I become alarmed. The car is moving way too quickly to take the corner. I start to stand, pulling Fudge away. We cannot back off; there is a bench right behind my knees.

At the last moment the driver becomes aware of the corner, braking heavily. He takes the corner but loses the road and the car smashes into the neat dry-stone wall edging the verge only ten feet or so away from me and Fudge. There is a deafening crash and Fudge bolts.

My first thought is of Fudge and I am about to chase after her when I realise that she has, with great common sense, dashed into the house. She is safe.

The car is a different matter. The front end is crushed, and somehow, the windscreen has been thrown clear of the car, lying whole on the road a few feet away. Two people climb out; a girl, late teenage perhaps, and a lad of about the same age. She is crying and he looks stunned.

"Are you hurt?" I ask. They are confused but after a few moments, shake heads and agree that they are not actually hurt. Albert and Edith, my next door neighbours arrive.

Albert looks at me and shakes his head. "Too fast for the corner?" I nod. Words are superfluous.

The boy now seems to come to. "My Dad's gonna kill me." he says.

I am unsympathetic. "You're alive. You're not hurt. Count your blessings." Looking at the girl. "Cup of tea?" She nods miserably and Edith dashes back into their house to put the kettle on. I leave Albert talking to the boy and offering the use of a phone. At Patricia's front door I knock loudly and press the bell repeatedly, until I get a response. It is late, and she looks frowsy and grumpy as she answers.

"Oh, hello Chris. What is it?"

"There's a car just smashed into your garden wall. It's done quite a lot of damage. I think you'd better get out here now if you want their insurance to pay for it."

As I return, the girl is sat on the bench cradling a mug, a blanket round her shoulders. The boy and Albert are not there; indoors perhaps making phone calls. I go into my house.

Fudge is nowhere in sight. Kitchen? Lounge? Back garden? I find her in the understairs cupboard, shaking like a leaf. She refuses to come out and so I get in with her, sitting down to hug her between my knees and arms, talking to her gently, until she calms down.

Twenty minutes later, when I go outside again, there is a panda car, flashing blue. Patricia is taking photos of her wall and the boy is stood, head bowed, in front of an older man who, judging by the gesticulations and finger pointing, is threatening him with dire consequences.

Minutes later, the boy and the man, with the girl, get into another car and go, as does the panda car. The following morning, looking out from my bathroom, the crashed car has gone. There is only a little broken glass, a headlamp perhaps, and this, Albert and I sweep up between us.

Fudge, in common with Labradors, has a serious relationship with food. Being elderly and spayed she tends to overweight and I have to keep tight control of her eating. This is not easy and Fudge is disinclined to co-operation. She will eat pretty much anything and everything she can get down her neck. This has consequences.

I am in the pub with my friends Howard and Laura. They ask me why I have arrived later than usual. "I had to take Fudge to the vets." I explain.

Howard and Laura are 'doggy people'. They have four dogs of their own and understand. One of their dogs achieved local fame by eating a two pound bag of sugar. "What's wrong with Fudge?" she asks.

I prevaricate with a lovely phrase I picked up out of one of the James Herriot books. "Oh just the normal consequences of eating every bit of rubbish she finds."

"Ah" says Laura. "You mean that she's got the shits."

I nod and pay close attention to my drink.

My Old Lady Fudge is getting on in years, happy enough, but she is slowing down. Low slung and with legs a little short for her frame, she has never been an athlete. When I adopted her, she was already well past her prime, and in her time with me, she has had two operations for mammary tumours. The tumours are growing again now, not malignant, but always returning, always growing. There are only so many times you can operate on an old dog.

Fudge no longer wants to go for long walks. If I try to take her anywhere too demanding, up Pendle Hill for example, her modus operandi, to bring the walk to an end, is to dash ahead of me, wheezing all the way, and then, place herself square on, in front of my feet and knees.

She may be short, but she is solidly built; there is a lot of Fudge. I can step around or over her once or twice to continue my hike, but it becomes wearing after the tenth or twentieth time.

I know that it is only a matter of time before I lose Fudge, sooner probably, rather than later.

She will live out her retirement with me, enjoying life for as long as she is able, but I want a young dog with fun and energy, zip and zing. I want a dog who will still enjoy walkies with me.

It is time to visit the Rescue Centre.

Seamus

~~~~~

I pull up at the animal shelter and wander into the reception. The girl on duty, I do not recognise, but as I sign myself in, Jean enters and spots me. Jean knows me of old.

"Hi Chris." smiling. "What can we do for you today?"

"I'm looking for another dog. Can I take a look around at who you've got in?"

"Course you can. You know where everything is. Just go in. We'll be around if you want to know anything about any of them."

In the kennels I try to take shallow breaths. The staff do the best they can for the dogs in their care, they really do, but it cannot be avoided that as the dogs arrive, many of them are terrified, a lot of them are dirty or unhealthy and all of them are unsettled by this new and frightening experience. The kennels stink of shit and puke and disinfectant and there is the sour smell of fear in the air.

I pass by the puppy shed. Pups are so cute that they are bound to be rehomed. They don't need someone like me. Neither do I want a pup. I need a dog who can be more or less autonomous from day one.

Entering the main blocks there are the usual suspects. As ever, there are far too many of certain breeds. Staffordshire bull terriers are always over-subscribed in the shelters in that area. 'Staffies' are one of the unfortunate breeds that attract jerks wanting to make an 'I'm a Big Man' statement without having a clue how to look after the dog properly or the inclination to try. Not all of them obviously. I know some exemplary owners of staffies. Nonetheless, my comment stands. Staffies draw a certain class of bad handler.

Result: after two or three or four years, the owner is either disappointed, because they are in fact, quite a sweet breed, or the dog has been made completely unhandleable by some moron who thinks it's clever to train a dog to be aggressive. They think that to be a 'man's dog', the dog should be taught that lunging at strangers is a correct way to behave.

German shepherds and Rottweilers have similar issues. It is not the fault of the dog. From the dog's point of view, he doing exactly what he was trained to, when being told he is a 'Good Boy'. When people are attacked or hurt by such dogs, the dog itself is also a victim.

There are a couple of runs with a label 'Not to be rehomed.', each containing a dog straining and snarling, trying to go for the throat through the bars. These poor creatures have been abused beyond help. Made utterly savage by either bad training or sheer cruelty, their wonderful 'doggy' natures completely erased, no risks can be taken with them. They are simply too dangerous to be adopted, and will probably be destroyed. My heart goes out to them, but I cannot help any of these dogs. I hope their previous owners are proud of what they have done.

I wander up and down the ranks of pens. Some of the occupants come running to the mesh to say 'Hello!', jumping up and begging for my attention, tails wagging and mouths open in doggy smiles. 'Talk to me! Talk to me!' These friendly dogs, cheerful and confident in themselves, should find new homes fairly easily.

Others lay curled up in baskets, miserable, apathetic. Some venture out towards me as I approach. I squat down to let them sniff my hand through the bars, but if I come too close, they back away, tails tucked in, desperate for attention, but too scared to accept it.

These nervous dogs have such a hard time in the rescue centres. The staff try hard to help, but the constant racket of barking, unfamiliar smells, as well as the familiar smells; disinfectant, urine, faeces and dozens of other frightened, apathetic and unknown dogs, makes the whole kennelling experience a tough trial for them.

I arrive at the end pen of the row and consider its solitary inhabitant.

I have a preference for crossbreeds and mongrels. They tend to be healthier than pedigrees, particularly in these days when so many of the breeds have been overbred, carrying genetic illnesses. These defects in the breeding and overbreeding of the pedigrees can produce an animal doomed to a miserable, and often, much shortened life; pugs with the faces so foreshortened that they cannot breathe properly, their nasal passages becoming infected, German shepherds and Labradors with hip dysplasia, their hind legs sagging and unable to support the weight of such hefty animals; syringomyelia in the Cavalier King Charles spaniel breed. Syringomyelia is a disorder of the brain and spinal cord resulting from breeding for a cute face to the point that the skull, quite literally, is too small to house the brain. The result is an agonising condition which results, all too often, in there being no option but to euthanize the dog.

So for health reasons alone, I steer clear of pedigrees. Crossbreeds and mongrels are my dogs of choice. I love that touch of uncertainty that means you never quite know what kind of dog you have. For example, the golden retriever breed, cheerful and glamorous dogs with magnificent personalities and glorious looks, but when I see people out walking four identical blond 'clones', I do wonder if they don't occasionally yen after a little variety in life.

I contemplate the occupant of the pen before me. This chap is my kind of dog. For a start he is 'dog-shaped', a kind of shrunken down wolfy/foxy shape. Sandy coloured and skinny, he is perhaps a German shepherd cross greyhound, or maybe German shepherd cross whippet, rather dingo like in fact. Bright of eye, lean and long legged, he meets me in the eye, looking straight up at me and smiling, laughing in fact. His otherwise upright and pointy, foxy ears, droop appealing.

Don't anyone tell me that dogs can't smile. They do smile and it is almost exactly the same expression that humans use. Dogs just don't have as many facial muscles as we do to pull it off.

The face goes up and back. The mouth also goes up and back and the eyes go with it. I will grant though, that most humans don't smile with a lolling pink tongue.

Going closer, I hold my hand to the bars. No problem. This guy wants to be friends. I like his devil-may-care sparkiness and his lop-sided doggy grin. The tail starts wagging and he yips at me excitedly, ears up, paws up at the mesh to make my acquaintance. Then, down again, he sets off running around his pen. Galloping full tilt around the run, he pelts round and around in circles, stopping occasionally to say 'Hello', but then almost immediately setting off running again. Time and again, he circles his small space, barking delightedly.

I read the information card on the front of the mesh. There is precious little on there.

"Sabre - I would like a good home as I have been in here far too long......."

I check the date. Sabre has been in the shelter for seven months...... As they say, far too long. 'Sabre'!?! Who called this dog Sabre? That's a name for ten stone of hulking Rottweiler, not for this dancing lightweight.

Sabre is still pelting around his run. The 'wall of death' routine continues for five minutes or so before Jean comes by. "What can you tell me about this guy?" I ask.

"Well, you're looking at the problem." she says. "He's a lovely dog, but anytime anyone comes close, or shows the slightest interest, he starts doing this. People take one look, and move on to another dog who's a bit quieter. So we can't rehome him. He's been in here for months."

"Do you know anything about him?"

"No not really. One of the inspectors found him tied to the hedge at the bottom of the lane. The vet thinks he's about two years old. He's on medication for a few things…."

"Medication?"

"He's got conjunctivitis. His stomach's iffy, and his bowels are loose so he's losing weight. Other stuff too."

I inspect the patient. Now I look closer, I can see a touch of matter at the corner of one eye. "Did he have that when he came in? Or is it just that he's been kennelled too long?"

"Mmm... yes, probably. He's a really lovely dog. Ever so friendly..."

"Can I take him for a walk?"

"I'll get a lead for him."

Swapping car keys for dog and lead, Sabre and I set off down the lane. He really is super dog, alert and bright. Everything is interesting. When I speak to him, he acknowledges me with a wag and a lick before returning to the important business of trying to piddle on every tree we pass. He is an absolute charmer. Why would anyone have dumped such a nice dog? Tied to a hedge and left! How can people do these things?

Returning to the centre, I pass the lead back to Jean. "I really like him. Put my name down for him and I'll be back on Thursday to walk him again."

"Oh that's lovely." Jean smiles. "He's such a nice dog. He doesn't deserve to be in here. I'll sort out the paperwork, but he will have to be cleared by the vet before we can release him."

"Okay. But I think the main thing this guy needs, is to get out of the kennels."

"Yes I know, but we have to follow the rules."

Thursday comes. The 'Rules' are that any prospective homer must visit a dog a minimum of two times, before being permitted to collect. There is no problem with a home check because the staff know me from previous occasions. Among others, I adopted Fudge from this shelter.

As I sign in to the register, Jean says "I should warn you that he's a bit different today."

"Oh?"

"Well, because we couldn't rehome him, what with all that running around and excitement, the vet put him on Valium to calm him down a bit. We thought if he was a bit quieter, he would have more of a chance of somebody taking to him. Anyway, when you put your name down for him, we took him off the Valium……"

"So….?"

"He's going through withdrawal, so he's not very happy."

At Sabre's pen, what I find is in complete contrast to my first visit. Instead of a bouncy, excitable, rubber-band of a dog, Sabre is standing in the middle of his pen, face to the ground, and is unmoving except for the shaking. His whole body is trembling as he pants and gasps at the floor. I kneel down and call to him. For a moment he doesn't move, but then he looks up at me with dark liquid eyes, one eye running with green matter. The plea is so easy to read. "Please, get me out of here."

I try to take him for a walk, but he is so apathetic that we just potter around the yard for a minute or so, then sit down together in the sunshine. I stroke and hug him, scratching his ears through smelly, spiky fur.

When we go back in, I make an appointment to collect him. "I'll be back on Saturday. That will give him the weekend to settle in."

"Alright, but he has to be cleared by the vet before we can release him."

I feel eggshells crackling under my feet. "What this dog needs is not more medication. He needs to be out of the kennel. He's been in there far too long and that is almost certainly at the root of his medical problems."

"Yes, I know, but he still has to be released by the vet."

I count to ten. "Fair enough. You don't make the rules. I'll call you on Saturday morning to check that you have the vet's clearance."

Saturday morning comes and I ring the shelter. "Has Sabre had his clearance from the Vet?"

"No not yet. He'll be doing his rounds this afternoon."

"What time will I be able to come over and collect him?"

"Can I ring you back?"

"Yes of course, but I would like to collect him today…"

It is the following Thursday before Sabre is released. I take the day off work, line the car passenger seats with newspapers and an old blanket 'just in case', and set off for the shelter.

As I walk through the door, Jean sees me. "I'll go and get him. Can you sign the paperwork?"

Two minutes later she returns with Sabre. He is obviously recovered from his Valium problem and is bright and bouncy. Jean passes over various bottles and packages. "This is for his conjunctivitis. Rub it in twice a day. These are for his loose bowels. Two, three times a day with his food. This is some of the food he's been eating. You can wean him off it gradually…."

She pauses "I wouldn't worry about what you put him on for feeding. Frankly, anything is going to be better than what he's been getting here. We always have to buy the cheapest. Here is his vaccination certificate. We can make an appointment for you to bring him in to be neutered, or you can use your own vet and we'll pay the bill."

I am surprised. I'd not actually looked that closely. "He's not already been neutered?"

"No, but we will cover the cost for you. It's built into the adoption fee."

i's dotted and t's crossed, Sabre and I walk out of the centre to the car. I have already decided that my new lad is not going to be stuck with 'Sabre' for a name. He deserves something altogether more appropriate.

I have been watching 'The Irish RM' on TV and I like the Irish names

Also, my first dog, the dog I grew up with, was called 'Paddy'. So, my choice of name has been hovering between 'Flurry' and….

"Come on Seamus. You come with me. Let's go home."

Tail waving like a pennant and head held high, Seamus inspects each car as we walk past, picking his way daintily past puddles and mud. Reaching my car, he gives me a 'So this is it eh?' kind of look, walks around the car, trailing me on the end of the lead, piddles on each wheel in turn, and then jumps straight in as I open the passenger door for him.

It is a twenty-minute drive home. All the way, I babble nonsense to him, just talking and making contact.

"What a good boy Seamus is. Seamus likes being in the car doesn't he. Seamus is a good boy…." As I pull onto the drive, he is alert and ready. I open the door for him and call. "Seamus. Come on lad."

He responds to his new name. Seamus steps down in a very gentlemanly fashion, placing each paw delicately on the cobbles. He follows willingly on the leash as I open the kitchen door, lead him in and then close the door behind him.

Now comes the test. Fudge is in the house and I know that Seamus will almost certainly, not be made welcome.

Fudge does not disappoint. I take Seamus into the lounge, still on his lead and let Fudge see him from the other side of the room. She looks grim, growling balefully from her basket, but makes no attempt to get out of her basket or approach Seamus.

I lead the newcomer past her to the back garden, keeping him as far away from Fudge as possible. Seamus wants to say hello and steps towards her, then pauses as the growling gets louder and turns into a snarling bark. He backs away. 'Blow that for a lark.' and follows me into the garden.

Seamus is ecstatic as I take off his lead, racing around my little garden, doing dizzy circuits in the restricted space. We need to do better.

"Here Seamus." I say bending down to his level. He stops and trots over to me, waggy and panting. In the sunshine I can see his infected eye and the coarseness of his blond fur. Snapping on the lead again, we walk up the road for five minutes to a nearby field. I have chosen this particular field beforehand, because I know it is properly gated and fenced and there are no sheep within. At about four or five acres, it is a good size for a dog to run freely, without being unreachable if there is a problem.

Clicking the gate closed behind me, I double check that there are no sheep and unclip Seamus' lead. For a moment he freezes, looking around the field, then he looks up at me. "Is this okay? I can do this?"

"Go on Little Boy. It's alright."

Seamus looks around the field again, then back up at me. "Really? I can really do this?"

"Go on Seamus." I say. "Enjoy yourself." and I wave him off.

Seamus sets off at a sprint. He heads for the nearest fence and then follows the fence all around the field. He does another circuit, and another. Head up, tail up and ears waving in the wind, he runs joyously, full pelt around and around the meadow. He is not running away. He is just running for the sheer joy of running.

Eventually he comes back to me and drops in a heap at my feet, panting and hot, but the tail still at full mast. We sit together on the warm grass for a few minutes, just enjoying the moment.

I know right now that Seamus and I are perfect together. Wrapping an arm round his shoulders, he leans into the hug, giving me a brief licky kiss as he does so. He rests his head against my chest and I hold him, talking quietly.

As we walk back home, for the sake of appearances, I clip the lead back on him. I know now that this is barely necessary.

Fudge has not moved. She growls menacingly at Seamus, but makes no other move.

Over a few days Seamus learns to kowtow to Fudge's moods. She never does learn to like him; quite the opposite, Fudge detests Seamus and always moves to push herself in if she thinks that he is going to get first food, or first hug.

However, dislike him as she might, having Seamus around rejuvenates Fudge. It has seemed to me that that I am going to lose my Old Lady in a matter of weeks. Instead, age falls away from her. She brightens up. There is a spring in her step again. Fudge's fur takes on a gloss that it has not seen for a couple of years. In every way she becomes a younger dog again. For me, this just proves the point that dogs are pack animals. They need to 'belong' and for a dog to be alone is a kind of cruelty. Despite Fudge's dislike and jealousy of Seamus, he is good for her. For a time, they are together, and Fudge, aged as she is, benefits hugely from Seamus' presence.

Seamus is also transformed by his new life. Within a week of arriving, his conjunctivitis clears up, his bowels steady, and the 'iffy' stomach I was warned of, never makes an appearance. So much for having to be released by the vet.

Tissues and Other Curiosities

I arrive home from work. Seamus has lived with me for about a month. It is bright warm sunshine; a lovely day, and I left the back door open to the garden to give the dogs chance to enjoy the fresh air while I was out. Parking up the car, as I walk to the door, Albert pops his head over the wall from next door, grinning broadly. "Someone's been having fun."

I pause. "Sorry? I'm not with you…."

The grin broadens. "You'll see."

Perplexed, I unlock the kitchen door and step in.

My immediate impression is of a snowstorm in my kitchen and I stop in my tracks for a moment, nonplussed, then take a deep breath and walk through to the lounge. The snow theme continues. The carpet, the furniture, every shelf and surface is covered in…. what????

In the centre of the maelstrom Seamus stands, laughing up at me - four legs planted firmly akimbo, tail up and wagging hugely. He barks excitedly, bouncing with enthusiasm and pleasure. "Haven't I done well!"

I finally plug my eyes into Planet Seamus. The 'snow' is hundreds and hundreds of tiny shredded pieces of tissue. A Kleenex box lies upside down on the floor, empty of all contents, cardboard semi chewed.

Continuing through the lounge and out of the back door, the garden is also extensively decorated in the blizzard theme. Albert leans over the back gate. "He's had such fun you know. He kept bringing them out one tissue at a time then throwing them in the air. He caught them as they came down, shredded each one in mid-air and scattered the bits around the garden."

Torn between laughter and annoyance, "I thought we were supposed to be friends Albert. You didn't think to stop him?"

"He was having such a good time. I didn't like to……"

~~~

This is not my only 'Home-Coming' from Seamus. A couple of weeks later my new lounge suite arrives, my first brand-new furniture, actually bought from a shop, not scrounged, begged or borrowed. There is a settee and an armchair, the reclining kind that tips back to lift your feet.

The settee and chair in the lounge, I unwrap the sheeted plastic and the new furniture is immediately declared by Seamus and Ginger the cat to be just what the house needs for optimum comfort. Ginger, in his role as ornamental feline, is clear that he needs an appropriate 'frame' for his beauty and adopts the armchair, with its direct line of sight to the fire.

Seamus stretches out full length on the settee. I take up my normal position on a couple of big floor cushions where I can settle down to read.

Perhaps it seems odd, to buy furniture but use floor cushions. However, I have always preferred sitting on the floor to read. Through most of my life, settees have been for dogs, guests and somewhere to put the magazines and newspapers.

A couple of days later, returning from work, I unlock the kitchen door, walk through the kitchen into the lounge and see…. the cushions from my two-day old settee stripped from the settee, strewn liberally over the floor and the stuffing scattered all over the carpet.

I close my eyes, counting to ten, and then so that I do not 'react' on the spot, call both dogs to the car to take them for a walk around the woods.

Back home again, I sadly conclude that the cushions are beyond saving, not just unstitched, but shredded. After some thought, I tack them back together well enough to hold in the stuffing and put them back on the settee.

Hopefully, by the time I acquire new ones, their novelty value will have diminished and they will have become 'background'.

The following day, I visit the furniture shop to order replacement cushions. Next I call by a pet shop and several second-hand shops, buying a variety of dog toys, squeaky balls, old teddy bears and other bribes for Seamus; things that are his, to give him something 'official' to destroy. This does work, and the disembowelled cushions are Seamus' last act of destruction.

Seamus is a lovely dog. He seems to have almost no hang-ups, so when I do come across evidence of his previous life, it unsettles me.

He is very, very playful and at the slightest encouragement comes bounding up, front legs outstretched in a flying play-bow, inviting me to join in and play 'Catch-Me-Chase-Me' or 'Let's be Silly Together'. He loves tennis balls, repeatedly dropping them at my feet and barking incessantly until my will crumbles and I throw the bloody thing for him one more time. If for some reason I do not launch his ball again, I find him batting the ball around the garden with his paws 'To make it go.'.

So, when we walk in the woods together, it seems the most natural thing in the world to pick up a stick and throw it for him. Nothing doing. Seamus is not interested. Quite the opposite; he actively avoids the sticks I throw for him. Then I realise that as I bend over to pick up another, his eyes roll and he shows the only signs of nervousness I have so far seen from him, tail drooping, body sinking and crouching. So that is the problem. Someone has walloped him, using a stick to do it.

Fair enough. I will not throw sticks if they frighten my Lovely Boy. However, Seamus' fear has other consequences. The floored loft in the cottage, which had sold me on the cottage, has a loft ladder, the kind that goes up through a trapdoor and is pulled down with a hooked rod to turn the latch to the access hatch.

I want something I have stored up there and so I pop upstairs to the landing to open up the loft. Seamus, by now my ever faithful shadow, immediately follows me to see what 'Mum' is doing. Picking up my loft opener, as I reach upwards with it to the hatch, Seamus yelps and cries, dropping to the ground cringing, then shoots off down the stairs.

I hare off after him, realising what has happened, to find him in the lounge, whimpering and shaking.

I sit down on the floor with him, hugging him and talking to him until he calms down, trying to explain that Mum would never hit him with a stick. After a few minutes, he relaxes, then cheers up entirely when I open up a special can of tuna as a treat, but I never again do I raise any kind of stick near Seamus.

୨∞෬

Several months on, Seamus is in moult, and he is changed.

I thought that I had a 'dingo'. During my first meeting Seamus in the rescue centre, he was blonde. His fur was short, spiky and really not very pleasant. Almost overnight, he has changed into black and tan, German shepherd costume. Until now, I have not realised that that when I first met him, Seamus was in such rotten physical condition. I assume that, through the trauma of being kennelled too long, and with his catalogue of minor ailments, he did not have a full coat of fur. Most dogs have an undercoat of soft warm fur and an outer, tougher coat of longer harder hairs. I think of it as body armour for dogs. Seamus has had only had the blond undercoat. Now as he moults, his new fur coat is fully developed, glossy and handsome.

I am becoming rather proud of him, my good looking boy. I notice also that he seems, oddly, to have grown in the last few months. At the rescue centre they said Seamus was 'about two years old', so I should have had, I thought, the fully adult sized dog. But I swear he has put on an inch or two at the shoulder since he first came to me.

I conclude that through being kennelled so long at the rescue centre, his physical development has been somehow delayed from when he was a 'teenager', or perhaps more simply, as a now happy and confident dog, he is 'standing tall' in the world. Perhaps both. Certainly when we walk together Seamus steps out beautifully.

I love watching him move. His slightly uncertain background of German shepherd/whippet/greyhound-ish cross has produced a lovely lurcher type dog. The combination of physical power from the German shepherd and the speed and acceleration of the greyhound means that I have a dog who is absolute poetry in motion. He is lanky legged but his shoulder muscles are developing. On those long shanks, Seamus moves like a dancer, or an athlete, or a horse trained in dressage. Accelerating, he moves through different gaits in the same way that a horse does; walk, trot, canter and full gallop. Sometimes he trots with diagonally opposite legs moving in pairs - front left with back right, front right with back left - and sometimes he paces with the two legs on the same side of his body moving together - left front with left back, right front with right back. In whatever way he moves, he is graceful and light on his feet. Dogs are very physical animals. They express themselves through body language, and everything about Seamus says 'Hey! Look at me! Ain't I just cool?'

I sit down in the lounge with my new purchases, nothing exciting, a couple of printer cartridges, some staples, a set of highlighters and a roll of sticky tape, all in a brown paper bag. I start rummaging through. Seamus notices and trots over. He sits squarely in front of me, watching with interest.

"Can I have that?"

I look at the printer cartridge I have just taken out. "Why do you want a printer cartridge Seamus? It's no good as a toy."

"No, not that. That" His nose and slightly droopy ear tips triangulate on the bag of stationary.

"No you can't have staples. They're dangerous."

"No Silly. Not those. That."

The purchases are now in a small heap on the settee and Seamus is pointing at the paper bag in my hand.

Ahh…. Got it.

I crinkle the bag slightly and it makes an intriguing, rustling sound. The triangulated ears twitch and Seamus' rump shifts.

"Would you like this, totally ace and cool, brown paper bag?"

Seamus smiles and wags his tail. "Yes please."

I make another small crunchy sound with the brown paper, then offer it to him. Seamus reaches forward and takes the bag, ever so daintily, from me with his front teeth, and then carries it in triumph, held aloft, out into the back garden. He settles on the lawn with his prize and starts to nibble it into minute pieces.

An hour later the bag has been processed into compost and I sweep it under a shrub where it can rot into the soil.

Out walking, it is a lovely Autumn day and Seamus trots cheerfully, just ahead of me. Leaves like golden flakes lift in brief swirls from the woodland floor and then settle again. The air is fresh and we both have a spring in our step. Seamus drops behind me for a minute. I glance back. He has stopped to 'do his business'. I wait for him.

Seamus takes longer than usual. I look back to see if all is well. Is my boy poorly? An upset stomach? Nope, he's been eating grass and is having trouble at his rear end. Not to put too fine a point on it, he has klingons.

He shuffle-bottoms across the grass, trying to rid himself of this troublesome load, but to no avail. He still has a dangler hanging from his rear end by several threads of grass.

He repeats the process, then he rubs up against a tree. He really is having trouble.

His annoying hang-ons swing to and fro between his back legs, refusing to be removed by shaking, tree trunk or 'flop-botting' across the ground.

Seamus really does trust his Mum to sort everything out for him. Looking over his shoulder, he backs up close, pushing his bum up to me, tail pulled to one side.

Oh no!!!

What do you do?

With a sigh I grab a handful of the largest leaves I can find, some rather tatty looking docks, a bit out of place here in the woods, and using them as a glove, pull the offending items out from beneath Seamus' tail.

He gives me a bright look, wipes himself on the ground again and trots off.

꼭

When he first comes home with me, Seamus is not neutered. Although he was in the shelter for so long, for some reason was decided not to perform the operation until he was rehomed. Part of the deal with the shelter is that, when adopted, the dog, male or female, is to be neutered, so when I collect Seamus, I am provided with a voucher to be given to whichever vet I choose to perform the operation. And I know that by all the rules I should have the operation performed as soon as possible.

Seamus is a lovely lad. I love him from the moment we meet. I adore his blithe love of life, his cheeky smile and the lopsided way he laughs at me when he returns from a run around, ears pricked, tongue lolling.

He has such a magnificent personality. He reminds me so much of my Paddy that I grew up with. I simply do not want to risk any change to his individuality and charisma, so much like Paddy's devil-may-care, sod-you independence, but at the same time loving and loyal, attitude to life.

I read of how neutering will change the personality of a male dog, indeed, that is often the point of the operation. I do not want to change Seamus' personality and so I do nothing.

At first, it does not seem that I have a problem. Seamus, whole and entire, settles in nicely and we develop our routine of work, walks, drives out to Pendle Hill, the coast, the Lake District or the Yorkshire Dales. Fudge cannot walk very far, so often I take a short walk with the pair of them until Fudge is tired. Then I settle her in her basket with a chew or a bone, and Seamus and I go off adventuring.

Seamus is the perfect companion for a walk. We set off together along whatever trail or track I have chosen. Wherever possible I make a point of choosing places where Seamus can be off the lead. I do not enjoy holding a lead and a dog needs to run free to be properly exercised. There is, initially, an issue with sheep. Seamus is far too interested in them.

There is only one 'crime' for which I will physically punish a dog. For the most part, I find that a far more effective punishment is to 'send him to Coventry'. A dog who craves your affection and approval can usually be brought into line by being, temporarily, ejected from the pack. Otherwise, either verbal discipline or a tap on the nose is enough to make the point, but sheep-chasing is an absolute no-no and there is no allowance for error.

I lead Seamus straight through the heart of a flock of ewes. He tries to play with them. He cannot actually chase as I have him on a runner lead, but he pulls, and tries to reach the woolly temptations.

I give him two warnings on-lead when he tries; a light smack on the nose, just to get the message across. After that, I know that he knows he is disobeying me.

The third time he tries to chase, I belt him, and I make sure it hurts. I don't like it, but it is better than his being shot.

Seamus never tries to touch a sheep again. On the contrary, if he notices a flock, even from some distance away, I see him actively divert around the sheep, swinging wide around them in a huge arc.

It is the only occasion I ever hit Seamus, and he gets the message loud and clear. He never again tries to even approach a sheep and our walks become a relaxed delight.

Setting off for our ramble, I choose some path or trail while Seamus wanders about enjoying himself in his own way. He might stay just within view, typically acting as outrider along a field edge, ridge or a wall, or he may vanish into woods or shrubbery, coming back to 'check in' every ten minutes or so. He loves his walks. He is young and fit and full of life. Everything is a joy to him.

At home it is a little more difficult. Seamus loves his freedom. Having been deprived of it for so long, he wants nothing more than to just potter along the lanes, investigating whatever he finds as he ambles along. The problem is that he jumps the front garden wall when my back is turned.

Other doggy walkers come past. "If you're looking for Seamus, he's at the end of the road heading for the woods."

So of course I take the car to collect him. I am not worried about him causing any trouble, but there is always some driver who does not drive with the care due on a narrow country lane. I do not want my lad getting hurt.

Adopting Seamus at 'about two', he is 'teenage', and has not had the opportunity to grow up. As time goes on and his confidence grows, I see him mature and become more adult. Sighting another dog, his responses begin to change. He takes to approaching other dogs in a very upright manner, proud; tail erect and chest pushed out. Males are assessed and informed that the Lord of the Manor has arrived. Bitches are courted and closely inspected. I am just a little bit proud that most of the bitches seem to find Seamus rather appealing.

It is less so with one or two of the dogs; they are no so enamoured of my Lovely Boy. While things seldom come to more than posturing, there is a definite competitive edge to meetings between the Boys.

It makes me laugh: two dogs meeting face to face, off lead, most of the time go through a 'Yah-Boo to You.' performance, more so if the girls are around to impress (Am I talking about dogs or humans here?). There is posturing, strutting and growling. It is essential to stand high, ideally high enough to look down on the opponent. However, importantly, there is a definite limit on how far this goes. Push the competition too much and there might be an actual fight. Very few dogs really enjoy fighting, so face to face encounters tend to stop at posturing.

When separated by a gate or a fence however, the gloves can come off. No one can actually be hurt, so everyone is free to make as much noise as possible. There are loud pronouncements of horrible fates for the other party. "If I can just get my paws and teeth on you...." Outraged abuse is expressed at the competitor's very existence. The situation moves from armed truce to Def Con Five in a moment. Open the gate again, and the Cold War resumes. Actions return to finger jabbing and swagger.

Every Hero of the story must have an Arch-Enemy and Seamus' Nemesis is Scrumpy. Scrumpy's Dad, Brian, lives about half a mile from my house. Most mornings, Seamus and I pass their door as we do our 'round the village' circuit before I go to work.

Scrumpy is a rough haired Jack Russell and resembles the love child of a scrubbing brush and a pineapple. He is a charming little chap but comes with the gritty obstinacy resulting from housing an eight-foot-tall soul in an eight-inch-high body. Seamus, while long legged, is not a particularly tall dog, but nonetheless towers over Scrumpy. Both Scrumpy and Seamus know a worthy foe when they see one and so we have the seeds of a years' long feud.

Brian is rather a nice chap and I always enjoy running into him. Ever ready for a bit of a chat and local news, he is a good laugh.

'Mrs Brian' is also a very nice lady, and once she establishes to her satisfaction that, single woman as I am, I do not have designs on her husband, is also usually around. She offers me tea and freshly made buns.

Scrumpy is never far away. He knows his task is to defend his Dad. Seamus knows that his, is to defend me. Face to face, Scrumpy and Seamus circle around each other, growling and muttering threats that everyone knows will never be fulfilled, but ensuring that Honour is Served with appropriate hostilities.

Scrumpy sleeps in the garage annex of Dad's house. This means that the up-and-over door of the garage, fronting directly onto the lane, provides Scrumpy's perfect listening post. He knows the sound of my and Seamus' footsteps and the barking starts, coming through the garage door, some hundred yards or so before we actually walk past Scrumpy's garage door.

With the gauntlet hurled thusly to the ground, Seamus cannot with honour walk quietly past, and so he responds by hurling himself at the crack at the base of the door, barking maniacally through it. There are no other houses nearby or I would have to start using another route to avoid upsetting neighbours. This canine racket could wake the village. As it is, we pass by in the early morning, and over the ear splitting noise of two dogs hurling venomous invective at each other through a half inch crack, I hear another weary voice from the bedroom above. "Good morning Seamus!"

Fortunately, Brian is a 'doggy man' and he and I both find this hilarious. We swap chitchat and plant cuttings whilst Seamus and Scrumpy conducted their Clash of Armies from three feet below, four feet in Scrumpy's case. Sometimes other dogs and their owners come by. We all know each other and the various canine political lines are being drawn and redrawn as butts are sniffed, wags and/or growls exchanged and every dog does its best to be the last one to pee on the sycamore fronting Brian's cottage.

Seamus becomes good friends with some of the other dogs in the area. One lady walks past every day with her dog, but I have never paid much attention before Seamus' arrival. The day after Seamus first moves into the cottage, she stops as she passes, staring at him.

After a moment, I realise why. Looking at her dog, Seamus and the stranger look enough alike to have come from the same litter.

We exchange notes. 'Maggie' who belongs to Olivia (one of the few 'Mums' whose name I actually learn), has come from a shelter close by the one Seamus had come from, but a couple of years earlier.

When adopted, Maggie had almost no fur and was starving. Now, a couple of years on, she is nicely recovered and she could be Seamus' twin sister.

Clearly she cannot actually be his twin due to their age difference, but the two dogs are sniffing interestedly through the gate at each other and tails are wagging enthusiastically.

Olivia and Maggie are heading up to the fields so Seamus and I tag along. It will do Seamus good to make some new pals.

Maggie and Seamus become best buddies. Maggie comes walking past the gate every morning and evening. If Seamus and I are about, then he wants to go along. If Seamus and I are in the woods at the top of the hill or any of the nearby walks we often run into Olivia and Maggie. Maggie introduces Seamus to the varied group of dogs who come with their owners to 'help' muck out the horses at the livery stables, a motley crew of assorted collies, Labradors, terriers and spaniels, along many of the kind of dog that you can only call mongrel. About two thirds of them have come from the same shelter as Seamus, and some of the others have been acquired by their owners after being found dumped in the woods.

Seamus is having the time of his life. Maggie introduces him to the joys of stable living. She tries to show him how to roll in muck heaps, but Seamus is having none of that.

Other dogs I have known, usually the white ones, come back plastered with pond slime, fox poo and essence of well rotted sheep, but Seamus is the cleanest dog I have ever known and rolls only in fresh clean grass.

His coat is always immaculate. And, if by some horrible mischance, mud splashes him as he goes by, somehow, the dirt simply slides off him as he delicately tiptoes through violets and roses. He refuses to roll in horse dung. However, when he finds it in the fields, like most dogs, he enjoys eating what I choose to think of as 'meadow prunes'. I can live with this, but prefer not to have a licky kiss afterwards.

It is not all trouble free of course. There are occasional run-ins and even fights with acknowledged enemies. When this happens, I choose another walking route for a week or so, to let tempers settle. Fortunately, in this lovely area, there is no shortage of marvellous places to roam. It does however disturb me that these fights happen at all. Along with Seamus' growing wanderlust, I am beginning to worry that he might be hurt or get himself into some other serious trouble.

It comes to a head one day with Rosa. Rosa is a very nice, middle aged lady with a passion for Yorkshire terriers. She has at least five or six of them. I am never sure of the exact number because they seem to change from time to time. I think she is a breeder, one of the better sort. Her dogs always look wonderfully healthy and alert. Her pack of tiny terriers, rather than being toys as many are, are real little dogs, just built on a smaller scale. Rosa comes to my door one evening, minus her collection of terriers, and holding a torn cardigan.

"I haven't come to complain." she starts. "I'm a doggie person too, so I know what the problems are."

My heart sinks. What has happened?

Rose continues. "I was walking with my dogs but Daisy is in season so I was carrying her. We ran into your Seamus. I know he's a nice dog, but he wouldn't stop following us.

He kept trying to jump up to Daisy. He ripped my cardigan trying to get to her. Look..." She holds up the evidence, displaying a large hole in one sleeve

I am mortified. My Perfect Boy has definitely sinned this time. I apologise profusely. I will of course pay for the cardigan. Rosa refuses. She only wants to tell me about it so that I am aware of the problem. She is not falling out with me, and yes, a cup of tea would be very nice, thank you.

I drink a brew with Rosa and then reflect on the situation. Seamus is mature and 'whole' and it is now a problem. He is a healthy, happy and very normal dog. Naturally he is going to follow where nature leads him. I can avoid it no longer. It is time to take Seamus to the vet for his operation, before he gets himself into real trouble with someone who is not as sympathetic as Rosa.

I hate the whole idea and desperately hope that this will not change my Boy's personality. I want a dog, not a subservient eunuch.

Reluctantly I book the appointment for him. Dropping him off at the surgery a few days later, I feel like a traitor, not just because he is going to be castrated, but also because, for the first time since we have been together, I am leaving him alone with a stranger. I hug him and say goodbye, hoping he understands me as I promise to back for him later.

When I return, the vet reports that all has gone well but that Seamus is still affected by the anaesthetic. This is certainly true. The staff walk Seamus into the surgery, but he is groggy and unstable. I try to lead him to the car, but a long legged dog, semi-anesthetised, is a sad sight. His lanky frame wobbles and staggers as he tries to keep his balance.

Finally, I pick him up and carry him to the car, then lift him out again when we arrive home. I tuck him into a basket to sleep off the rest of the anaesthetic. He whimpers a bit, so I carry him upstairs and put him on my bed to sleep with me, covered in a warm blanket.

The following morning, I wake to find Seamus standing, straddled over me on the bed, nose in my face, laughing and wagging his tail. He shows no signs of discomfort, or of even noticing the stitches between his back legs.

It all looks rather swollen and uncomfortable down there to my eyes, but Seamus apparently disagrees. He continues blithely through the day as though nothing has happened.

There is a brief episode of discomfort a week later when the stitches come out. Seamus is not at all happy about this and I sit on the floor with him cradled in my arms and legs to allow the vet access. Seamus yelps and tries to shuffle-bottom backwards into me as I hold his upper half clear and the vet tweezers out the stitches. Five minutes later the job is done and we leave, Seamus dancing on his toes as we depart. He does not like visiting the vet.

The next time I run into Annie from the big house she asks after Seamus. "So why was he at the vets?"

I tell her the tale. "Oh dear." she says. "So he's not your little nut cutlet anymore?"

Over the next few weeks I wait for signs of change in my Boy. There is almost none. His personality is the same. He still likes his same friends and still dislikes old enemies. There is a very slight reduction in his tendency to wander, but my Seamus is essentially unchanged. But when Rosa's next little girl comes into season, she is able to walk through the village unmolested.

Seamus and Fudge

Travelling with dogs is fun. I am single and I make my own holidays. I have no desire to travel abroad to hot places, lie on a beach or get a tan. What I want is to set off and explore. The UK has some of the most beautiful countryside in the world and so much of it is within an hour or so's drive of my home.

On Friday night I pack my car with tent, camping stove and other equipment, a few days' supply of food, and of course, two dogs. I drive a big estate car, so it is not too crowded; not fast or glamorous, but easy and comfortable to drive and roomy enough to sleep in if the weather turns really unpleasant.

Fudge is an old hand at travel. I have long ago learned that travelling with a dog, security considerations aside, is an easy conversation starter and a reliable ice breaker.

Quite apart from weekends away, Fudge has accompanied me on business trips, the car doubling as mobile office and mobile kennel. I have found that she will unlock doors I cannot. Many a pub landlord, upon meeting Fudge, has bent the rules regarding dogs by the lounge fire.

I am in Glasgow. I have appointments the following day, but right now I need somewhere to stay overnight, somewhere that will accept both me and Fudge. I cruise the streets awhile until I see a house with a B&B board outside. The area is a bit seedy, but it is late, already dark, and I am ready to get my head down.

Leaving Fudge in the car, I ring the doorbell of the guesthouse. After a few moments the door is answered by an unkempt individual wearing a baggy cardigan, ornamented with the remains of his last meal.

He does not wear the face of high intelligence, but he does at least, look friendly. I wonder if this is a good idea, but, it is late. I cannot be too choosy.

"I'm looking for a room, single, just one night. Do you have anything?"

He replies in a strong Glaswegian accent. "Yeah sure, no problem. C'mon in." He starts to wave me into the porch.

"Er, before I come in, I have a dog with me. Is that okay?"

Storm clouds wash over his horizons and I feel the temperature fall. "Oh! Sorry, no. No dogs. We're not allowed." He shakes his head firmly, and then again. "No."

I turn up the charisma a notch or two and don my Charm. "She's absolutely no trouble I promise. She's quite old and she's very clean."

He is unmoved. "No sorry, definitely no dogs. The boss won't let me." He folds his arms and stands, blocking the way in.

I take one final shot. "She's just in the car over there. Can I at least bring her over for you to take a look, then you can decide properly."

He wavers and I seize the opportunity. *Carpe Diem.* "I'll just bring her over then."

I fetch Fudge out of the car, promising her a pork pie if she can charm us in. Fudge obliges and, wearing her most ingratiating smile, trots over to the door, sweeping the air with her otter tail. She looks up at the man, radiating bonne amie.

He melts instantly. "Oh what a lovely old girl. What's she called? Come on in. Do you think she would like a Weetabix?"

I know that Fudge would sell her own grandmother for a Weetabix, but say "That would be lovely. It's been a long day and I've not had chance to feed her yet."

As I bring in my suitcase, the man is calling down the corridor asking if Fudge would prefer warm milk on her Weetabix.

༻✦༺

With Seamus along too, it is even more fun. His whiz-bang enthusiasm has him ready for anything. The three of us stop in a 'Dogs-Welcome' guesthouse in Ambleside.

The landlady makes Seamus and Fudge very welcome indeed, slipping them bits of sausage.

"Only two rules, Love" she says. "They can't come in the dining room, and you can't leave them in your room by themselves." Fair enough. Neither of those is exactly an unreasonable ask. The room is basic, but clean and comfortable and is supplied with thoughtful extras such as old towels for dogs, a boot rack and an airer to hang wet clothes and jackets. I have purchased a map of the local walking and we set off to explore Loughrigg Fell. It is pleasant stretch of the legs, not over strenuous and the three of us return for a good night's sleep.

The following morning, I pop Seamus and Fudge into the car for a while, so I can have my breakfast in the dining room. Entering the guesthouse from the rear, I hear a commotion coming from close by. The landlady's voice rises to a screech, with words I cannot make out over the rumbling sound of some kind of machinery.

"You okay?" I call. "Are you alright?" There is no answer, so I follow the noise to find myself in a utility room. The rumbling sound is an industrial sized washing machine churning its load of bedlinen. The landlady is, as we say in the North, 'Going off on one.' Her arms are flailing in all directions, as she sorts through an enormous pile of sheets, issuing what sound like death threats, to someone I cannot see.

She spies me and calms down. "Oh sorry Love. Did I disturb you? You see what I have to deal with; here's me trying to run a business an' all...."

She gestures at a gigantic tumble drier, door stood open. Peering into the bowels of the machine, hot and dry, I see, sat atop a tumble of sheets and pillow cases, a large ginger cat, purring contently and kneading the sheets.

I laugh "Well you do advertise as pet friendly."

A few minutes later, as I sit down to an excellent breakfast, the cat joins me at my table, sitting on the next chair and clearly waiting for bacon and sausage to gravitate towards him. No pets in the dining room? Everyone knows that rules do not apply to cats.

The landlady provides me with a packed lunch. I weigh it in my hand. It is quite a heavy packet. "Well there's three of you int' there love." is all she says and then she gives me a small carrier bag, which I find contains the 'doggy bag' leftovers of a dozen or so guests. "You're the only one with dogs today. I don't like it going to waste." Fudge's tail thumps agreement with this sensible statement and Seamus' nose hovers delicately past the bag.

At lunch-time, sitting by Grasmere, I offer Seamus some ham. He sniffs at it. "No thanks. It's that smoked stuff. I'll have some of the pork sausage though." His ears and nose indicate the desired item. "Yes that's it. Not the one with tomato sauce on it."

Fudge is nothing like so discriminating and manfully gromphs everything passed in her direction.

Farewell Old Lady

It is three years since the arrival of Seamus and Fudge is failing. For all her dislike of Seamus, his arrival injected new life into my Old Lady. However, her rejuvenation can only delay, not avoid, the inevitable. Fudge is, I think, about fifteen and that is a good age for a Labrador.

Her mammary tumours have grown and grown. Three times now, she has had the operation to 'strip them' but each time they return. These are not malignant tumours. They do not invade her system, cancerously stealing her life away. Instead they simply grow, becoming huge and unwieldy. The tumours swell and keep swelling, developing into a huge mass under her belly. They may be called 'benign', but they are crippling her and making her life miserable. Fudge cannot walk properly because of the bulk dragging under her. I have already made the decision for her that she is too old to go under the surgeon's knife again.

I try taking the two dogs together out in the car, giving them a short walk together before returning Fudge to the car, to continue with Seamus alone. This is not a success. Fudge howls and wails despairingly as we walk away. When I return five minute later, she is still crying; shaking and miserable inside the car.

Soon, the monstrous tumours are so large that they are dragging on the ground, sore and bleeding. I can no longer claim the Fudge has a good quality of life and I know the time has come. It is an awful thing, but the last duty we dog owners have to our friends, is to ensure that they die pain-free, cuddled and unafraid.

I call the vet in. Fudge has a huge breakfast of fried liver and is still gulping it down as the vet arrives.

I sit on the floor with Fudge, hugging her and talking to her as the vet slips in the needle and eases her on her way.

Later I take her body up to the woods and bury her in a quiet corner under the beech leaves.

Sophie

And so we are two. Seamus and I are a team and he is everything I wish for in a dog. However, dogs are social creatures and I feel strongly that Seamus should have a friend. My own preference is for dogs over bitches; I simply like the dog personality. That devil-may-care cockiness that comes from the male personality appeals to me. However, since this is to be Seamus' friend, I feel that it should be a 'girlfriend'.

So I return to the rescue centre. I wander up and down the aisles, examining each inmate in turn, automatically rejecting the dogs and weighing up the bitches.

Would this girl be a suitable friend for my Lovely Boy? Spaniels, collies, greyhounds, staffies, and all the mix and match versions that come in between, stare out at me from the runs. Their eyes range between soulful, joyful at being noticed, despairing, and simply numb.

It is still for me one of the most painful experiences there is, walking up and down those corridors, knowing that it is simply not possible to help all the animals in there. You can only do your best for one or two.

I stop in my tracks at the sight of the next dog I reach, and I make one of the biggest mistakes of my life. I fall in love with the *look* of a dog, and I choose her on that basis.

'Muffin' is, judging by her appearance, a collie cross spaniel. She is white with markings in the most amazing shade of foxy red I have ever seen. She is lithe and agile, with that long bodied, slightly low slung, build that you get in the collie types. Her eyes are bright and attentive. She is simply amazing to look at.

Muffin wags excitedly at me and comes to sniff.

I do not read her card properly. I notice some notes about her having been in several previous homes and saying that she is not house-trained. I more or less dismiss that. Dogs like to be clean.

In my experience the problem sorts itself out with time and confidence. Neither do I question the attendant closely enough about her background. I simply fall for her on the spot and say I will take her.

I walk her a couple of times, always on the lead of course at the shelter, and she seems fine. A few days later I call to collect her and bring her home. This time the collection is not so straightforward. Muffin does not want to get into the car. I try drawing her to the car on a lead but she refuses to get in. I walk around the car a little, to allow her to accustom herself to it, but she still refuses to get in. Eventually I simply lift her onto the passenger seat and close the door on her. During the journey home she is anxious, panting heavily. I repeat my formula of talking to her constantly, to get her to answer to her new name of 'Sophie'. Despite her unease, she is brightly intelligent and has no difficulty with her new name. She answers to 'Sophie' as I lead her out of the car.

Seamus is delighted to meet Sophie. She is small and quick and pretty, and is equally delighted to meet him. They charge around the house together, and is quickly clear that Sophie is already the leader; Seamus is following. They run in dizzy circles, becoming more and more excited, Seamus yipping and yelping, becoming more and more hysterical.

I try to calm them down and take control of the situation, but Sophie is paying me no attention and Seamus follows her. I decide that I need to get them out together to run off some energy.

Catching Sophie by the collar, I snag a runner lead onto her and we three walk up the road to the field where I first took Seamus; my nice enclosed field with gates, walls and fences, a perfect place to first release a dog. Since however, the two seem so wound up, it seems better to walk them for a while under control.

I amble up the hill, following the footpath through and beyond the stables, across the fields to the woods, the circular walk around the woods and back again.

I have walked perhaps a couple of miles. Sophie has done probably five times that, constantly weaving backwards and forwards in front of me, always at the full extent of her lead. And Seamus has followed her.

By the time we reach my safe field again, the main rush of excitement seems to have worn off, and checking that gates are closed, I let Sophie off the lead.

To my horror, Sophie takes off for the far side of the field, reaches the dry stone wall, flows over it like quick-silver and heads for the horizon in the next field.

Oh Shit!

I give chase, calling her frantically, praying that no one has sheep nearby. Fortunately, Sophie is distracted by a cowpat, and I catch up with her, wheezing and red faced, as she has rolled herself green. I clip the lead back on and we walk, at a more sedate pace, back home.

I am reluctant to bathe Sophie, it being her first day with me, but there is little option. She is oozing. I close the doors, open the windows and shower her down in the bathroom.

Joy of joys! She loves being showered down. After two shampoos (only the best, Pantene for silky hair is all I have handy) and several rinses, I have a clean dog again. Towelling her dry, we return downstairs.

I open the back door to the garden. Much as I love 'em, wet dog is not my favourite fragrance. Sophie considers she is not sufficiently dried off and finishes the job to her own satisfaction rubbing along the side of the settee, the armchair, the curtains....

Eventually she is clean and glossy, her lovely white and foxy fur shining. Then she and Seamus spend the rest of the afternoon romping out in the back garden. By the end of the afternoon, Sophie is tired and Seamus is on his knees.

Having been warned that Sophie is not house trained, I have decided that, at least for a night or two, Sophie can sleep downstairs in the kitchen, until we establish some ground rules and habits.

She has been entirely clean in the house all afternoon and each time she has needed to 'go', has used the garden. I do not believe we are going to have a long term cleanliness problem.

So, come bedtime, I set Sophie up with a basket in the kitchen, plenty of water and a little snack of chicken to help settle her. I have scattered newspapers over the floor to deal with any 'accidents'.

Completely happy with all this, Sophie nestles into the basket, until the moment I leave, taking Seamus with me, turn off the light and close the kitchen door behind me. Immediately she starts barking and jumps up against the door.

I decide to ignore it. Best to start as we mean to go on. I go to bed and Seamus takes his accustomed place on the bed at my feet.

The barking becomes more and more frantic, turning to howls and yelps. I can hear the thump of her jumping against the kitchen door. The thumping turns to crashes as Sophie hurls herself against the door. She is by no means calming down in the dark and the quiet. Instead she is becoming more and more desperate.

Eventually I go downstairs. From the lounge, I see the kitchen door rattling under the impact of Sophie beating herself against the other side.

As I open it, she collapses in a heap at my feet, lying there, shaking and crying. She is filthy, caked in her own faeces and the kitchen is worse.

Newspapers are scattered and shredded. The floor and all the walls up to a couple of feet from the ground are splattered and a good amount of the excrement has splashed higher on the walls and upwards onto the table and work surfaces.

Picking up the whimpering Sophie, I carry her to the bathroom, cuddling her while I run the shower warm and then we have a shower together. I towel her and then wrap her in another dry towel. Putting a couple of large towels over the bottom of my bed, I lay her on them.

She is calmer now. Seamus jumps up beside her. I cannot face dealing with the kitchen at this time of night. I open the windows and close the door on the situation. As I get into bed, Sophie is sound asleep and does not stir all night.

The following morning, I wake to bright sunshine, Sophie's paws on my chest and her tongue working its way over my face. In my sleep befuddled condition, she succeeds in a direct hit inside my mouth; don't you just hate getting a French kiss from a dog?

Sophie appears entirely recovered from her night-time trauma. Seamus is also stood by, eyes bright, tail wagging, awaiting Sophie's attention. He yips and she leaps down to him. They spend a crazy half hour playing Chase-Me-Catch-Me around the bedroom.

I sit up in bed, sipping tea. I have a golden rule of not getting up until I have my morning brew inside me, and am not looking forward to the morning's first chore.

An hour later I have wiped down walls, mopped the floor and disinfected all my kitchen surfaces. Having achieved as much as I can with a single cleaning, I pop the lead on Sophie and, Seamus trotting alongside, set off.

A short way up the road, two doors along, the gate to my neighbours' drive is swinging open. Through the gate Sophie spies a run containing two rabbits, their little girl's pets, on the lawn.

She lunges through the gate to the run, and only by luck, the runner lead pulls her up short before she can reach the rabbits. I have to physically haul Sophie away, straining and coughing against the leash, to get her out of the garden. Only when we are another hundred yards or so up the road and her attention is distracted by a passing bird, does Sophie cease to fight against my control.

I am uncertain now how to exercise Sophie. She is a collie cross spaniel. This is not a dog that can get adequate exercise on a lead or running around my little garden. She needs serious amounts of activity to deal with her energy levels.

Walking up to the woods, this time I do not let Sophie off the lead until we are safely inside the woodland, where she can be entertained by squirrels.

This works perfectly, and she and Seamus spend a happy hour chasing through the undergrowth, treeing squirrels, barking loudly upwards, demanding that the squirrels play fair and come down.

At length, satisfied that the two should be happily tired, we return home, again with Sophie safely on the lead.

Back home, I make myself some lunch while the two dogs, indefatigable, bounce around the house and back garden together.

Needing something from the car, I open the front door to step outside. Sophie appears from nowhere, darts between my legs and dashes up the road, with me running behind, trying to catch up. She does not go far. Running into my neighbours' garden, she is haring round and around the run, trying to get into the rabbits, yapping dementedly.

Fruitlessly I try to catch her, an utterly pointless exercise. There is no way I can catch this speeding canine scofflaw. I try squatting down to persuade her to come to me, but she simply keeps the run between me and her, yapping at me and the rabbits equally.

Terrified in case my neighbours return, or some passer-by sees what is happening, after nearly fifteen minutes I catch her by the scruff of the neck. I have no lead on me, so I one-handedly remove the belt from my jeans and loop it over her head. As I close the door behind us, she lunges forwards to play with Seamus, so I set her loose.

While making lunch I do some hard thinking as to how to deal with the situation.

Whatever has happened to Sophie in the past, she is delinquent. I am already of the opinion that, contrary to what I have been told, she is perfectly house-trained. Her problem is psychological. Someone has well and truly screwed her up.

Lunch is one of my favourite meals; mince, mashed potatoes and peas. Sitting in my armchair, plate of food on a tray on my lap, I settle down to watch the news while I eat.

Seamus also likes mince and mash. He knows there will be some for him in a few minutes and he chills out on the settee, waiting for his share. Sophie sits squarely in front of me, utterly focussed on the food. Looking at her, I can see her control cracking. As she stares at my plate, she wriggles and twitches, then at last, launches herself to land in my lap, on the tray.

It had to be mince of course. A cheese roll would have simply dropped to the floor. Chips would have scattered across the carpet. But the plate of mince and potato splashes across the floor, the walls, Sophie and me. The only one unscathed is Seamus who, at my yell of outrage, has made a sharp exit to the back garden.

Taking the practical approach, I let the dogs clean up the gravy besmirched carpet and walls, then get down with bucket and suds to finish off the carpet. I'll have to touch up the paintwork later.

Garry, my boyfriend, arrives. I have already told him that Sophie is coming and invited him up to meet her. It is an instant success, love at first sight. Garry and Sophie are made for each other. I pop out to make a pot of tea and return to find Garry bouncing Sophie up and down on the settee.

The next difficulty is car travel. At first I think that Sophie suffers from travel sickness. Even on short journeys, only ten minutes up the road to the woods, Sophie throws up every time. The two dogs sit together in the back section of my estate car, so the worst effects are contained, but Seamus is not at all happy.

The first time it happens, from my driver's seat, I hear a noise from the back, but in the rear view mirror, all I can see is that Sophie is out of sight behind the car seat and Seamus is looking down at her with an odd expression.

Then, something he never does, Seamus jumps over from the back section to sit on the rear seats. When we reach the woods and I open the back of the car, I see it awash with vomit, Sophie shaking and trembling, cowering in the stinking fluid. Seamus is wearing his best 'It's nothing to do with me.' expression.

Sophie and Seamus enjoy the run through the woods, romping, playing and trying to climb trees after the ubiquitous squirrels. As we approach the car, I put Sophie on the lead again to be sure that I can get her in. I have an old blanket I always keep in the car and I drop it over the mess so that the dogs do not have to sit in it, but on the short journey home, Sophie vomits again.

This is a problem. If I cannot freely take the dogs out in the car, then our lives must be much more circumscribed. With dogs, as with much else, cars spell freedom. Sophie must learn to travel.

I decide to experiment with very short journeys. Two minutes or so, no more. It makes no difference. On even the shortest journey, Sophie is sick and is close to collapse when I open up the car.

After a couple of weeks of trying various combinations of travel, time and destination, I reach the conclusion that Sophie is not suffering from car sickness at all. She is terrified of travelling.

What has happened to her, that a car journey is such a devastating experience? Has she been taken somewhere and abandoned? Taken somewhere and beaten? I can never know.

I change tactic. I travel to my routine 'doggy places' but allowing for Sophie being sick. The back of the car, containing Sophie, is well lined with old newspapers and I have a fresh supply with me for the journey back. Seamus sits on the passenger seat next to me; no need for my immaculately dapper lad to get his fur soiled.

For three weeks, travel is Hell. I visit Pendle Hill, the Ribble Valley with its rivers and green places, and the woods at least once a day; all to no avail. Sophie continues her terror-stricken vomiting.

If she has already thrown up, I hear her retching and coughing, trying to vomit with an empty stomach, crouched down out of sight.

I begin seriously to consider Sophie's future. This is not kind to her. Perhaps she would be better with someone who will simply walk her to the park every day?

It is Saturday and I decide that we will visit Lytham St Annes. The weather is beautiful and the sand dunes by the sea shore are the perfect walk for the perfect conditions. Perhaps Sophie will enjoy the sea; and I can have fish and chips out of paper while I watch the dogs play.

I make the usual travel arrangements. Newspapers, water bottles, flask, no picnic this time, fish'n'chips are calling me.

The dogs in the car, I set off. Within five minutes, Sophie produces a Niagara of vomit. The day is warm and with an hour's journey ahead of us, the car is distinctly whiffy. I open the sunroof.

After a couple of minutes, in the mirror I see Sophie sitting upright and sniffing the air. She looks brighter, much brighter. Fresh air? Is that all she needs? Sophie flows over the back seat and raises her head as high as she can, trying to reach the sunroof. It is too high for her, but now she is smiling. A moment later, there are two paws on my shoulders, one squarely either side of my head.

Sophie is resting on my shoulders to stand with her head out of the sunroof. God knows what this looks like to the car behind me.

Glancing up, Sophie's red ears are whipping behind her in the wind, her mouth wide open in a canine laugh. She is clearly loving it and, since she is not interfering with my driving, I see no reason to stop her.

At least she is enjoying travel. Driving down the motorway at speed I think she will probably come down, but no, she remains there, enjoying her 'flight'. Looking up I see that the rush of air is now actually forcing open up her eyelids, ballooning them out from her eyes.

This is not a good idea. However much she revels in her new experience, drying out her own eyeballs is not sensible. I decide though, not to bring her down. Instead, I slow the car until the air flow ceases to perform facial reshaping on her.

As we approach the coast, the air acquires that tang of the sea. Sophie is sniffing at the breeze, circling with her nose, trying to locate the source of this new scent. Parking up by the dunes, I pop a lead on her, wanting her well away from the busy traffic here before I risk releasing her. She needs to know where we are, to be safe.

I need not have worried. Sophie is straining at the lead to reach the sands. I cross the dunes onto the main beach.

The tide is out and miles of open sand stretch before us. Seamus gives a little yip – he knows this place well and loves it here – and goes tearing off towards the sea. I unclip Sophie and she follows.

They run, and they run and they run. And then they run some more.

I walk out towards the sea. Lytham has fine beaches and the tide a long way out. It is a fair walk to reach the sea. The two dogs are still racing.

I pass the strandline, always an interesting part of the beach, with the usual mix of seaweed, plastic bottles, odd feathers, shell and bits of rotten fish.

Sophie shows Seamus how to roll in the remains of a putrefying seagull and then offers him use of this amazing facility. Seamus sniffs at it briefly, shudders and walks on. Sophie learns how not to drink seawater, gulping some down and then bringing it up again a few minutes later, with I note, some bits of seagull.

I pour water from the bottle I am carrying, into a collapsible bowl I have for this purpose, letting them lap it up so they can enjoy some more running.

This is wonderful! Just what Sophie needs. By the end of today, she should be so knackered that she will sleep all the way back. Seamus is flagging, so I take them both back to the car for the couple of minutes it takes me to buy my fish and chips.

As we walk back into the dunes, Seamus informs me that he will be happy to assist in the matter of any leftover chips or spare fish.

Seamus and I flop down onto the slope of a dune while Sophie dissects a dead crab. When we find ourselves being covered in a spray of sand as she buries the crab, we move along to the next dune to discuss the important matter of the equable division of a large haddock portion with extra chips on the side. I am permitted to eat the mushy peas unmolested.

Driving home, Sophie does not in fact, sleep. She sits on the rear passenger seat with Seamus, looking out of the window with alert interest.

The day is cooler and I do not open the sunroof, not wanting a repeat of the morning's circus performance. Stopping at some traffic lights, I semi-turn to check up on them; "You okay Sophie?" She leans forward and licks my ear.

༄

Garry adores Sophie. And it is quite mutual. She loves him beyond question. Garry connects with Sophie in a way that I never quite manage. She loves everything about him and endlessly wants to play with him. I find them one day in my bedroom.

Garry is picking Sophie up and, not just dropping, but hurling her down on the bed for her to bounce up again like the world's biggest elastic band, up and all over him, demanding that he do it again. I can see she is having the time of her life.

"For God's sake be careful with her." I say, half angry, half amused. "If she lands badly she could break something, wrench a shoulder or something."

Garry is laughing out loud at this performance as he bounces Sophie down again. "I've never had a dog before that wanted nothing more than to be thrown about like a rag doll."

I shake my head. "Whatever it was that happened to her, it can't have been physical mistreatment."

I leave them to it as Sophie comes up off the bed again like a jack-in-the-box.

༄

It is Winter, mid-Winter. In the night snow has come down and, lies as they say, deep and crisp and even.

I am preparing to take Seamus and Sophie out for their morning constitutional. Seamus has prepared for this by bolting down his breakfast. Sophie is preparing for it by charging to the closed front kitchen door, u-turning right back through the house to the closed rear door and u-turning again. Rinse and repeat.

I don hat, scarf, coat and gloves and as I approach the front door, Sophie is one about the twentieth re run of her round-the-house marathon.

I reach for the door handle as Sophie re-enters the kitchen at speed. As the door opens, she sees the white world outside and screeches to a halt. "WTF's that!?!" Certainly she has never seen snow before. She is perhaps four or five years old and we have had several snowy winters. How can she not have seen snow before?

৩৵

Sophie is adorable, but in human terms, unhinged. For her, to think and to act are one. There is no consideration, no introspection, no awareness of consequence.

She flies headlong at everything. When she gets herself into trouble she has only her pure unwavering doubt that 'Mum' and 'Uncle Garry' will rescue her.

Garry and I are walking by the canal, Seamus and Sophie enjoying themselves pottering about, as we all stroll along the towpath. The canal is well constructed and for the most part, the water level is a couple of feet below the stone and brick edging. Only in areas where the side walls have collapsed is it safe for a dog to enter the water.

Around these tumbledown areas, silt and mud builds up among the broken bricks and rubble, reeds take hold, and small peninsulas develop where wading birds stand spying for frogs and tadpoles, and tiddlers shoal around, taking the shelter of the reeds. In these areas, there is a way out again for the dog who ventures in the water.

Seamus likes these micro-headlands. He tiptoes between the reeds, being careful not to go more than ankle deep; he does not like swimming. And he is also careful not to splash mud on his immaculate fur. He laps a little water and then, ready for action again, jumps back onto the bank to go hunting rabbits in the brambles.

Sophie is not so prudent. She loves swimming. She did not know how to swim when we first met, but has learned to do so by running into the water and simply continuing, showing no recognition that her surroundings have changed.

She sees a duck and hurtles towards it, continuing over the edge of the canal into the water as though nothing has changed.

"Sheer drop? No way out? No problem. They'll pull me out." After this happens a couple of times, I no longer dare walk by this stretch of canal without Garry.

If Sophie gets into the water and has to be rescued, I can lift her out if it is no more than a few inches down, but when the water level is two feet down, it needs Garry's size and muscle to pull her up by the front paws, dripping and unrepentant.

On another occasion, we are all taking our usual walk along the towpath. This time we are on a stretch where the footpath runs between the canal on one side and open fields on the other.

The fields are not very attractive; very rough grazing with just the occasional shaggy pony to be seen. They are too marshy for decent pasture, scattered patches of bog grasses and rushes with scraggy looking hawthorns interspersed. However, there are no sheep and so the route is a 'safe option'.

Seamus and Sophie run ahead of us while Garry and I lag behind. The canal is thronging with tadpoles, swimming through the murky waters in swarming, black, wriggling flows of thousands at a time. Very occasionally, there is the electric blue whizz of a kingfisher flying by.

The two dogs have vanished from sight. This is not unusual. They know the route well. Up ahead there are thickets and brambles, full of rabbits and other enticements. Typically, they will meet us there. We walk on to the spot where we would expect to find the dogs again but there is no sign of them. We do not worry but continue walking. The dogs will catch us up.

Garry and I reach a point where we normally turn around; a small bridge where the path might lead a dog onto busy town roads. Still, we have not seen the dogs.

I begin to worry. We walk back on the same route, waiting to encounter the dogs. Eventually, Seamus runs up to meet us. He is alone, panting and anxious. Now we are both seriously worried and we step up our pace.

There is a strange noise in the distance. I take it at first, to be the sound of a flock of geese. Still we do not see Sophie. The odd sound gets louder. Still, it sounds like the shriek of geese, but now I start to wonder. Where are there geese around here?

There are no close-by farmyards for domestic birds, and wild geese tend to call only when they are flying. I see none of the V-shaped formations above us.

We arrive at the scruffy fields and the noise is even louder. I stand staring out, trying to identify this weird sound. Then I see Sophie, a flash of foxy red in the distance.

It is too far to make out the detail, but the sound, the horrible sound, is being made by Sophie. She is not moving, but screaming.

We scramble down the embankment, through tangles of gorse and bramble, wading through mud and puddles. I am nimbler than Garry and pull ahead of him. Although I can see Sophie, I still cannot see why she is not moving, why she is screaming. We are both shouting to her, telling her we are coming, telling her that, whatever has happened, we are coming. Sophie sees us and falls silent.

Finally, I am close enough to see what is wrong. Sophie is hanging, upside down, trapped by one back leg in a barbed wire fence. Somehow she has caught herself between two strands of wire and twisted, so that the metal strand is now looped right round her back leg and she is hanging, quite helpless, by that one leg in the barbed wire.

"I'm here Sophie. I'm here." I yell and bend to take her weight, lifting her to take the strain off the back leg just as Garry catches up with me. Like me, he is appalled.

Thank God. If I were by myself, what would I have done?

Taking Sophie's entire weight, my hands are full and I cannot move. "I'll hold her. Can you get the wire off her?"

Garry is in tears. He is a big man, but it takes all of his strength to prise open the loop of wire to release the leg as I lean inwards to take the tension from the loop. Finally, the leg is free and Sophie lies limp in my arms like a ragdoll, while Garry untangles the beautiful fur of her foxy tail from the barbed wire. Sophie is clearly in shock and is not able to walk.

We are perhaps a mile from the car. "I'll carry her." he says. Garry picks up his Little Girl and stolidly, carries her back to the safety of the car. It is a long walk and we stop several times to let him rest.

Sophie is not a large dog, but she is still a heavy load over that distance.

Back home, we assess the damage. By some miracle, the wire has not cut into her leg and her toes are pink and healthy looking. The blood supply to her foot is intact. She does appear to be basically unhurt, just shocked and frightened. We put her in her basket and she sleeps.

The following morning, she is up and about, manic as ever. In Sophie's world, nothing has happened of note. Her skies are blue and she flows onto 'Uncle Garry's' lap completely unchanged.

Sophie now relishes travel. She understands that getting in the car means going for walks! And I take the two dogs on as great a variety of walks as I can.

Visiting the Lake District and taking the Windermere ferry, we learn together that Sophie adores boat rides, as she slips her leash to sit on the prow of the boat like a small ginger figurehead, her ears rippling in the breeze.

I discover a new set of rambles on the network of canals running through the area. There are a number of them, The Lancaster, The Rochdale, and nearest to me, only a ten-minute drive, The Leeds-Liverpool Canal.

Originally very much an industrial resource, the Leeds-Liverpool has now 'gone wild'. Wikipedia tells me it is 127 miles long, but in my immediate ten miles or so, it meanders to and fro, crisscrossing the route of the M65 motorway.

This is not really a co-incidence; the construction engineers are always going to pick the easiest route they can for these big civil engineering projects and the canal and motorway both follow the line of the valley between Pendle to the west and the great line of hills leading to the famous Howarth Moors (of Wuthering Heights fame) to the East.

Here, down in the valley it is lush and green, and the canal with its flat easy walking is a pleasant stroll for as many miles as you could wish to go.

There are plenty of parking places for the start of my walk, but I usually choose a spot just by the bridge where the canal is crossed by Barden Lane. From here I can walk South or North on the canal, and either way is a pleasant ramble.

Today I choose to walk North. The walk is almost completely rural, apart from a short stretch where the waterway runs close enough to the motorway to hear the roar of the traffic.

Another advantage to this walk, is that I can relax a bit. The whole side of the canal for some miles is fenced off and so I know that Sophie's madder exploits are curtailed; she can only be by the canal, and the drop to the water is shallow enough that I can fish her out if need be.

After a while the canal opens to an area which I think must have once been a boat repair yard. A wide pool, once industrial, it is now overhung by willows, reeds and lily pads by the edges.

There is the rotting hulk of a barge of the far side and the remains of some moorings, but the scene now is blissful and still under the cool green shade of the willows.

A flotilla of ducks approaches. They know a rucksack when they see one and they know also that rucksacks reliably contain bread rolls. I am quite friendly with the landlady of a local pub and she regularly gives me her stale bread. The ducks feast.

Seamus and Sophie protest at this discriminatory treatment and are also given a bread roll apiece. They sit blissfully dismantling their rolls whilst I munch on a cheese sandwich. Tea from my flask completes brunch.

We continue. Ahead of us, some way down the path I see a family of swans. This is unusual. The swans are generally on the water. This time they are blocking the way and I hesitate. The path is not wide and I cannot go around them.

Seamus and Sophie sight the swans; Mum, Dad and a trio of cygnets. I read their thoughts. "By 'eck! Them's big ducks. Let's go chase them!" Despite my calls, the two dash down the path towards the swans. I am not worried for the safety of the swans.

The swans see the dogs racing close and turn, square on, to face them. One rears, spreading its wings like the Angel of Death bearing bad news, and hisses.

The dogs skid to a halt, "Blow that for a game of soldiers!" and reverse out at speed, not turning their backs on the swans until they are a safe distance away.

The swans, unmolested, resume their vigil of the path. I decide that today, we will turn back at this point.

☙❧

The swans of the canal have attitude. Like the ducks they know all about walkers, rucksacks and bread rolls. Unlike the ducks, they are prepared to make demands rather than requests.

Again, I am sat by the canal, in a different spot, enjoying my picnic lunch. There is a small ramp into the water for canoeists and rowers to launch their boats.

A swan glides over and walks up the ramp towards me. I am happy to let him have some of my egg sandwich. However, instead of waiting to be offered some, the swan suddenly runs towards me, wings outstretched, head outstretched low, hissing like a pressure cooker ready to blow. This swan has experience of menacing innocent walkers into giving up their lunch.

Sod that!

I stand straight up with my arms outstretched and hiss back. "Aaaarrrggghhhhssssssss...." The swan, classic schoolyard bully that he is, turns tail and scarpers.

☙❧

Seamus aside, Sophie's best friend is Kerry. Kerry is a blond Labrador who comes by at least twice a day being walked by her 'Dad' Craig.

I first meet Craig shortly after moving into Whinshill Cottage. While sitting on the bench on the little green outside my house, they pass by on their final walk of the evening. Fudge is underwhelmed by Kerry, but Craig and I exchange a few words.

Craig and I become quite good friends over time and exchange gossip and small talk most days. However, when Sophie arrives, she and Kerry strike up an instant friendship. If I am working in the house, no matter what I am doing, Sophie informs me that Craig and Kerry! are out there. We must go out now. Yes, stop that. We must go out now! I put on the kettle and take out two cups of coffee. Craig is sat on the bench and he and I chat, whilst Sophie and Kerry chase each other round and around the little grass triangle.

I am tired one day. It has been a tough week and I am working all hours. Feeling a bit depressed, I tell Craig that I envy him the holiday in Portugal he and his wife are about to take. He looks at me a little concerned. "Don't overdo it." he says. "You know what they say. No one on their deathbed ever regretted not spending more time at the office. It's not worth it, overworking. You don't know what life's going to bring you."

I agree with him. We finish our coffee and Craig walks down the hill with Kerry. I do not expect to see him again for a week or so as he leaves for his holiday tomorrow.

Three weeks later I have still not seen Craig, only Kerry, being walked by a friend while they were away. Suddenly, up the hill, comes Kerry, being walked by 'Mrs Craig'. She is a nice lady who I barely know because Craig always does the dog walking.

"Hi Lynn." I say. "Long time, no see. Good holiday?"

As she comes closer, I can see her eyes are red. "Hello Chris. Er, no I'm afraid the holiday wasn't so good. Craig had a heart attack by the pool and died. The doctor said it was stress relief from not being at work."

My dog walking friends Ronny and Eva walk by one day, with their usual pair of lurchers and another dog I have not seen before. He is a sprightly little chap, some sort of terrier mix, and he looks like classic rescue dog material.

"We've called him Billie." says Ronny, smiling with pride.

"From the shelter?" I ask. "I didn't know you were looking for another."

They exchange glances. "No we weren't." says Eva. "We saw him being dumped."

"You saw it? That's unusual..."

"We were in Accrington in the shopping centre. We'd parked up just off the pedestrian zone. From the car, we could see a young couple arguing over the dog. He was trying to get her to tie the dog up outside a shop and leave it...."

Eva is quite animated in her description. I can see her emotions running high. She continues ".... the girl was very upset, but we could see that he had the upper hand. Eventually, while we were watching, she tied the dog up to the bollards outside one of the shops and they started to walk away."

"We got out of the car then and chased after them. We asked if we could have the dog. The lad......." Eva pulls a face. Ronny mirrors her expression. "....he looked dead rough, said yes and he'd never wanted the dog in the first place."

Ronny interrupts. "I didn't want them changing their minds later. So I insisted on paying them £10 for the dog, and I made him give me a receipt to prove we'd bought it and that the dog belongs to us now. It was only scribbled on the back of a bit of paper, but it was a receipt." He draws a breath. "There was a bit of a crowd by then, and they didn't like it much."

I nod. "I can imagine."

Ronny continues. "Eva took him, Billie I mean, and went to put him in the back of the car. But I went back to the girl. I told her she was a fool to be with the man. I said to her, 'If he does that to a dog, he'll do it to you.'"

"True." I say. People can be heroes. They can be complete bastards. And they can be utter fools.

⁂

I am working two or three days a week in Yorkshire, not too far from my mother's house. An hour and a half from home, I cannot just pop out at lunchtime to let the dogs out.

"Mum, if I bring Seamus and Sophie with me, do you think you could look after them during the day for me?"

"Of course I can Love. No problem at all."

My mother and Seamus are very fond of each other. She has not met Sophie yet. Her garden is not huge, but there is plenty of space for two energetic dogs to bounce around freely, and it is really well fenced. There should not be too many problems.

So, I call in there, around nine one morning, to drop off the dogs. Mum is there to meet her 'Best Boy' and Seamus is thrilled to see her. He jumps up for love and hugs. Sophie dashes into the house, whizzes around everywhere in a flash, invited or not. This includes my grandmother's mini-flat downstairs.

Part of the reason that I fell for Sophie, being a pretty spaniel type, is that my grandmother, having had dogs all her life, has recently lost her little old lady, Katie. She refuses to get another dog because she is afraid of outliving it, worrying about what would happen to another dog if she dies; as though either I, or my mother, would have not have adopted the dog on the spot.

But Grandma is elderly and her thinking is not always so clear. In her life, she has had a long line of spaniels.

She does not like Seamus, despite his loving, loyal and reliable personality, because he 'Looks too much like a wolf.'. Grandma does not like dogs with pointy ears. However, I am sure that she will like Sophie and am looking forward to their meeting. I must go to work and so I leave.

I return at about five o'clock. "How did it go?"

My mother looks thoughtful. "That Sophie's a bit of a Madam isn't she…"

Oh dear…… what has happened?

It transpires that my mother, also thinking that Grandma would enjoy Sophie's company, has left the two of them together for an hour or so while she went out shopping. She has returned to find that Grandma has turned Sophie out of her rooms and will not let her back in.

Grandma had made some lunch for herself, a bowl of tomato soup. The phone had rung; she had gone to answer it. When she returned, her soup was gone.

Now I think back, my grandmother's spaniels, and her later dogs, a Labrador, and Katie, a collie cross, have all been sweet, submissive dogs. None of them would ever have been allowed to cross Grandma's will.

Sophie, with her utter lack of thought with regard to consequences, and her heedless attitude to any form of discipline, is not Grandma's kind of dog.

Sophie has been exiled from Grandma's rooms. I remember my mince and mash, reflecting that perhaps this is for the best.

Seamus on the other hand, has spent most of the day mining in the garden. Mum has thrown out some bird food, bread crusts, bacon rind and similar; also, a dried out scone which accidentally fell between a small retaining wall and the garden fence. Seamus has spent most of the day trying to get it out, jamming his head down the three-inch crack.

After some hours, it has been retrieved for him with a knitting needle so that he does not rub all the fur off his nose. He is now smiling and contented and has a small number of scone crumbs hanging off his whiskers. Seamus is always welcome at my mother's house.

Over the next few weeks, Seamus and Sophie spend a couple of days a week with my Mum. It is Summer and they spend most of the day playing out in the garden. It works well for everyone.

I notice that Seamus is putting on a few pounds, more than a few in fact. He is becoming quite portly and his dainty waistline is vanishing under rolls of fat.

"Are you feeding him during the day Mum?" I give the two dogs a meal twice a day and they do not need more food.

"Well, not actually feeding him. He does share a ginger biscuit with me when I have my coffee."

I think about this for a moment. My mother takes two or three coffee breaks a day, stopping off from her work as a dressmaker to sit out in the garden and enjoy the fresh air.

"Is that, you share a ginger biscuit every time you have a coffee break?" I probe this issue further. It transpires that Seamus is getting several biscuits a day. How many? Well quite a few. How many? I learn that Seamus is being fed the equivalent of a packet of ginger nuts every day he visits. Seamus loves his 'Ginger Biscuit Grandma'.

Garry and I take a day out to Bolton Abbey in Yorkshire. We are in late Winter, moving into Spring. The weather is glorious and the Great Outdoors is calling. Putting together a picnic, I fill the flasks and tell the dogs that we are going out. They don't have to come if they don't want to. They can stay at home if they prefer.

I suck my bruised fingers where the door has slammed open on my hand as Seamus and Sophie exit the kitchen to the car. Seamus is trying to show me how to use the keys to the back of the car. We all pile in and set off for the Yorkshire Dales.

Bolton Abbey is a blissful trip out for the dogs. Set in the heart of the Dales, from the huge carpark there is a walk of perhaps a mile down to the River Wharfe, over green turf and passing the beautiful ruins of one of Henry VIII's demolition jobs.

Down at the water's edge there are miles of walking along the river banks, at first clipped, neat and civilised, then turning wilder on the far stretches. The path never becomes difficult to walk and a bridge over the river about three miles upstream enables a circular walk and fresh ground to tramp all the way. It is wonderful.

We walk through woodland in sunshine by the side of sparkling, rushing waters. Interestingly, the feeder streams to the river come in from different directions.

On one side of the river they bring water from the high fells and the limestone 'pavements' so classic to the area. The water runs white with the silt it carries. On the other side, the water drains from moorland peat and is golden amber as whiskey. In places the two separate steams can be seen running side by side within the river before they mingle to a single flow.

The dogs love this walk. As ever, Sophie leads and Seamus follows. They explore thickets and stands of broken bracken, brown now before the new fronds curl up from warming earth.

She swims in the calmer stretches of the water, going in time and again to retrieve sticks that Garry throws for her. Again and again, she plunges into freezing waters. Despite her heavy exercise she is shivering in her wet fur, but shows no sign of wishing to stop.

I say to Garry that since Sophie has no common sense of her own, we need to have common sense for her. Reluctantly he stops throwing sticks and Sophie simply starts running again, ahead and along the path for miles, while Seamus tries to keep up. Then she turns and runs back again.

Eventually Seamus drops to an exhausted stagger at my heels. Sophie just keeps running. She has no sense of 'enough is enough'. She is still running as we arrive back at the car. Garry and I have walked perhaps seven or eight miles. Sophie must have done thirty or forty. Collapsing into the back of the car, she immediately falls asleep.

Driving back, she is so still that I stop the car to check on her, seriously wondering if she has actually run herself to death. But no, she is only sleeping deeply. Garry takes her onto his knee in the passenger seat and so Sophie drives home being cuddled by Uncle Garry.

Two days later, it is a cold evening. I have finished work and, it already being almost dark, I drive the dogs to Spring Woods.

With Sophie's heedless temperament, these woods are a favourite walk for me. I can park up, open up the back, and the dogs just dash off into the woods, well away from the dangers of traffic.

If Sophie, oblivious as she is to danger, keeps running, then at the edge of the wood she will simply encounter fields and more fields. These in turn are edged by only farm tracks, or at most, country lanes where traffic is minimal and slow.

The woods themselves are a dog's adventure playground, with lots of undergrowth, a pond, paths to explore and fascinating diversions like streams and a waterfall.

If I am really lucky, Sophie will find some fox or deer poo to roll in.

By the parking area there are levelled lawns, gravelled tracks and tarmacked paths, complete with lighting. I can idle up and down this area under streetlamps, whilst Seamus and Sophie play in the woods, unbothered by the dark. When they have enjoyed themselves for a while, they will return, hungry for their tea. Under these wintry conditions, with their early nights and boggy, uneven walking out in the fields, it is as safe an environment as I can give them.

I set the dogs loose and the two run merrily out into the trees. I hear them crashing around in the undergrowth for a while then the noise subsides into the distance and is drowned out by the swishing of branches in the cold wind.

I give it twenty minutes or so, walking to and fro along the pathways, back and forth from the car park, moving briskly to stay warm. Then I call the dogs. Seamus appears quickly enough, bounding out of the brambles, panting and happy, but there is no sign of Sophie.

I do not worry. This is hardly unusual. Shouting again for Sophie, I encourage Seamus to run around a bit more, but keep him close by for when his companion reappears.

Ten minutes go by, then twenty minutes. There is still no sign of Sophie. When an hour has passed, I am beginning to worry. I call Garry. "Got a favour to ask. I'm in Spring Woods and Sophie hasn't come back. Could you drive round the lanes at the back and see if she has managed to lose herself. That way I can wait here in the carpark for her."

Garry doesn't hesitate. "Of course I will. I'll set off now". Twenty minutes or so later, he pulls into the car park. "I've driven all through Back Lane and round there. No sign of her?"

I shake my head. I am really beginning to fear for my crazy little girl.

"I'll set off and have another look." he says. "And I'll see if she's turned up at home. How long has it been since you saw her?"

"About an hour and a half now."

Garry nods, positively. "Yeah, she could easily have got home by now, your place or mine. I'll go and check."

I wait another half hour. It is cold and dark. I am numb with chill and I need to eat. I try to call Garry, first his home number, then his mobile. No reply.

I drive home, intending to grab a sandwich, fill a flask and then drive out again to look for Sophie. As I turn the key to my front door, I can hear the phone ringing.

I dash to pick it up. "Hello."

A man's voice. "Hello. Er…. I'm calling about a dog. Is Sophie yours?"

Relief washes over me. She's been found! "Yes, she's mine. Have you got her? I'll come and get her."

The voice hesitates. "Well, yes, I've got her. But I'm afraid she's been run over."

I swallow, frozen for a moment. Is this the moment that I have always known was going to come to Sophie? My mad little dog. "Is she badly hurt?"

"I'm sorry, but she's dead. I'm so sorry."

I well up and must force out my words. This man, this stranger, is trying to help me. "Thank you for calling. I'll come and get her. Where are you?"

He tries to give me directions, but I am dazed and confused and I cannot think straight to understand him clearly. Quickly he asks "Where are you? Where do you live? I'll bring her to you."

I give him my address and, crying, call Garry's mobile number again. I still can't get a reply. I wait in my kitchen.

It is cold. I am cold, and I think that I should have a hot drink. I put on the kettle, but when it boils, find that I do not want the coffee.

A quarter hour or so later, there is a knock at the door. A man stands there with a large cardboard box in his arms. Swallowing hard, I manage to invite him in. "Please, put her down there." He lays the box on the table, and there inside, laid on a blanket, apparently asleep, is Sophie. There is little visible sign of injury, but a trickle of blood runs from her nose, and when I feel her chest, there is no heartbeat. "What happened?"

"I'm sorry. I don't know. I was driving past on the dual carriageway and she was lying by the side of the road. I just picked her up and rang your number from the tag."

I blink. "You found her by the side of the road? Someone had hit her and just left her there?" He shuffles awkwardly, clearly unwilling to say anything more upsetting. I try to be polite. "Thanks for taking the trouble you have. Would you like a cup of tea?"

He shakes his head. "No, er, no. Thanks anyway. I don't think you really want me here do you?" I don't like to agree with him. "It's okay. I'll show myself out."

He closes the door, pulling it quietly shut behind him, leaving me alone with my dead little girl.

I try Garry's number again. This time he answers.

"Sorry, just had to dash for the phone. I was out shouting for her." He sounds breathless. "Have you found her yet?"

"Garry, I'm at home. I had a phone call from someone to tell me he'd found her. She's been run over."

"Christ! How bad is it? Have you called the vet?"

I interrupt him. "Garry, I'm sorry. She's been killed. The man who found her, he's brought her over."

There is silence for a moment, then "I'm coming over."

Garry walks in less than five minutes later, eyes streaming. "What happened?" Then he falls silent as he sees Sophie. There is nothing either of us can say.

Neither of us wants to eat or drink. It is too dark to bury her. Eventually Garry leaves and goes home.

Seamus stands in the kitchen with me. He looks sad and neglected. No one has spoken to him or made a fuss of him for some time. What has he done wrong? He stands, head hanging, tail low. I feel I must try to explain to him.

Lifting the box down to the floor, I show him Sophie's body. Seamus does not understand. He looks down at his playmate, ears pricked and tail slightly wagging, then paws at her. Why will Sophie not get up and play?

I do not want to explain to Seamus what death is. I lift Sophie back up onto the table. The next day, Garry and I bury her together in his garden and plant crocuses on her grave.

Shannon

After the death of Sophie, I am in shock. Never have I failed a dog before. I keenly feel the guilt of her death, but do not know how I could have prevented it. Sophie's mad ways were always going to doom her to disaster. And as before, it is important to me that Seamus has a friend.

Garry is distraught over Sophie's death. If Seamus is 'my' dog, then Sophie was his. Garry really loved Sophie and she in turn, had simply worshipped him. This time, I am getting a dog for Seamus and Garry both. If I can, I want to find a dog who physically resembles Sophie. This is not going to be easy with Sophie's unusual appearance. Her particular mongrel mix had produced film star looks, and I have never seen another dog quite like her.

At the rescue centre they are sympathetic. Sophie had been a known 'problem dog', ruined by previous owners. I had done well by her to keep her alive as long as I did. This helps me feel a little better, but only a little.

In the kennels I have barely started searching, when I am attracted to one of the inmates. It is not immediately obvious just what she looks like, lying in her basket at the back of the run, a curled up ball of misery. Everything about her looks defeated, no spirit left.

She gazes blankly at the wall and only responds to my presence when I speak to her through the bars. I have never seen a dog cringe whilst laid down before, but this one manages it.

She looks vaguely white with brownish patches, some kind of collie mix, and she is filthy. Her fur is matted and the look in her eyes is beyond desperation.

There is no hope there. I try to talk to her, the usual nonsense I spout when talking to a strange dog, "C'mon, nice girl. Nice girlie......" She just curls up tighter and looks away.

I read her card. She is called 'Poppy' and has only just come into the shelter. Jean comes by. "You interested in this one Chris?"

"Mmm. Could be. What do you know about her?"

Jean pauses, hesitating before she speaks. "Umm... how interested are you? There's a bit of a story and it needs to be confidential."

This takes me aback. Normally the shelter staff are only too willing to tell all they know. "Well she's caught my eye. I'm looking for a friend for Seamus. And if I don't take her, I promise my lips are sealed."

"Okay." Jean stares up at the ceiling, clearly choosing her words. "You know that thing that's being going on in the tabloid papers, with the naming and shaming on paedophiles...?"

"Mmm... Yes." I begin to see where this is going.

"Well her owner was one who was named. The neighbours caught on, and they chased him out of the country, more or less just before the police got there apparently. He'd cleared off and left the dog behind. The police brought her to us. We are told that he was using her as a lure for kids."

I look down at the dog in the basket. Behind the bewilderment, the fear and the misery, there is a potentially beautiful dog there. She looks, perhaps, quite young. I can see how children might have been attracted to her.

"Anything else you know about her?"

"The vet thinks she's about two. She's not spayed and she only came in yesterday so we've not had chance to do it yet. She'll be getting her jabs over the next few days. And er... we're kind of assuming that she's good with kids."

"Alright. Let's try taking her for a walk."

On a lead, Poppy is timid in the extreme, crashing to the ground anytime something strange comes by; a car, another dog.

She spooks like a thoroughbred at passing shadows.

Painfully thin, she totters as she walks and has no muscle tone to speak of.

Has she been kept locked up all her life? No exercise at all? I take it very easy walking her, only going a few hundred yards and then turning back.

I discover that at the sound of her name, Poppy hits the deck, cowering, her eyes rolling. 'Poppy' is a word that frightens her in the extreme. Whatever her previous owner was guilty of with children, the condition and the state of mind of his dog tells me most of what I want to know about him.

Poppy is a problem dog, but this time I am taking it on board that she is a problem dog. There will not be a repeat of the Sophie catastrophe. Back at the shelter, I see no reason to hesitate. "Put my name down for her. The best thing for her, is to get her into a normal home as quickly as we can. And another thing, she's frightened of her own name. Next time I visit, I'll have a new name for her."

Jean smiles. "That's great. You know the routine. I know it's you, but two more visits and then she's yours."

"Don't worry. I'll be back."

A few days later I have the vaccinated and chipped dog previously known as Poppy, on a lead, walking her to my car. Taking it as easy as I can with her, I squat down to stroke 'Shannon'.

"Now then Shannon. Let's go home. I've got a friend waiting to meet you." I stroke her for a minute or so, over her rump, back and shoulders, but not going too near her face. Touching a face is as personal for dogs as it is for humans. After a little while, she relaxes a bit and her eyes soften.

Opening the car door to see if she will get in willingly, she does so, climbing obediently onto the passenger seat.

Driving home, I go through my usual patter of doggie nonsense, constantly repeating Shannon's new name. Pulling up to the cottage, I turn to her and for the first time she looks me in the eye

"Good girl Shannon." I say, and slowly reach to stroke the side of her face, giving her the opportunity to reject the caress if she wishes to do so. She accepts the touch, but is not thrilled by it, so I withdraw.

I hope that she will start to settle in quickly. For a start, she really does stink and I want her to start cleaning herself up. I do not want to give her a bath; that would be entirely too much for her in her present state of mind. In fact, I never bathe a new dog if I can avoid it. Yes, they smell terrible when they come out of the shelters, but they will start to groom themselves soon enough. It is one of the first signs in rescue dogs that they feel life is looking up.

"Now then Shannon." I say. "Let's go and meet Seamus."

As I step out of the car I hear Seamus' chaotic doggy welcome from behind the door. Shannon's ears prick and she cocks her head at the noise.

I open the door and Shannon freezes. However, she does not appear nervous or frightened. Her ears are high and her eyes brighten. Seamus stands inside the kitchen, looking startled. He is also stood, frozen to the spot, one front paw slightly lifted and again ears up, eyes sparkling. Then the spell breaks and Seamus pokes his nose forward, tail up and waggy.

The tail is a little stiff; a 'This is my house.' tail, but it is still a welcoming tail. I encourage Shannon inside, walking ahead to lead her. "Come on girlie. Seamus wants to meet Shannon."

Closing the kitchen door and now safely inside, I take the lead off Shannon. It is my experience that dogs do better if they feel they control their own destinies (who doesn't?), so I always take leads off whenever possible.

Shannon and Seamus introduce themselves to each other in the usual canine fashion. Noses meet and bums are inspected. It is going well. I can see they like each other.

I have often wondered, and never had a satisfactory answer, as to how it is that dogs who are complete strangers know that they don't like each other from a hundred yards away? And other times they know that they do like each other from a hundred yards away; but in this case, nose to rump, both of them, Seamus and Shannon definitely like each other.

Where have Shannon's nerves gone? She seems completely happy and relaxed. It looks very much as though my Seamus-Shannon planned friendship is going to be a hit. Suddenly Seamus goes into 'Romp' mode. He yips and jumps, and Shannon responds. Seamus starts playing, paws up and outstretched in a play bow, then starts whirling gyroscopically around in silly circles. And Shannon joins in. I cannot believe it. Shannon is transformed. She is wobbly and ungraceful with her appalling muscle tone, but the will to play is there.

My kitchen is a tight fit for two dogs in silly mood so I lead them through to the back garden to complete their introductions, abandoning any idea of standing over them to ensure no problems. The two dogs are an instant hit with each other and there is little I can contribute to the situation. I leave them to it. This is the best possible therapy for Shannon coming out of her terrible previous life.

Later on I take them out for a walk, to the same field where I had first let Seamus off the lead. I do not believe that Shannon will try to jump walls as Sophie did, so it is a good safe environment for that first 'out in the big wide world' experience. And it is just as successful with Shannon as it was for Seamus.

The two dogs simply continue their romping and running, but with more room to do it in. Seamus runs ahead, looking back with a 'Catch me if you can.' expression, and Shannon follows, lolloping clumsily after him.

For all her joy, Shannon's poor physical condition is obvious. She is more than willing to run and chase, but her muscles are so underdeveloped. On her hindquarters, under horrible dirty fur, where there should be a smooth convex curve of thigh muscle, it is actually concave.

When I get a rear view of her running, she flounders and lurches from side to side, staggering like a drunk. Her leg muscles are almost atrophied. She is not in fact, properly dog-shaped.

I will never know of course, but I strongly suspect that her previous owner, when not using her for his own purposes, has simply kept her locked up and unexercised.

Shannon has never had the opportunity to build up a proper physique. But there can be no better cure for her than what Seamus is now providing.

She tires quickly. After only five minutes of cavorting enthusiasm, she flags and drops to a walk. I like to end on a high note so I pop them both back on their leads and walk them home, where Seamus makes himself comfortable on the sofa and Shannon joins him. They drop off to sleep together.

An hour or so later, Shannon wakes and starts cleaning herself. I give a silent 'Hallelujah'. Things are going very well indeed, far better than I had expected after the trauma of Sophie. When I go to bed, Seamus takes his usual spot by my feet and Shannon joins him.

The following morning, I wake to the sound of licking. Through sleepy eyes, I see a transformed dog. Shannon has cleaned herself overnight and her previously matted, stinking fur is now soft and silky, gleaming in the sunlight streaming through the panes. She has changed from mucky white and 'orrible brown to an almost pearly white with very beautiful black and tan markings. She has not quite managed to clean up her face, but since Seamus is licking her around the mouth, eyes and ears, it will not be long before this is sorted out too.

Things continue to go well over the next few days. So as not to overtax Shannon's limited physical resources, I take the pair for a lot of short walks with Shannon on the lead. We wander through the village where she is introduced to the other dogs in the area.

This always involves a protracted discussion with the owners, exchange of opinions, anecdotes and advice.

At first, Shannon is very nervous of meeting strange men, backing away and showing her teeth, but over time she improves. After a time, I notice a pattern. She is particular nervous of men in jackets and caps. I feel I could give the police an identikit description of her previous owner. Rescue dogs know that there are monsters in the world, and some of them look like real people.

One small problem begins to rear its head. Seamus is very protective of Shannon. 'Proprietorial' is perhaps a better word. She is 'his' and Seamus protects his rights. Bitches are no problem. They are permitted contact and even friendship, with Shannon. Dogs are altogether different. Any male dog approaching Shannon is supervised by Seamus, head up, chest out and tail up straight. He hovers over the meeting, issuing low rumbling growls and threats of mayhem. It does not help that Shannon loves meeting other dogs and welcomes them all. Not to put too fine a point on it, she is a right little tart, and starts fawning and rolling on her back if she likes the look of the dog approaching her. There is no 'I am submissive to you.' feel about this, more a mood of 'Take me Sir Jasper.'

This does not sit well with Seamus. He takes to 'marking' Shannon as his. For a few weeks Shannon's beautiful white fur bears yellow stripes where Seamus pees his ownership stamp on her. I try to prevent this 'Kilroy was here.' approach to Seamus' graffiti-ing of Shannon but to no avail. If I wash her down, Seamus firmly replaces his mark on her.

I can only hope that as time goes by, the habit will run its course. Fortunately, it does.

After a few months together, I think it finally dawns on Seamus that no matter how much Shannon frolics with other dogs outside the house, she comes home with him. I suppose it is the canine equivalent of 'You can look at any menu you want, so long as you eat at home.'

If there was ever True Love between dogs, it is between Seamus and Shannon.

As time goes on and other dogs join us, the group functions beautifully as a pack, but there is always something special between Seamus and Shannon. Watching them together is a joy. They play together, walk and run together and often just sit together.

The bond between them is remarkable and is lifelong. In the end, they die within a couple of months of each other, with Seamus extremely elderly at the age of seventeen.

Now however, they are young and full of the joys of life and, so far as I can express it in human terms, they are in love with each other. And Shannon is unspayed.

Interlude – Paddy and Sadie

I know that I should get Shannon neutered as soon as possible. She is a gorgeous dog, and a house full of 'little Shannons' is an appealing idea, but it is simply not fair to randomly produce puppies.

When I was a child, one of our dogs was 'Sadie', a German shepherd who had belonged to my grandfather, then foreman at the local waterworks. She had been trained as a guard dog for the site and was very much 'his' dog. However, when he retired, he lost the house that went with the job; an on-site bungalow, set in twenty or thirty acres, and had to go into a flat. There was nowhere in such a place for a dog like Sadie, trained to be aggressive to strangers, and so on my grandfather's retirement, Sadie came to live with us.

At the time we lived in a bungalow in a small village near Selby in Yorkshire and had a huge garden. There was plenty of room for all of us, 'us' being myself and my sister, my mother and father, half a dozen ducks, about fifty rabbits, a bad tempered parrot, a farm cat we never saw and our dog, Paddy.

Paddy was the dog I grew up with. He was my combined best friend, cohort in crime, and guardian. If I wanted to go out, and this was in the days when children were allowed, almost expected, to roam, it would be "Mum can I go out?"

"Yes, take Paddy with you."

I cannot remember a time that was 'Before Paddy' but I do remember coming home with him as a puppy, in the back of the car, wrapped in a towel on my Mum's knee. She could hold him in her cupped hands.

Paddy grew up into an amazing dog. A collie cross Labrador, he had the steady reliability of the Labrador, the quick wittedness of the collie, the high intelligence of both breeds, and the mind of a criminal genius.

He was completely self-willed. If he did as you asked him, it was because he damn well felt like it. But he was loving, adventurous and exciting to be with. He always wanted to be part of anything the family was doing.

If we went camping, Mum, Dad, my sister and I, were all packed in with tents, camp stoves, ground sheets and other camping paraphernalia, into a Reliant Robin. Paddy would be crammed in with us, in his assigned square foot of space by the back window, and willing to suffer *anything* rather than be left behind.

If we went out for the day for a picnic, say to Roundhay Park in Leeds, Paddy would be there with us, to charge into the lake after the ducks, chase them off and then come out to shake himself dry over all the other picnickers (Mum: "Come on kids. Pack up. We're going. Be casual. He's nothing to do with us.").

I grew up in Yorkshire in a village surrounded by countryside, and would just set off and go. Paddy would accompany me, and together we would explore, play hide and seek, go scrumping for apples, and hunt for caterpillars and frogspawn.

Paddy loved frogspawn. There was a bucket of it sat by the front door one day, waiting to go into its tank, so that we could all watch the tadpoles hatch (every year, we did this, releasing them back into the pond when they started to grow legs – how many children do it now I wonder?). Paddy drank the lot, then sat on the doorstep burping for the next hour.

Paddy was constantly in trouble with someone. Accompanying my mother to the village butchers one day, he took a fancy to a pig's trotter he saw in the shop and helped himself. This would have been bad enough, but the trotter was, at the time, still attached, by a bit of skin, to the rest of the pig hanging from a ceiling hook.

A quick yank from Paddy and the trotter came loose, but everything else came crashing down too. Naturally uproar resulted. Paddy however, did not hang around to face the consequences of his actions, instead he legged it away through the village with his ill-gotten gains.

Another time, he returned home with a chicken, oven ready. My mother quickly hid the evidence, before anyone else saw it. She said afterwards that it went into the rubbish bin, but I'm sure there was roast chicken for lunch the following day.

Paddy disliked strange men, men in uniform in particular. As far as he was concerned, these uninvited strangers turned up at his house and it was his job to send them packing. Postman were seen off with baying and a gnashing of teeth behind the letter box. Woe betide the Salvation Army officer who knocked at the door shaking a tin. Even the milkman, in his neat white tunic, was persona non grata to Paddy. But Paddy's Nemesis was 'Gas Meter Man'.

This unfortunate individual arrived at our door every few weeks, and came into the house to empty the gas meter. Paddy was beside himself at this behaviour and had to be tied up so that 'GMM' could do his job and leave the house with all his fingers. He would calmly empty the gas meter, the sound of rattling coins drowned out by the canine uproar coming from the back room.

After a couple of visits, Paddy came to know the sound of GMM's van engine, and would be waiting for him behind the door as he was let in. GMM responded by coming to the back door on his next visit.

A kind of arms war broke out, with GMM and Paddy each trying to outguess the other; GMM trying to decide between doors and Paddy dashing around inside the house, darting to and fro, between the two doors, trying to get to the right door in time.

But Paddy had a heroic side too. He was brave, dependable and utterly, utterly loyal.

Once, taking a walk as a family through the fields, some bullocks decided to chase us. They didn't mean any harm I'm sure, but bullocks are a bit on the large side to play with, and given that I was perhaps six years old, and my sister four, we had to get out of the way, and fast. To this day I can remember Paddy holding the entire herd at bay, barking and snarling whilst my father threw me and my sister over the fence. It was into a patch of nettles unfortunately, but you don't make an omelette without breaking eggs. Paddy was tossed over the fence last before Dad did a Mexican roll over the fence. Perhaps five years old,

Always a wanderer, I was out roaming once, perhaps five years old, Paddy with me as usual. We came to 'The Horse Field' where there were a couple of horses grazing. The horses were normally no problem at all, but on this occasion, one of the mares had just had a foal. Being that age, I thought the foal was the most wonderful thing ever and went straight up to it to stroke it. The mare did not like this at all and came charging in to attack, teeth bared, screaming fury at me. Paddy placed himself between me and the horse, and again, held her at bay whilst I made my escape over the stile.

It is worth commenting perhaps, in these days when children are kept in because it is 'dangerous' out there, risking the certainty of lifelong obesity, instead of the small chance of running into trouble whilst growing up and learning to deal with life, that while a dog may be 'just an animal', it is an animal with an adult mind.

Dogs understand that children are 'people puppies'. They ken what is happening, and their point of view is one of 'Us and Them'. I am quite sure my mother did not know where I was a lot of the time; these days I would probably have been taken into care. However, she did know that I had a proven guardian and, when called upon, he came ready, armed and dangerous.

Paddy's weakness, his 'fix' as it were, was the Ladies. If there was a bitch in season within ten miles, Paddy would respond to the call.

This was in the days before dogs were routinely neutered and Paddy was 'fully equipped' and poised for action. The first indication that there was an available lady in the area was that Paddy would vanish, and his vanishing would be for anything up to two weeks; staking out 'The Site' and waiting for his 'Opportunity'.

I have no idea how many times my mother was called out to a local pound, police station or simply the home of some outraged owner. Neither do I know how many terminations she paid for.

I do know that Paddy fathered the most enormous number of puppies. Right through my early life, if I saw a dog with a vaguely collie/Labrador look, a certain set about the body and a glint of cunning in its eyes, I could be pretty certain that I knew who 'Dad' or 'Grandad' was.

I recall being with my mother when she was chatting in the street with the lady from 'The Posh House' in the village, Mrs Barker.

Mrs Barker was also 'posh' and she spoke differently to everyone else I knew. Looking back, I suspect that she hailed from Surrey or similar, but at the time I just knew that she was posh. And she had a 'posh dog' too. All the other dogs in the village were rather rough and ready types, either farm dogs, game and shooting dogs or other workers. But 'Jemima' was a pedigree and obviously so. A King Charles spaniel, she was never out without her pretty pink collar and lead. Her collar had sparkly bits on it and Mrs Barker treasured Jemima above rubies.

The conversation between my mother and Mrs Barker was interrupted by some obvious kafuffle just down the road. A small crowd parted, to reveal Jemima and Paddy in full conjugation in the middle of the pavement, both wearing large smiles and an air of intense concentration. Mrs Barker's cry of "Jemima! Oh my Jemima……!!!!" as she ran down the road to interrupt proceedings, carried a haunted tone. Caught in flagrante as it were, and both thoroughly enjoying themselves, Paddy and Jemima were in no mood to stop, and when Mrs Barker tried to separate them, they had already tied.

So that was another trip to the vet for one of Paddy's widespread harem.

Paddy would do almost anything to get out when The Call came. No amount of refusal, discipline or containment could hold him.

For a given Opportunity, he would have a window of a week or so in which to make his break, and in that length of time he always found a way to escape. He would go over the fence, or he would dash between your legs as you opened the door. One time, we came back to a house empty of Paddy when we knew that all the doors had been closed as we left. The mystery was solved the following day, with the discovery of some of the garden rose bushes, directly below the bedroom window, almost completely flattened. Paddy had made his escape through the top, small opening light of the upstairs bedroom window. The roses bushes had broken his fall, but it must have been a very spiky landing.

He never changed. Even when he was very, very old he would still leave when he decided to. The only thing that altered was the length of the trips. As a young dog he would disappear for two or even three weeks. As he grew older this dropped to a few days, then a day and then a couple of hours.

He was canny about coming back too. Once, when I was quite small, Paddy's romantic tours kept him away for a fortnight. My mother had worried about him that time, because it was the dead of winter and very, very cold. One night, the lament of a blizzard outside, we were all woken up by the sound of howling. Paddy had returned and he wanted in. And he wanted in *now*.

Through my bedroom wall, voices could be heard. "Bob, the dog's back".

A grunt.

"Bob, Paddy's back. He wants to come in."

Another grunt.

"It's freezing out there, Bob. We've got to let him in."

There were a few moments of silence, then a crash, as my parents' bedroom door was flung back on its hinges. A stomping noise of feet on wooden stairs and another crash as the outside door was opened, followed by a yelp as Paddy went into the kitchen on the end of my father's foot.

This was in the days before central heating. The old farmhouse we lived in, with its stone flag floors and single lightbulb rooms was very cold. Most activity in winter took place in the kitchen, where an old black range was constantly lit, only being damped down at night so as to spring back into life in the morning.

That particular morning, as we all moved down into the kitchen, we learned how Paddy had been keeping warm the past couple of weeks; bedding down in a manure heap. Overnight he had thawed himself through by leaning against the range. The spot where he had been leaning was clearly visible as an almost cartoon style, dog shaped cut-out on the range, made of, let's be polite and call it pig-muck, stoved on to the metalwork.

Paddy himself, had also dried out nicely overnight, and was now completely encrusted in a baked-on layer of said muck, desiccated and hardened to the consistency of Kevlar.

The stench was unbelievable. Had he chosen the heap behind a stable it would not have been bad enough. Or even if it been a cowshed it would have been too bad, but pig muck it was and the stink it produced was just astonishing.

Despite the freezing conditions, all the doors and windows had to be flung wide. The range had to be wire-brushed clean and Paddy was taken out, chained with his collar two inches from a drainpipe, and hosed down. The hose water was of course also freezing cold and set to ice as it ran over the path into our little front garden. Judging by the colour of the water though, the garden was going to be the most fertile spot in the village come Spring.

I grew into a teenager, but Paddy was essentially unchanged. He would do his disappearing act, vanish for several days, and then, as I was walking back from school, a walk of perhaps a mile, I would suddenly find that Paddy had dropped into heel with me and was accompanying me home. I was so accustomed to the click of dog claws behind me that usually I would not notice him until say, my sister, pointed out to me that he had appeared.

When Sadie came to live with us, the situation was complicated. She was already quite old by the time we got her, perhaps ten, and vet said she was too old to be spayed. So, when she came into season, all that could be done was to try to separate her from Paddy.

This was problematic. Anyone who doubts that bitches want sex as badly as dogs might note that that the first time she came into season with us, Sadie and Paddy were kennelled (each had a giant beer barrel, a flap of carpet on the opening and rugs inside; great kennels and great kids' dens) and chained, out of range of each other, in the back garden. Sadie wrenched her chain free. This resulted in nine puppies.

The second time, Sadie was on a more secure chain and Paddy managed to slip his collar. This time it was eleven puppies.

The third time, Sadie was locked up in the pre-fab concrete garage at the bottom of the garden. Her response was to take the door apart, complete with door frame, wrenching the whole lot free of the main building. Thirteen puppies resulted.

Sadie was pregnant again when the vet declared that she was simply too old to take any more of this and she had to be put to sleep.

Shannon and Seamus

So, it is bearing Sadie's history in mind that, having had Shannon in the house for two weeks, she comes into season. At the shelter, I have been told that they do not think her heat is due for several months. Perhaps the change in her circumstances has triggered something in her. Perhaps it is relief of stress. Perhaps it is Seamus' presence. At any rate, her season comes like a bolt out of the blue.

Seamus has at this point, been neutered several months before. In theory he should not be interested in Shannon's season. People may tell you this. I can tell you it is Utter Rubbish.

As Shannon comes into season, Seamus thinks all his birthdays have come at once. His princess, his prize possession, his pearl.... his Shannon, suddenly takes on a completely new level of delight and attraction. However, it becomes rapidly clear that Seamus, for all his keen interest, has never 'had' a bitch before.

Shannon is all co-operation. She presents herself to Seamus, almost prostrating herself before him. She tries to give him hints, advice, like shoving her rear end in his face.

I let all this continue, because, remembering Sadie and her appetites, I want to keep Shannon occupied with the 'safe sex' option. If she stays with Seamus, there can be no puppies. But can Seamus pull it off?

Yes, he can.

There is about a day and a half of what I can only describe as adolescent fumbling. There are probably specialist web-sites handling some of the things Seamus tries to do to Shannon; in her ear, at her chest, in her eye, then he gets it.

I am in the kitchen, half listening to the scrabbling, jumping and thumping sounds from the lounge indicating that Seamus and Shannon are having another go at getting it together, when suddenly I hear a yelp, followed by hysterical whining. Dashing through, I find that the two have tied.

Shannon is in raptures, gazing skyward with a look of delight, but Seamus clearly does not know what is happening and is panicking. He is trying to extract himself and, worrying that he is going to hurt himself, I kneel down, wrapping my arms around them both, trying to hold Seamus still, so that nature can take its course. Speaking softly to him, I mentally reflect that I never expected to have to nursemaid a dog through his loss of virginity.

Feeling rather ridiculous I hold them together for a couple of minutes until Seamus calms down. Once I feel he has settled, I let go and stand back. Calmer now, Seamus quickly decides that this is all pretty good stuff and begins to look a lot more enthusiastic, until Shannon, rather heartlessly I feel, decides that she is calling time and pulls free.

Seamus yelps loudly and starts to lick the sore bits. Shannon goes into an ecstasy of leaping, running and swirling round in circles, barking all the time as she does so. Seamus, his first aid administered, sits and looks at her, and me, with a quizzical expression. "So that's what it's all about is it?"

After this, there is no holding them. For most of a week, I have two humping dogs in the house, joyously expressing themselves wherever and whenever, takes their fancy; the lounge, the kitchen, the garden. I cannot move in the house without falling over them. My route to the bathroom is blocked, because they are half way up the stairs. I have a joiner in, my long-time friend Jeff, working on my built in wardrobes (at long last!). He finds his work blocked by the ecstatic canines bonking in the bedroom.

I avoid going out with them more than necessary because I have noticed the arrival of another Shannon fan, one of the ugliest mutts I have ever seen, lurking around the house.

Remembering Paddy and his talents for achieving entry and exit in Will-o-the-Wisp secrecy, I keep the front door closed and the garden closely watched.

After a few days of course, Shannon's season passes and life returns to normal. Shannon is gratified, satisfied and pupless. Seamus meanwhile has learned some valuable life skills.

Minnie

If you have an addictive personality, do not start collecting rescue dogs. The 'Habit' is difficult to control. And do not visit rescue centres unless you intend to adopt. You will not be able to resist getting a 'Fix'.

Seamus and Shannon are doing famously. I am stunned by how well it is working out and not a little proud of the result I am getting from my doggy household. So, I decide it is time to pay a return visit to the rescue centre, to show them how well two of their previous guests are doing.

Jean is pleased to see them both, especially Seamus. Having been in the centre for so long, he had become a favourite with the kennel girls. They all want to make a fuss of him. Seamus is equally pleased to see them and jumps up to be hugged. Shannon is indifferent to it all. She was only there for a few days and I am not sure she even remembers being in the centre. But the girls are pleased to see her anyway, happy and healthy. I conclude the visit is a success.

"I'll take a look around while I'm here." I say, not really intending anything by it other than interest. Big mistake, as I realise when I step through the doors to the sheds.

Scanning the ranks of wagging, barking, whimpering, cowering, romping and jumping dogs, I know that one of them is going to be coming home with me.

How can it be otherwise? I have the space, the lifestyle and the budget to suit myself, and if I want a third dog, who is to gainsay me?

Wandering up and down the corridors, I am assailed by that same horrible smell; urine, faeces and scared dogs, all overlaid with disinfectant.

There is the usual collection of the cute, the afraid, the appealing and the ordinary. Dogs who will find a home quickly because they are young, healthy, cute and not too large. Dogs who will struggle to find a home because they are too old, or too ordinary looking, or because their card says that they are not to be homed near children or other animals.

Some may never be rehomed, because they cower at the back of the runs, refusing to connect with, or even acknowledge visitors. And there are the dogs who doomed to be destroyed, their card announcing that they have been assessed as too dangerous for rehoming, betrayed by the humankind they trusted.

Nothing changes.

I stop by a run whose occupant is a small sheltie type. She looks elderly; small and barrel bodied, but quite charming. Crouching down to the mesh, she toddles up to me, wheezing slightly but friendly and approachable. She sits next to me, panting, but tries to poke her nose though to me.

Reading her card, I make out her name, Muffin, but I cannot make a lot of sense of the rest of it. There are so many crossings out, scribbles and extra notes, that the whole thing is unreadable. I go to the desk and ask Jean about her.

"Oh that one." she says. "She needs re-homing fast or she's going to be put down in seven days."

Shock! "What's the problem? She seems like a sweet little thing."

"She's been in and out of several homes. Each time, they bring her back because she can't get on with other animals. Gets quite aggressive apparently. The instructions are that she's not to be rehomed where there are any other animals...."

She purses her lips, considering the options. "You've got, what, two other dogs now? Still, you're experienced, and frankly her chances of finding someone else now that the clock's ticking...."

"But she's okay with people? Children?"

"Oh yes. Fine in that respect. Maybe that the problem? She's possessive perhaps? Wants all the attention?"

What can I do? Leave this friendly little old age pensioner to be destroyed in only a few days? I can take her home, try her out with the others. If it works, I can give her a retirement at least. If not, then she's no worse off.

"Sign me up." I say. "That will buy her a few days. And if you pop her on a lead, I'll take her for a walk and we'll get to know each other. Is there any chance of someone else taking one of the other dogs for a leg-stretch with us so I can see what the problem is?"

"Good idea." says Jean. "I'll find someone."

Muffin is brought out on a lead and handed over to me. One of the kennel girls, Suzy, comes out with another dog, a big placid Labrador. "This is Ben." she explains. "He's nice and bomb proof. Nothing bothers him. We thought it would be best to use a dog who isn't likely to react to her."

I nod. This seems sensible. I let Suzy walk out ahead of me with Ben, and I follow with Muffin.

The walk is calm enough just so long as Ben keeps his distance. Muffin completely ignores him. But if I draw closer to Suzy and Ben, or if they approach me and Muffin, a low growl emanates from Muffin, getting louder and more menacing over a few seconds. Then she turns and snaps at Ben, straining at her leash to reach him. This happens several times during the walk. Ben is underwhelmed by the threats being issued by the pint sized geriatric, and continues serenely with his stroll.

I return Muffin to Jean. "Okay. Let me think about how to deal with her. I'll definitely have her, but I'll take a few days over deciding the best way to do things."

At home, I ponder the problem of how to deal with a seriously antisocial dog, one who dislikes all other dogs.

I do not want to leave Muffin in the shelter, with only seven days' grace.

But how to integrate her into my household? Seamus and Shannon are such a perfect team. Is it fair to do anything that might disrupt their friendship?

Then I laugh inwardly. Nothing is going to separate Seamus and Shannon. Their love for each other is too great. Then I think of Fudge, and how she was when I first adopted her; a real Jekyll and Hyde. Brilliant with people, but totally unable to deal with other dogs, Fudge was almost completely unsocialised. She tried to kill a pup I had at the time (I rehomed the pup for her own safety) and would launch herself at any dog we passed.

I cured her habits by taking her to training classes, just basic training; sit, stay, come, recall and so on. I was not overly concerned about her training, although it was helpful. What I wanted was that she be thrown in at the deep end with a lot of other dogs. Fudge reacted badly at first. On her first evening at the classes, she had a panic attack and collapsed, so I took her to the edge of the hall and we sat on the floor together, watching the rest of the dogs with their owners, Fudge being hugged between my knees for a sense of security.

It worked. After a couple of months' attendance, Fudge was a different dog. She was never thrilled by the company of other dogs, but she learned to cope with it, and that made her a happier dog.

Her experience with Seamus was a case in point. She never liked Seamus, but having him there added years to her life. Dogs need each other as much as they need us.

I am decided. I will collect Muffin from the shelter and, as with Fudge, I will 'chuck her in at the deep end'. With her seven-day life expectancy, she has nothing to lose and it could be the making of her.

Also, I will change her name. A little rebranding may help her break with her past; whatever it is.

So Muffin, now known as Minnie, comes to Whinshill Cottage. I have told Seamus and Shannon before leaving that I will return with another dog. I am never sure how much of this they understand, but have acquired the opinion over the years, that dogs understand a lot more human language, and certainly body language, than they are given credit for.

Shannon in particular, I am realising, is super-bright. When I talk to her, she is listening; not just paying attention, but listening. Looking into her lovely amber eyes, I can see the wheels turning. However, I always chat with all my dogs. Sometimes it is just doggy-nonsense (Good Boy. What a Clever Girl), but a lot of the time I simply talk to them like another human. So now, even if Seamus and Shannon do not understand exactly what I have said to them, they know I have told them something. There is a new thing of some kind about to happen.

I enter the house with Minnie. Seamus and Shannon bounce over to investigate, and Minnie bristles, bottle brushing her fur, hedgehog style. She is much smaller than the other two though, and restrains any murderous impulses she might have. Her eyes roll a little, but she neither panics nor turns aggressive. It is a good start.

I keep Minnie on a lead for a few minutes whilst initial excitement wears off. Seamus tries to approach for a sniff but has his nose snapped at. With a 'Blow that!' air, he disappears off to the garden and Shannon follows. Taking Minnie off her lead, I let her potter about.

And so it continues. Minnie joins our household, but lives on the margins as it were. I quickly learn that it is not just dogs she keeps at a distance. Whilst friendly enough with me, she is nervous, unused to affection.

I do not know Minnie's background, but I can speculate. She dislikes other animals of all kinds, but does like people, sort of. She is will let me touch her, so long as the touch is not too personal. Coming to know each other over a few weeks, she shows all the signs of a dog who wants to be loved, but when I try to be close, she is almost schizophrenic.

Sitting next to her by the fire, she leans into me, and then away. If I caress or cuddle her, ever so gently, I hear her groan of pleasure, but she is trembling. Minnie wants to be loved. But love and close contact are scary.

I do not believe that Minnie has ever been given the affection she should have had, and certainly not physical affection, which is all-important to a dog.

I come to think that Minnie has perhaps been owned by a single person, who, while not showing her outright cruelty, has not offered her the bond that should be between dog and human. And maybe there were no other animals in her life, other dogs or cats even, who might instead have offered her affection.

Over weeks I try to acclimatise Minnie to emotion; kindness, closeness. If I pass her, I give her a scratchy ear, or a soft rub on the face. She responds with her strange mix of craving and fear

It has been perhaps two months since Minnie came to me. Sitting on the floor, I am leaning back against the settee, watching TV. Seamus is lying on the sofa behind me, blissfully upside down, legs in the air, doing his 'dead bluebottle' impression.

Minnie approaches me, submissive, head down, almost belly-crawling. She slides towards me, and for the first time, slips her head under my hand, wanting to be loved, asking for a caress.

Of course, I stroke her softly, rubbing her head, gently scratching her chin and ears, giving her the love and the closeness that she wants. I talk to her gently, telling her she is a Good Girl, and, as I look into her face, one of those 'Eureka!' moments happens, that are so rewarding with rescue dogs.

I see the scales drop from Minnie's eyes. It is alright to ask for affection. It is allowed to ask for hugs.

This moment marks a transition for Minnie. From here on, whilst she is never a perfectly behaved pooch, her progress is ever upward. I see her developing understanding of being part of a group, of belonging. This is the start of Minnie's new life.

Even after her Paulian moment of discovery, Minnie's body language can be a little strange. She never quite learns to behave in standard doggy fashion and it is only because I come to know her idiosyncrasies, that I know how well she is progressing.

I drive to Harrogate to pick up my sister, Carol, as she is coming to stay with me for a few days, taking the three dogs with me for the journey. They enjoy stopping off at a number of the places en-route. On the way there we call in for a walk by the canal through Skipton. On the way back we stop off at Pendle Hill for a walk down a track. I open the back of the car and the three leap exultantly out, haring off over the moor

Carol has come sensibly dressed and is wearing trainers. As she picks her way past the puddles and through the mire she comments. "Bloody typical of a stay with you. I've not been here five minutes and I'm already knee-deep in mud."

My sister knows me well. The first time she visited me at Whinshill Cottage was for my first Christmas there. At the time my hospitality consisted of her sleeping on a blow-up mattress in my unrenovated loft, just by a huge gap in the floor where my replacement staircase was to fit, once funds allowed. Her comment then, was that she felt like a Victorian scullery maid.

Carol also loves dogs and is much taken by the fluffy, barrel shaped Minnie. She finds a toy and starts to play tug-o-war with Minnie, then drops it in alarm at Minnie's ferocious growling as she tosses her head from side to side, shaking the toy like a rat. I reassure Carol.

"That's just how Minnie talks. She's enjoying herself. It's quite safe."

This is borne out by Minnie's pushing the toy back into Carol's hand, in an attempt to restart the game. This time Carol carries on tug-o-warring regardless of the alarming noises emanating from Minnie and the two have a fine old time, becoming good friends.

Although Minnie is female, Seamus never displays any interest in her, the way he does with Shannon. Of course, Minnie is spayed whereas Shannon was not when she arrived. But I think that it is more than that. Shannon is a natural femme fatale whereas Minnie is the spinster aunt. She is always welcome, and is part of the family, but if you look for her at the party, she will be sat at the edge of the dancefloor, or in the kitchen serving lemonade. However, she has found her place, and is happy.

Duncan

Life settles for a while, my canine triad and I, living in a sort of domestic bliss.

I am visiting my friend Tessa one evening when she pipes up. "Oh I've got something for you. I thought it was your kind of thing."

Tessa produces a local newspaper, riffling through it until she finds the page she is looking for. A dog's face looks out at me from the page; young, almost a puppy, vaguely foxy looking, cute as they come and quite pathetic.

The headline reads 'Can you help? Duncan is in urgent need of an operation. We need to raise £600.' It goes on to say that Duncan, found as a stray, has been run over and needs to have a leg amputated.

I look at Tessa. She looks back. "Well? I know you like that kind of thing. I thought you might want to donate."

"Of course I'll give them something. I'll call them in the morning."

The following morning, I ring the number. "You have a little dog in the paper. He needs donations for his operation?"

"Oh yes, Duncan. Yes, we do. Actually, he's already had the operation. We have an agreement with the vet. He does the work and he's not in too much of a hurry to be paid. But we do need to raise the money to pay him sometime."

"Yes that's a good arrangement. So how many offers of a home have you had for him? He looks really appealing in the paper." I have assumed that this little chap has them cueing up to adopt, with such good publicity for him and his adorable face. I am shocked at the reply.

"We haven't had any at all. We don't understand it. Usually we get a really good response to these adverts, but this time, you're the only person who has rung."

"No offers of a home for him?"

"No, none at all."

"And he's just had a leg amputated?"

"That's right. The day before yesterday. We castrated him at the same time."

I sigh to myself. What do you do? "How old is he?"

"The vet thinks about eight months. Might you be interested?"

I pause and hold my breath. I already have three dogs and a cat. And my little cottage is not getting any bigger. "Where are you? I'll come and take a look at him."

Later that afternoon, I visit the surgery. Duncan has been given the run of the place and is limping pathetically about, barely able to walk, but determined to follow the girls around. He is small, but not tiny, and is constructed on the theme of 'terrier'. He is a bit underweight, but was clearly at the head of the queue when they were handing out the ears; they are huge; upright and pointy, sitting atop an expressive face with brightly black, button eyes.

I learn that he had been 'playing with the traffic' when he was run over. A member of the public handed him to the police, who passed him to the dog warden. It is dog warden who has the arrangement with vet. I also learn that the dog warden and the vet work with the local animal rescue charities, and they have a deal with the local newspaper for a weekly column. Each week, a different charity takes its turn to advertise a needy case.

All of this has led of course, to my seeing the advert for this poor little chap, who in just a couple of days, has been lost/abandoned/thrown out, run over, had his leg amputated, along with his 'crown jewels' at the same time, and who is now homeless except for the kindness of strangers.

I watch Duncan hobbling around the room. I already have three other dogs. There is something indomitable about him. Still more or less a pup, but just past the 'cute puppy' stage (which is when a lot of dogs are abandoned or thrown on to the street), crippled and only just out of major surgery; nonetheless, he is wagging his tail.

He is not feeling sorry for himself. Quite the opposite, he is making the best of what he has. This one is a fighter and a trier.

Working his way around the three girls staffing the surgery, he goes to each in turn to have his ears scratched and to be told he is a Good Boy. My arrival simply means there is someone else there to tell him he is nice. I ask "Where did the name come from?"

'Duncan' is an unusual name for a dog to say the least. One of the girls shrugs. "Bill said he looks like a Duncan. It stuck." I look down at the face, dark round little eyes and oversized ears, gazing fixedly up at me. I have to agree. He does look like a Duncan.

I have never had a terrier before and have yet to learn of the 'Take on the World.' attitude of the type. All I can see is this pocket sized fighter, who despite everything thrown at him, is nonetheless refusing to stay down, and who is game for more. I've still got three other dogs.

I think about it. Shannon will not be a problem at all. She loves other dogs around her. Seamus? He is very possessive of Shannon in the presence of other male dogs, but Duncan is small, crippled and still basically a puppy. Seamus shouldn't have a problem with him either. Minnie? Well Minnie is making great progress with the other two. One more couldn't hurt. It will be good for Minnie to learn to cope with a bit more change in her life.

I reach my decision. "Well." I say. "He seems game. If he can get along with my other three, he can come home with me. When will you be able to release him?"

This time, to Duncan's carers, I am an unknown. I have never used this particular vet and neither have I met the dog warden. They insist on a home check. We arrange an appointment for the warden to visit and to bring Duncan along, on a provisional basis, to see how he and my Gang of Three react to each other.

I do not know what I expected from the dog warden. Some little chap in green overalls maybe, or perhaps a civil servant type in a suit. When I open my door, the man who greets me could have been found standing over the entrance of any ten clubs, bars and boozers you care to name. He is huge, well over six foot and built like a brick outhouse; he sports a skin-head haircut and tattoos up his arms. "Hi." he says, with a disarming smile. "I'm Bill. You're interested in Duncan?"

Bill is a very pleasant chap. He obviously takes his job seriously and asks all the usual questions you would expect for a home check. Seamus, Shannon and Minnie all introduce themselves, and then jump all over and around him, clearly healthy and happy. I can see him, upside down, filling in his forms, but I know he is going through the motions of ticking off the boxes on his list. It feels a little surreal. This enormous, macho looking man looks cut out for anything from the SAS to extreme sports to gang warfare. He just doesn't seem the type to be rehoming the lost and the lonely.

We agree that Duncan can try living with me and the Gang but that it is probably better if they all meet for the first time on neutral territory. I suggest a stretch of road I know, about half a mile away, open to walkers but private for cars, so there will be little or no traffic and the walking will be as easy as possible for Duncan.

We drive both cars to the road, mine containing my barking, rowdy gang, and Bill's transporting Duncan.

I release my three and then walk them a hundred yards or so just to burn off the initial excitement and de-gas some of their enthusiasm. "Okay Bill. Let's give it a try."

Bill lifts Duncan out of his car and very gently places him on the ground, supporting his weight for a moment or two extra while Duncan sorts out his legs and balance. Seamus, Shannon and Minnie all spot the newcomer and bound over; Seamus to the front in case anyone has the effrontery to make a move on Shannon, Minnie with her furry coat bristling, and Shannon lolloping over with her usual 'Hi Stranger.' charm.

Duncan goes into 'puppy mode'. He stands his ground but starts trying to lick the mouths of all the three at once. Probably this is the best thing he could do. A puppy is no threat to any of them. In fact, after a minute or so, it is all rather boring. The Three lose interest and rush off in search of other diversions.

"I'd call that a success." I comment. "Shall we try back at the house now?"

We drive back to the house, again with Duncan in Bill's car and the Gang in mine. Bill carries Duncan into the cottage.

"Just sit with him on your knee." I suggest. "That way he's with you, not me and if there are any problems, you have it under control. Use that chair." I point him at the seat normally not favoured by the other dogs. Bill sits down, Duncan cradled on his knee. The little dog looks a bit lost, sat on the vast lap.

The Three pile into the house with the usual hairy, enthusiastic bouncing and slobbering. They all slop down some water, check the food bowls to see if they have miraculously filled while we were out and then drop into their accustomed places in the lounge, Seamus and Shannon together on the settee and Minnie onto the big floor cushion which is supposedly mine. I put on the kettle. "Tea or coffee?"

"Tea please."

The Three all ignore Bill and Duncan. They have met on the walk. The little dog is pretty unimpressive. 'Been there. Done that.' their attitudes say.

Bill and I exchange looks. "Seems okay to me." I say.

"Mmm yes." he agrees. "Mind if I just take a look out back? I can see how these three are living, so it's only a formality, but I've got to be able to say that I saw your garden."

I wave him out through the back door. He carries Duncan with him and lets him hobble around the postage stamp sized lawn. "It's pretty small." he comments.

"So it is." I agree. "But a hundred yards away, I step into open fields where they can run off lead. There's ten acres of woodland up the track and Pendle Hill is a five-minute drive away. This lot get at least a couple of miles a day and usually more. At least, I do a couple of miles and they probably do ten or twenty. Weekends, they get more."

"Fair enough." he smiles, "But I don't think this little chap is going to be doing that much any time soon."

We sit outside, drinking tea and chatting. "So how did you become a dog warden?"

Bill gives an ironic smile. "I was looking for a change in lifestyle." he said. "It wasn't too good, my old life. I wanted some Soul Food."

"Yes? What were you doing in your previous life?"

"I was a money-lender."

৯৵

I have made preparations for Duncan's arrival. Conscious of his frail condition, the boisterousness of Seamus and Shannon, and the possibly toxic attentions of Minnie, I have set up a dog crate by the radiator. Inside is a nice cosy little bed with warm fleecy blankets. Even convalescing as he is, I think that Duncan will be toasty and comfortable in there.

He has a bowl of water and some dry food, so he should have all he needs. I sit Duncan on my knee for a while, but not for too long. I do not want any jealousy issues with the Three. Seamus and Shannon seem completely relaxed about the whole thing, whilst occasional rumblings can be heard coming from Minnie, but she is behaving herself.

Duncan is exhausted. In his current condition, it has been a long and tiring day for him, so I pop him into the crate and tuck him up into the blankets. Touching the radiator to check the temperature, it is nice and warm but it won't roast him. Then I leave him to sleep and I settle to watch a movie.

I have a method for successfully watching a film. The knack is to get the movie playing first and to have the controls, TV listings, glass of wine, peanuts, ham sandwich and apple, in the right place on the coffee table. Then I pull out some treats or snacks, some bits of cheese perhaps, to get the dogs off the settee I want to sit on. While they wolf down the cheese, I get myself on to the settee and into a comfortable position before they all pile back on top of me.

Once in place, I am hemmed in by Seamus in 'his' position on top of me, Shannon squeezing her way down between me and the back of the sofa (over time this will put her into a position where she can wriggle a bit and gradually lever me off the edge of the settee) and Minnie on my feet. With the central heating on as well, it is really quite hot.

After a while, I realise that not everyone is warm and comfortable. Even under his blankets I can see that Duncan is shivering. Poor little mite. All his physical resources are used up. In trying to heal himself, there is just nothing left to keep warm with.

Going through to the kitchen, I make up a hot water bottle, wrap it in an old towel and put it in the crate, nestling against Duncan's back. That ought to do it.

An hour later, at the end of my movie, he is still shivering; shivering harder if anything.

There is one time honoured, and pretty much guaranteed way to warm up a body. When I go to bed, Seamus, Shannon and Minnie take their usual spots on the bed and, as I slide down between the sheets, thinking of phrases like 'Rod for one's own back', I pull the violently shivering Duncan in with me and hug him to my stomach. Sure enough, after ten minutes or so he stops shivering and sleeps peacefully through the night.

❦

I keep up the 'Three dogs on the bed. One dog in the bed' regime for a week and then decide that Duncan has recovered sufficiently to go it alone. This is easier said than done. Duncan, for all his knocked about appearance, traumatised condition and half-healed physique is turning out to be a tough little cookie. Not having had a terrier before, I am only just beginning to learn of the hard inner core that is part of the remit. Duncan is quite unconquerable, and struggles on long after exhaustion should have knocked him out.

He is beginning to play with Seamus and Shannon, who are in their turn, beginning to treat Duncan as one of the team. He avoids Minnie; she has made it clear that she wants nothing to do with him. But for everything else, even as he is, Duncan is a little trooper. No matter what happens, he gamely goes on.

This tenacious attitude transfers itself to my efforts to eject him from my sheets. I want him on the bed. He wants to be in the bed. I have become his Mum. Where else would he be?

I set him on a corner of his own on the bed, then, trying to quietly read a book, constantly have to push him away as he edges between the sheets. I go to sleep, only to find on waking, that Duncan has inserted himself and is in his chosen place cuddled against me.

This goes on for some weeks and Duncan shows no sign of losing his inclination for sleeping under the sheets. Eventually, I buckle and let him. He is not actually unpleasant to have as company.

He is warm and cuddly, if a little spiky; Duncan does not have fur, but hair fit for a second life in shaving brushes. Perhaps this is why he had so much trouble keeping warm in the first place. He does not have that warm inner coat of fur that gives a dog good insulation. Instead he has just the outer protective coat that acts as body armour to terriers. This is a dog bred to go down holes after prey (hence the name terrier - earth dog). That kind of breeding produces an animal with courage, stubbornness and defence against sharp teeth and claws, but it is like cuddling up to a toothbrush.

With the arrival of winter, I have second thoughts. Perfectly house-trained right from the start, when Duncan feels the call of nature in the night, he makes his way, three legged, down the dark stairs and through the dog flap into the garden. Returning, soaking wet from the rain, hail or snow, feet gritty with mud, he wriggles his way back between the sheets. The first I know of it, is when an icy cold, wet body snuggles against my warm stomach. This brings me to startled consciousness, and an awareness of Duncan's continuing efforts get into just the right spot, wriggling and shoving until he has himself, the bed and me, all arranged to his own exacting specifications.

When Duncan first arrives, he spends most of his time sleeping. Only a youngster, his much abused body needs to heal. Certainly, he cannot walk far. The other dogs must have their exercise, and so while I go out with them, I put Duncan to bed in his crate.

The first time this happens, he snuggles down happily enough to snooze, but the second time, he has wised up to what is happening and is not impressed. I persuade him into the crate with some cheese, but howls and wails follow behind me as the front door closes.

As I leave the house, his cries rise an octave, penetrating the foot-thick stone walls of the cottage, and I see heads turn in gardens. A voice calls out to me, Patricia from across the road. "You'd better get that puppy off the spit. He doesn't like it.".

Returning an hour later, Duncan's wailing cries are audible several hundred yards down the road. Leaving him in the house is not going to be a long term option, or for that matter, a short term option.

I scour the local second-hand shops and find what I am looking for, an old child's buggy. Making sure first that it will fold up to fit into my car, I buy it for a few pounds. I line it with some old blankets and pop a handful of treats into the little side pocket, then fold the whole kit and caboodle onto the back seat of the car. Normally this seat is down, to give the dogs more space at the back, but they are just going to have to squeeze up for a few weeks.

Kitted up, I call Seamus, Shannon and Minnie. They scramble into the back of the car, grumble a bit at their reduced space and then play canine origami while they slot themselves comfortably in.

Duncan, in his basket, is placed on the passenger seat, strapping the basket firmly in with the seat belt. Duncan is all co-operation. He is coming with us.

Driving slowly to my chosen spot, I chat to Duncan and the others, just asking them to bear with these odd arrangements until Duncan is fit for normal duty. The Three pant a lolling tongue agreement at me. They will agree to anything if it means going for a walk. Duncan fixes me with his button eyes, his great ears triangulating on me as I talk. Despite his battered condition, he is cheerful and waggy. "It's fine." he says. "This is great!"

For my walk I have chosen one of the backroads off the A59. This road, the main East-West route joining Yorkshire and Lancashire, was once a windy, twisty, turny road. When I was a child in the 1960's, trying to drive from, say Harrogate to Skipton, or Skipton to Clitheroe, if you were unfortunate enough to be behind a wagon or a tractor, or worst of all, a caravan, the journey would take hours. Even as young adult in my twenties, the Harrogate to Blackburn journey took about three hours.

Over the years the A59 has had its kinks straightened out, corners cut off and dual carriageways added. The same Harrogate-Blackburn journey now takes a shade over an hour. But many of those old kinks and curves are still there, running vaguely parallel to the now, main road. They carry almost no traffic, and despite, in places, having twenty wheeler trucks thundering past, separated only by a hedge, are ideal walking routes. Still tarmacked, albeit a bit pot-holed in places, these old roads, even when the rain is pelting down and the fields unfit for man nor dog, are a mud-free zone where a dog can happily run about in safety. My interest on this occasion is that I have a buggy to push.

Releasing the Three from their shameful captivity in the car, they spring out en mass, informing me that it is good to be back. "We've not been here for a while have we?" They rush off to 'read the news' in the verges and on the trees. "Mmm...... Butch was here yesterday. Don't think he's feeling so well – they've been feeding him tripe again - better widdle on it just in case."

Extracting the buggy, I pop Duncan in, to his protests. "It's a bit undignified. I'm not a baby!" Then he discovers the treats in the side pocket. This settles him long enough to discover that he is actually quite comfortable. For a hundred yards or so he rides in his carriage, slightly lording it over the Three.

The Three are busy. Things to do. Places to go. People to see. Piddling to be done. Birds to be barked at. Duncan wants to join in. He starts struggling to jump down, so I lift him down before he hurts himself. He hobbles along to join the others, joining in with the sniffing, the peeing and the barking, enjoying himself.

Five minutes later he is close to collapse, visibly sagging, so I lift him back into the buggy. He settles in for perhaps a minute, before deciding that he is ready to get out again. Once more I lift him out and my little Tripod joins the team. Sure enough, another five minutes and he needs to be lifted back in.

In this stop-start-stop-start way, we walk a mile or so. Everyone is happy and Duncan sleeps like a top all the way back home.

I continue this regime for perhaps a month. Duncan is a ruffty-tuffty, hard cored little hero. He never gives up and is always game for more. His stump heals and his physique develops. After only a few weeks more he is healed. His body has transformed into a solid, muscle packed mass with not an ounce of spare fat.

He can walk, nay run, ten miles over Pendle Hill with the Three and when he wants to move, he pilots like a bluebottle, making twists and turns I do not think possible in a three-legged 'crippled' dog.

In fact, Duncan is not crippled. He is 'differently-abled'.

The Gang of Four

And so now I have my Gang of Four. There is a touch of 'The Three Musketeers' about them, with Duncan in the role of d'Artagnan. After the first few weeks of Duncan's arrival, they begin to work as a seamless whole and, with occasional disputes, settle into a pecking order, which changes according to circumstance.

Seamus is Number One, Head Honcho, but he only exerts his authority outside the house. Out in the big wide world, if another dog approaches the Gang of Four, it is Seamus who meets them, front on, welcoming bitches and fending dogs away from Shannon. In woods or fields, Minnie, Shannon and Duncan stay close, but Seamus is scouting, patrolling boundaries, walls and ditches, exploring, just within sight and generally putting the world to rights.

In the house it is different. The girls are in charge. Or rather, Minnie would like to be Top Dog, but Shannon actually rules the roost. This does not happen easily or instantly, but it does come to be. The fact is, that Shannon is far larger and more powerful than Minnie. There is no real contest between them, but Minnie learns this the hard way. Minnie is a bad-tempered little minx and constantly tries to queen it over Shannon. Shannon is having none of this, and there are some testy sessions between the two.

It climaxes one day when, as Shannon brushes by too closely, Minnie snaps at her, bristling and radiating attitude. In one smooth movement Shannon turns and with her nose, flips Minnie over onto her back.

Agog, I watch as, with a gesture any big game hunter would recognize, one foot on the fallen prey; Shannon places a single front paw on Minnie's upturned belly and holds her there, staring hard into her eyes as she does so.

Not for long, a few seconds, but the message could not be clearer. Shannon is not going to be told what to do by Minnie.

There never is any more trouble between the two of them. Minnie accepts her subordinate role completely. I admire Shannon's handling of the situation; there are many humans who could learn a lesson from her diplomatic skills. She has applied the exact amount of force necessary to make her point, and no more.

Shannon is Top Dog between the two girls, and since Seamus never exercises his authority in the house, this means she is Top Dog in the home.

Seamus gets his own way in the house by more devious means. If I am sitting on the sofa, the space next to me invariably contains one or other of the dogs. Possession of this space 'Next to Mum' is hotly contended; prime real estate. I never interfere with who gets to sit there. The dogs must always sort out pecking order issues between themselves.

Sitting on the settee reading one day, Minnie occupies the space next to me. Seamus moseys in from the garden, obviously heading for the same spot, then stops as he registers Minnie already in 'his' place.

He wanders up and down the room a couple of times, looking sorry for himself and out of sorts. Then he pauses, looks around the room and spots a ball. He jumps up, pouncing onto the ball, tossing it in the air.

Minnie is extremely possessive of all toys. As far as she is concerned all the toys in the house belong to her. As Seamus throws the ball into the air she leaps off the settee to claim the ball for herself.

In a motion smooth as flowing cream, Seamus jumps up into the position next to me and settles himself. His expression is smug as he places his head on my lap. Minnie, not the sharpest knife in the drawer, does not seem to realise that she has been had, simply toddling off with the ball to hide it in in some safe place.

Duncan is at the bottom of the pecking order. His youth and his disability putting him squarely in the role of 'pack puppy'. He forever plays the puppy card with Shannon and Seamus, licking at their mouths whether they want it or not, driving them to distraction sometimes with his constant attentions.

Minnie does not get her mouth licked. The first time Duncan tries it with her, is the day after his arrival, in his surgical aftermath and in poor condition. Minnie attacks him, rolling him on his back, trying to bite.

I shoot across the room to intervene and rescue Duncan, who is in no condition to protect himself. As his frantic yelps draw in the other dogs, I administer one of my very rare punishments to Minnie, not smacking her. Pain would only frighten her and be counterproductive. Instead, I pin her to the ground, eyeballing her hard "No! No!"

Reflecting back as I write, I suddenly realise that this is exactly the same tactic Shannon used when Minnie's behaviour was unacceptable; complete demonstration of dominance when a crime has been committed.

Minnie leaves Duncan alone after that, and Duncan has the good sense not to vex the grumpy old lady. Over the years, after Duncan's style settles down a bit, and Minnie continues her lifelong journey of self-improvement, they become good pals, but for the moment they are simply the two junior members of the Gang of Four.

I am visiting Sunnyhurst Woods in Darwen. This is one of my favourite walks for The Four. Darwen town itself, it must be admitted, is pretty dire. So much employment has been lost here over the last generation that Darwen, once a thriving Lancashire mill town, is now all but poverty stricken. Many of the houses in the poorer areas are slums and whole areas are being bulldozed. It is not a tourist spot. However, every town has redeeming features and Darwen's is a beauty.

The town is built into a valley to the West of the Pennine Hills, 'Old Darwen' being built of red brick terraced houses running up steep sided hills which eventually turn to bleak moorland at the crests. Continue South or East from Darwen and you will quickly arrive at some of the harshest land in England: wild, gaunt moors where the sensible walker checks the weather forecast first.

It is very beautiful there, but it is the austere, brittle beauty of nature at its wildest and which, while you may sit and admire for an hour, you will then answer civilisation's call to some softer option.

However, Darwen has a park, Sunnyhurst Woods, and it is a Victorian gem. A sharp sided valley stretches down to the edge of the town. At the top end of the valley is a reservoir, constructed in the mid eighteen hundreds. An outflow from the reservoir runs magically down through the valley, through woodland and wild rambles at first, then, tamed, into a series of ponds, pools and channels that are an absolute joy to stroll past.

There is something for everyone; a paddling pool for kids and dogs, easy wheelchair access, plenty of seating over lovely views. The park is a delight. Small stone bridges allow the visitor to amble either side of the stream, and here and there, are plaques giving tribute to industrial philanthropists who provided funds for works, or volunteer mill-workers who, putting in their own time, built the bridges for the enjoyment of the whole community.

The Gang of Four love Sunnyhurst Woods. Driving through Darwen, Shannon sees me click up the indicator switch to turn into Earnsdale Road, where we can park up. She yips excitedly to inform the rest of the Gang and chaos breaks out. I am not sure when Shannon learned what the car indicator switch does, but she regularly issues information reports to the other three, that we are turning off the main road into some favourite area.

Opening up the car, The Four drop out in a waggy, panting, hairy heap, then charge down the little track that leads into the park.

I have chosen this spot to park because, with a hundred yards or so of track to follow before reaching the park itself, accommodating the initial canine 'bursting at the seams', the excitement will have worn off just a little before the Gang is loosed on unwary wayfarers.

I saunter through the park, deciding to make my way all the way through and up to the reservoir. It is a beautiful day. Perhaps I will walk further.

The Four will then be well exercised and I may be able to take command of the settee myself this evening.

The Four walk ahead of me in a loose pack. Seamus, as ever, is to the front, with Shannon and Duncan at his side. Minnie potters along to the rear, like a clockwork pincushion. It is a weekday and there are a lot of young mums out with toddlers in pushchairs. A couple of youngsters are showing how brave they are, with trousers rolled up and skirts tucked into knickers, paddling in the waters.

Coming towards me is a young woman, with a little boy running ahead of her. I vaguely note that she does not look as if she from the top of the heap. Most people on this walk are either chatting with a companion, or, if alone, are generally looking around, at the flowers, the ubiquitous ducks or the lovely landscaping. This woman does none of these things, not reacting to anything around her. Hers is not the introspection of those who spend more time living inside their own head than out in the real world (I live with one of those). She simply looks vacant.

Her little boy however, is anything but vacant. He runs along, shouting and pointing at things, trying to tell his Mum about the little waterfall, the daffodils, the fish. He spots Duncan.

Duncan always draws the 'Awww...' reaction from strangers. He is a sure fire conversation starter as people ask about how he came to lose his leg. I have had a lot of practice regaling Duncan's tale, and have lost count of the number of people who point. "Hey look there. There's a dog with one leg."

That was not a misprint.

One leg? Folks baffle me sometimes.

The little boy comes running up to Duncan, wreathed in smiles. Duncan is overjoyed to have a new friend and frolics around him, being made a fuss of. I call to reassure his mother "Don't worry. They're all perfectly safe with children."

The woman comes out of her trance and notices Duncan. "Awww…. poor little thing. What happened to him?"

I launch into my well-rehearsed tale of Duncan being a stray as a puppy and run over. I explain that his leg was smashed in the accident and had to be amputated.

"Awww…. poor little thing." she repeats. "Won't it grow back?"

༄

The Gang of Four occasionally has extra members. One of these is Gracie.

I am sleeping peacefully, when in the wee small hours, I am woken by the sound of kafuffle and disturbance downstairs.

Normally at this hour, I would wake to find myself pinned to the mattress under the weight of dogs, and probably clinging to the edge of the bed for good measure, being gradually jimmied over the brink. My bed is now king sized, purchased specifically so that there is some space for me. In fact, it has not made much difference. The extra space has simply allowed the Four to stretch out a bit further.

However tonight, Shannon, Minnie and Duncan are all up and about, pacing around, responding to something outside. There is no sign of Seamus.

I check the time: three a.m. What on earth could be going on at this hour?

It is a small village. The pubs are all well down the hill on the bottom road. There are no clubs or discos, and if there were burglars or prowlers around, the dogs would be releasing all Hell. Instead, the three of them are simply very unsettled.

I go downstairs, where as usual, I have left the dog-flap open to the garden so the dogs can relieve themselves in the night if they need to. With my four-dog-security-system, I have no fears of household invaders.

Out in the garden I am treated to the sight of Seamus with another dog, one of the fattest and ugliest Labradors I have ever seen.

The pair are madly bonking away in the middle of the lawn.

A head leans out of the window next door. Albert takes a look at what is happening and cracks out laughing. "You've got your hands full I see."

I spread my hands wide. "Do you recognize her?"

Albert peers down. "Nope. Don't think so. What are you going to do?"

I can see in the darkness that the strange dog is wearing a collar with a tag, but do not think the romancing couple will respond well to being interrupted. Still, since Seamus can only fire blanks, he can safely keep the stranger from seeking alternative entertainment until I can contact her owner. "It's pretty late. I'll bring them inside and ring her owner in the morning. That's assuming the rest of the dogs don't object."

I wait for a break in proceedings, sipping a cocoa until the preoccupied pair are willing to give me a little attention. Then I call them in, keeping a weather-eye on the other three dogs. Shannon sniffs a bit at the strange bitch, then strolls off with an expression of disgust. Minnie gives a warning grumble across the bows at the stranger loose in her home and Duncan is entirely uninterested.

Leaving Seamus and his paramour downstairs, I take the other three back to bed with me, falling asleep to a dim background noise of thumping.

The following morning, I get a better look at Seamus' new flame. She is truly the most uncomely Labrador, and one of the unattractive dogs, I have ever seen. Labradors routinely tend to excessive eating and overweight, especially spayed bitches, but this one is demonstrably not spayed. She is simply, and hugely, fat.

I look at Seamus. "I think you had one too many lagers when you brought this one back mi-lad. Let's find out who she is."

Seamus gazes levelly back at me with no hint of apology. "Sometimes you wake up with a dog." his expression says.

An investigation of the collar tag reveals that Seamus had been hosting 'Gracie' (Gracie? I've never seen a less graceful dog.), and there is a phone number on the back. Dialling, I am answered almost immediately. "Hello. Is this Gracie's owner?"

"Yes." says a male voice, full of worry and relief. "Is she alright? Have you got her?"

"Yes, she's absolutely fine. I found her in my back garden last night with my dog Seamus."

"Oh my God!" Panic in the voice. "I'll have to get her to the vets."

I try to calm him down a bit. "No need. Seamus has been neutered. He just kept her occupied and I brought them both in here overnight. Where are you?"

The tone of relief returns. "I live near Sabden at the bottom of the hill. She must have broken out of the garden last night. I'm forever having to repair the fence. Where are you?"

"At the top of the hill. Would you like me to walk her down?"

"No, I'll come and collect her. I'm at work right now so I'll be a few minutes."

"No rush. I'm in all day and the dogs are getting along fine. As I say, Seamus will entertain her. She'll not go looking for alternatives."

There is a moment's silence as Gracie's Dad is digests the possibilities of this. "Um, would it be okay if I left her there 'til about six o'clock? That would give me time to get home and patch up the fence."

"No problem at all." I give him my address and ring off.

'Dad', Dan, turns up as promised at six, thanks me profusely and takes Gracie away with him. I assume that is the end of the matter.

That night I am woken again by restless dogs and I know that our nocturnal visitor has returned.

Again I bring Seamus and Gracie into the house and go back to bed.

The next morning, I ring Dan again. He is horribly embarrassed and starts apologising "I really don't know how she does it. This happens every time she comes into season. She breaks out and goes roaming the village."

"Then it's as well that she's discovered Seamus isn't it? He's the safe option."

He laughs, relief in his voice that I am not annoyed. "Is it alright if I pick her up later again? Is that difficult for you?"

"Not in the least. I'm working from home for a few days so an extra dog is no problem at all."

I do have one more visit from Gracie that week, but then she calls no more and I assume that either she has finished her season, or that Dan has 'Gracie-proofed' his fence.

And that is that.

Until, six months later I am woken in the middle of the night by familiar sounds of humping and thumping below. And again six months after that.

In fact, for some years, every six months, Gracie calls by to renew her relationship with Seamus. I don't think Dan ever stops trying to repair his fence, but memories of Sadie and the garage door frame ripped from its socket remind me that when there is a will, there is usually a way.

☙❧

We are walking up Pendle Hill. The Gang of Four have raced up the hill ahead of me. I bring up the rear, purple faced with effort as I haul myself up the precipitous slope.

Pendle's flatish top and sheer sides give the hill its distinctive shape. Viewed from the West, Pendle rises out of nowhere, looming over a landscape which stretches flat as a billiard table to the coast, almost thirty miles away. Atop Pendle, on a clear day, the sea sparkles afar, and on a clear night, Blackpool Illuminations glimmer in the distance.

However, to reach the top of Pendle, I must first scale it. The path is breath-stealingly steep and no matter how often I take this walk, I never seem to build up the muscles to breeze my way up.

Stopping for a moment, I hold in my sides. Duncan turns, sees I have halted, scampers three-leggedly down the slope to check that all is well, then scampers three-leggedly back up again, as though the ground were flat. I curse him and all dogs under my breath, such as it is.

Some air back in my lungs and my heartbeat dropping below crisis levels, I continue up the track.

I trudge up, every so often stopping, partly to breath, but also turning to take a look at the landscape opening up before me as I rise. It is spectacular. The day is bright and clear with a stiff breeze. Scudding clouds cast light and shade over Clitheroe below me and beyond, to the green of fields and flatlands fading to the far West. From the North, the flat topped outlines of Longridge Fell and others lead the eye eastwards where, distantly, I can see the snow-crowned peak of Inglehead.

I have long suspected that the distinctive shape of the local fells, long and flat topped, all more or less aligned and similarly shaped, points to their glacial past, long lined edges to valleys scoured out by the ice. Certainly the glaciers were here. But I am no expert and may well be wrong on this.

Half a dozen paragliders wheel and turn like eagles above me in the wind, and the bite of the cold air brings my temperature down rapidly.

Reaching the top with a gasp, I walk a few hundred yards further to flop down on a dry stone wall for a coffee, my wind-raw face glowing with cold. The dogs mill around me, checking out the availability of ham sandwiches, sausages, cheese or pork pies. Since nothing more interesting than my flask emerges from the rucksack, they wander off again.

I sip my coffee, warming stiff and chilly hands on the comfortingly warm metal mug and pondering whether to head for the trig point or to stay close by this edge for the view.

I split the difference. I will walk to the trig point, have my lunch there, looking down over Barley, then return by the longer route, looping round the far side of Pendle to catch the Clitheroe views on the way back.

The route to the trig point is a brisk half-hour's hike cutting directly across the plateau to the far, southern side of the hill. The dogs gambol around me, sometimes tagging behind, sometimes stretched out in front, until they settle on our direction. Having decided that they know where we are going, they are all out 'following from the front', leading me towards the pathway of enormous stone slabs which comprise the route to the highest point of Pendle Hill.

This path has been laid some years previously, in response to the calamitous erosion that was taking place on the fragile moorland. Bleak and hard as it looks, these upland environments are delicate. Heather and hard grasses mingle with peat bogs, reeds and cotton grass on the poorly draining soil.

It seems strange to have bogs here, on a hilltop almost two thousand feet up, but the millstone grit heart of Pendle is impermeable to water, and rain here is absorbed and held by the peat. In places, high up as we are, there are not just bogs, but actual ponds. It is counterintuitive, but so.

A thousand walkers, a thousand pairs of boots, on a pathway across the plateau, tore away at the frail turf, exposing the peat below, making walking unpleasant and laborious as the peat degraded to a muddy slop.

The walkers responded by moving to the side of the track, wearing away at a new patch of turf. Pendle is famous in its way, and the sheer numbers of tramping feet destroyed the surface of the high moor, leaving only naked peat, disintegrating in the rain, then washing away.

A pathway was laid. Huge stone slabs, three, four, five feet long, laid end to end across the bog, giving the walkers a firm tread. The gaping wound in the landscape around the path was planted out with cotton grass and other appropriate plants and in an astonishingly short time, a few months, the ground healed. A landscape that had turned to naked earth as far as the eye could see, suddenly flourished, and new turf reknitted the surface.

It was such a simple solution, and it worked perfectly. I do not know who was responsible for the work, but it is a credit to him. The stone slab pathway now guides the walkers safely through the stunning, if austere, beauties of Pendle, without damaging it.

We arrive at the trig point, a stone obelisk perhaps four feet high, and yet another astonishing vista.

This is perhaps the widest of all the views from Pendle top, with spots where, looking out and standing with the bulk of the hill behind me, the wind in my face, I feel as though I am flying. Remember that scene from 'Titanic'?

The Four are unimpressed by the views. I suppose having a world's eye view eighteen inches from the ground makes a difference, but they are far more interested in quartering the area for any forgotten egg sandwiches, abandoned crisps or other lost delights and dainties.

Only Seamus is not involved, busying himself instead with a careful inspection of the obelisk itself for 'news'. Having circled it carefully, in an exacting nasal inspection, he cocks a leg and declares Pendle Hill to be his.

He then joins the others, gathered around me and following my hand like the crowd at Wimbledon, from lap to mouth, as I eat my sandwiches. I distribute the last sandwich between them and polish off my meal with a banana, except for the last inch. Seamus always has that and knows that the last inch of the banana is his inch of banana.

Finishing off my coffee, we set off to follow the path off to the left that will take us circuitously, back to the northern edge of the plateau. As we reach the far side, the wind has risen and is biting cold. My fingers are numbing again and I step up the pace to warm myself up.

Looking down over Clitheroe, it is difficult from this height to make out the castle, so prominent when in the town. The A59 is far below, but even here, I can hear the hum of traffic. There are very few places in England anymore, where it is possible to not hear traffic.

I become aware of internal pressure. My coffee is completing its journey and nature calls. In deference to other walkers and personal modesty, I did not join Seamus in his marking of the trig point.

Casting around for a private spot, there is nothing growing taller than shrubby heather, but there is no one in sight; the plateau is deserted. Apart from myself and the dogs, the only movement is from the dozen or so rooks wheeling in the updrafts from the steep slopes close by. I hunker down, not trying to hide. Even if I wanted to, there *is* nowhere to hide.

Nature takes its course and I am half-way through proceedings when, jeans around my ankles, there is a whoosh, and a paraglider rises up from the gulf, scattering startled rooks from his path.

The rider is close enough that I can see him gape as he spots me, before, with a twist, he turns and disappears gracefully down out of sight. I stand up, pull up my trousers and brush off a couple of strands of spiky grass, then continue along the trail.

◈

This is not my only paraglider event on Pendle Hill. A similar day, fine and breezy, and once more we walk Pendle. Today we are on the lower slopes just off the Clitheroe-Sabden road that leads the driver through 'The Nick of Pendle'.

Approaching from the Clitheroe side, this road is gentle at the base, getting progressively steeper, until at the summit, around fifteen hundred feet, the gradient, almost abruptly, reverses suddenly downhill and a glorious vista opens up over the village of Sabden.

We stroll hillocky ground. The paths weaves and twines in awkward twists where generations of walkers have worked easy footing into awkward ground through the drumlins. Away to my right the land inclines upwards towards the more precipitous slopes of the hill and gathered there is, once again, a group of paragliders.

This is an ideal spot for their sport. The breeze comes straight in from the coast and is almost always blowing. From here there is an unbroken flat plain out towards Blackpool, a brief stop by Ireland and then not much more of anything except ocean until the Statue of Liberty. This clean wind strokes the lower slopes before being driven skywards in powerful updrafts. The paragliders have only to run into the wind to be taken up into the air.

I enjoy watching them. It is one of the most graceful of sports, the chutes making elegant turns, sliding through the skies, spiralling up, wheeling and turning, like seagulls over waves. I find a comfy hummock and open my flask to enjoy a little vicarious flying. Shannon, Minnie and Duncan all continue ahead to splash in the stream, but Seamus stays with me, settling companionably down a few feet away.

I watch the air show for a few minutes. A couple of the fliers come down to land. This always seems to me to be the dodgy end of the sport. The ground over these slopes is very uneven.

Even in my boots and only walking, I must watch my step. What must it be like landing at a run with a parachute on your back? Still, it's their choice.

Another glider is coming down, and in our direction. Has he seen us? Yes, he has seen me, in my bright jacket, and he veers slightly away. But Seamus' brown and tan coat is well camouflaged against the dull heath grasses. The glider is coming down straight onto him.

Seamus is looking at me and has not noticed. I stand up, pointing at him, trying to alert the descending flier. At the very last moment, the flier sees Seamus and lifts his feet to miss his head by inches. I can almost see the fur between Seamus' ears ruffle as the flier whooshes over him to land only forty or fifty feet away.

Seamus is not a happy bunny. From his point of view, a giant bat has suddenly materialised in the air above him. Barking wildly at the apparition in the dayglow jump suit which is folding up its wings, he reverses away, not turning his back for a moment. The flier takes off goggles and waves at me, trying to apologise. "Hey I'm sorry, I just didn't see him there."

"Don't worry. No harm done." I laugh, but Seamus does not agree. Walking on to follow the other three dogs, I try to coax Seamus away.

He follows me, walking backwards, eyeballing the flier as he retreats, growling lurid threats at this danger to civilisation he has so narrowly escaped. He refuses to turn his back on the figure until we are good hundred yards or so away, then with a final burst of invective, he turns to join the others, all the time carefully watching the other gliders above us.

This is the end of any relaxing walks on Pendle if the paragliders are flying. The moment Seamus spots one of them in the air, all chances of peace vanish. They must be seen off, made to understand that they are Not Welcome.

As long as he can still see them, Seamus delivers a nonstop offensive of barking, cursing and defiance, which only ceases when they are out of sight. After a couple of occurrences, if the gliders are out, I take the car to the far side of the hill and we walk there instead.

However, for Seamus this event has far reaching consequences. He has now been made aware of the deadly hazards to life and limb of airborne objects. If it is in the air, it must be dealt with. This is unusual. In my experience, dogs do not generally look up. In their heads, they live in the two dimensional world of the ground dweller, but Seamus has learned his lesson. *Up* is dangerous.

Lamp posts are an easy target. During the day they are fine, clearly slumbering, but at night, they wake and so, must be warned off. As we past under each glowing lamp, Seamus fires off a volley at it, barking madly for a good half minute before deciding that this threat has been neutralised, then moving on to the next. I alter my night-time walking pattern so as not to wake up half the village.

The full moon is clearly a threat, and for four or five nights a month, the moon is given a good 'sorting out' by Seamus. Stubbornly it hangs over him, refusing to move or back down and Seamus paces up and down the lawn in frustration, baying up at the enemy.

A balloon glides over the cottage, rather low for comfort even to my human eyes, and as I wave to the people in the basket, I am restraining Seamus from his snarling attempts to leap and bring the offenders down.

Bright blue skies become a bit of a trial as aircraft at thirty thousand feet trail their silver rafters across the heavens. Seamus does not like these white lined trespassers in his sky. Fortunately, in the English climate, this does not happen too often and Seamus does not seem to notice clouds.

I maintain that dogs, whilst genetically a kind of wolf, if compared directly with humans, behave very much like children of age perhaps two or three years old. They may have adult reasoning minds, but emotionally, the owner is 'Mum' or 'Dad', or less anthropomorphically perhaps, the pack leader.

People laugh when I say this, but it works in practice, not just theory. And both ways.

I am walking with a friend, and The Gang of Four. The weather is threatening; with that egg yolk quality you get to the sky before a big storm. The Four are all walking as a group, a hundred yards or so ahead of us, when there is a rumble of thunder.

The Four, as one, turnabout and gather around my feet, tripping me up and asking for protection. My friend laughs. "They are just like children aren't they. Running to Mum if there's a problem."

I am with my God-children. They are seven and five years old. I am 'Auntie Christine' and am looking after them in the garden for a bit while Mum and Dad make a meal inside the house. They are running, helter-skelter around the garden, and I am wondering what Auntie Christine is supposed to do if one of them trips up and breaks a leg. Dogs don't have this problem. They are more sensibly designed with four, or occasionally three, legs.

'Mum' calls from indoors. "Tea's ready."

I assume I am expected to call in the troops at this point, so I shout for the girls to come in to eat. They slow down a bit, but otherwise, do not take a lot of notice.

"Well, I'm going into eat." I say. "Mum told me that it's spaghetti bolognese and chocolate trifle today." This gets their attention and they, kinda, meander in my direction.

I stand up to head into the house and, reflexes working, pat my thigh for them to follow me. It works perfectly and the kids coming running.

I will confess to, occasionally, doing this also to adults. While not naming those on whom it has worked, honourable mention where it is due; when I patted my thigh for Garry to follow, he was mortally offended.

My gardens are small. To the front and rear of the house, the front garden is for display and the back garden is for the dogs. At the back there is a tiny lawn, a flower bed to one side and shrubs at the far end.

After much deliberation I buy a small shed, just large enough to take my bicycle, the problem now being, that having put the bike in the shed, there is no room for anything else, such as a lawn mower, or garden tools. Even a small garden needs some care and I need to be able to cut the lawn.

I toy with the idea of a rabbit. A rabbit in a mobile run which I can move around the lawn, would eat the grass. The lawn would never need cutting and the grass would be automatically fertilised. On the other hand, how would The Four react to a rabbit in the garden? They have a well prescribed set of rules. They know that sheep, cats and chickens are sacrosanct, but that rabbits and squirrels are fair game; not that they ever catch either, but it's fun to try. And so the idea dies a death.

I am visiting my mother and we have stopped by a pet shop so that she can collect her dog food.

Hanging around outside, I idly scan the various goods on display out on the hard-standing; dog baskets, bird cages, flower pots, various bedding plants, all the usual paraphernalia. Towards the back of the display is a rabbit hutch. Bending down to examine the occupant, he is a medium sized rabbit of very unusual ginger colouring. I have never seen a rabbit quite like him and I wander in to ask the shopkeeper his breed.

"Oh that's not his breed." She says. "It's a mineral deficiency, copper I think, but we're not sure. He's a starvation case. We rescued him and we are trying to find a home for him."

As I drive back home, with 'Bramble' nestled in a cardboard box on my passenger seat, I wonder if I have been rash.

Realistically, yes, I have been rash. Introducing a rabbit to a household which already has four dogs and a cat, is a bit of a long-shot. Ginger will not be a problem in himself. His only interest in life is in exercising his sofa rights. But the smell of a cat might distress a rabbit. And The Four, how will they react?

Still, Bramble does need a home, and at least I can get him out of a hutch and into a nice run. I check inside the box. Bramble is contentedly currently working his way through a selection of carrot chunks, apple slices and some wild greens I pulled from the verge when I stopped for a break.

Arriving home, the day is cool and overcast, so I can safely leave Bramble in the car whilst I take The Four out for a quick walk and a de-energising session. If they are calm when they first encounter the new lodger, so much the better. Twenty minutes later, we return. I give the dogs a large meal and root out the dog cage from the attic, where is has resided ever since Duncan stopped needing it. I do not yet have a run for Bramble, temporary accommodation is required for him. Setting up the cage on the lawn, over a bit of nice, succulent looking grass, I pop in a water bowl and some food pellets, then go in search of some plastic sheeting to give him shelter against rain, pending my acquiring a proper run for him.

The dogs, having bolted down their food, appear in the garden to inspect proceedings. Seamus sits watching me, bemused. Duncan tries to get into the cage with Bramble, after all, it is his cage is it not? Minnie sniffs at the cage and then wanders off, bored. Shannon watches me for a while before disappearing back into the house.

A few minutes later, having covered half the run in waterproof sheeting, I go through to get Bramble from the car. Shannon is waiting by the kitchen door. She follows me to the car, inspects the box as I lift it out, and then follows me back to the garden, where I decant Bramble into his new quarters.

Bramble is entirely unfazed by having three dogs sitting around watching him. He flip-flops around the crate, nibbles a bit of grass and then sticks his nose through the bars to exchange sniffs with Duncan.

Seamus, Shannon and Duncan all swap introductions with the rabbit in amicable fashion, just as though he were another small dog. Minnie potters up, also sniffs, and then potters off again, still uninterested.

Seamus has ears pricked, fascinated but certainly not aggressive. Duncan seems nonplussed and Shannon simply watches interestedly, gazing at Bramble with liquid eyes.

I watch this performance for an hour or so, sitting out on the bench with a cuppa and doing small jobs around the garden. While I deadhead roses, cut back some nasturtiums that are getting out of hand and pull up nettle roots that are trying to stage a garden comeback, Bramble trims the lawn within the cage, and the dogs loll about on the lawn.

Decision time. Carefully watching the dogs, I open the cage door and clip it back, leaving Bramble to decide for himself what he would like to do next.

After a few moments, he lollops out into the open. At an unhurried pace, he circles the lawn, stops to say 'Hello.' to Seamus, tries out a dandelion and then discovers the pile of nasturtium clippings. He applies himself to their hygienic disposal while the dogs take not a blind bit of notice. They seem to regard Bramble as 'just another one of us'.

I stay with them all in the garden for another half hour or so 'just in case', but the peaceful scene continues.

Teatime. Going through to the kitchen to make myself a meal, I leave the back door open so that I can keep an eye on things outside.

After a few minutes of scrambling eggs, making toast and brewing tea, I turn to find Bramble in the kitchen with me. Slightly disconcerted, I step carefully around him, not wanting to frighten the little fellow by towering over him. Bramble is unbothered by my presence. He does a circuit of the kitchen floor and then stops by Ginger's litter tray and uses it.

I am dumbfounded, partly because I have never considered a rabbit as a house-pet, but mainly because I would have thought that the scent of a cat's litter tray, would be the most frightening thing imaginable to a prey animal like a rabbit.

Still, if Bramble is prepared to behave like this indoors, he is very welcome to join everyone else in the house if he wants to.

On reflection I should not be surprised at the success of Bramble. Seamus is always as good with other animal species so long as he knows that he supposed to be good.

Formal introductions have been made and so Seamus knows that Bramble is officially a part of the household. The other three dogs tend to take their lead from him, and so Bramble is accepted.

Outside the house, rules are set for other species. Sheep, no problem. We know the rules for them. Horses and cattle, no problem, and anyway they are too big to play with anyway. Others....

We are walking along a lane edging the village. It is dusk and Seamus is off-lead, trotting ahead of me.

He stops suddenly, fairly quivering with excitement, one front paw lifted and nose and ears triangulating in on some object on the ground in front of him. As I draw closer he pushes his nose forward and yelps, then backs off a couple of feet. He gives me a helpless look, tail in 'nervous wag' mode. "What the Hell is that?"

I look closer. Seamus has just had his first encounter with a hedgehog. I can see its enviable collection of fleas scrambling among the spines, poised to pounce onto larger, improved quarters at a moment's notice. I pull Seamus back a little. We all know how far fleas can jump. The little beastie is in the middle of the road, so I carefully scoop it up, and deposit it in the hedgerow.

We are walking along a lane edging the village. It is dusk and Seamus is off-lead, trotting ahead of me. He stops suddenly, fairly quivering with excitement, one front paw lifted and nose and ears triangulating in on some object on the ground in front of him. As I draw closer he pushes his nose forward and yelps, then backs off a couple of feet. He gives me a helpless look, tail in 'nervous wag' mode. "What the Hell is that?"

I look closer. Seamus has just had his first encounter with a hedgehog. I can see its enviable collection of fleas scrambling among the spines, poised to pounce onto larger, improved quarters at a moment's notice.

I pull Seamus back a little. We all know how far fleas can jump. The little beastie is in the middle of the road, so I carefully scoop it up, and deposit it in the hedgerow.

Duvet Day

I wake. It is dark and rain is lashing against the window. Checking the clock, it is seven am, not late, nor early, but it is January and will not be light for at least a couple of hours. Judging by the weather, it may not be properly light at all today.

Extending one arm outside the blankets, I flick on my teas-made, then withdraw back underneath again to cosy warmth. Duncan is stretched against my stomach under the sheets and, spiky hair aside, is rather comforting. Clearing my throat, it is sore and my head is stuffed. I have a cold coming on. I hear the rising hiss of the teas-made, then realise that it is the wind wailing outside. Getting out of bed seems like an uncommonly bad idea.

Nature calls, so I visit the bathroom, collecting my dressing gown on the way back. Calling the dogs, I open the back door to let them out into the garden, the wind lashing sleet at me. Minnie, Seamus and Shannon jointly examine the weather, dash out for less than a minute and dash back in again.

I shoot upstairs to put a cover over the bed before they cover the bedspread in muddy paw prints. The three of them shake briskly over the paintwork and then pile onto the bed. Duncan has not moved.

Wrapped up warm, I sit up in bed as my tea brews. More awake now, I realise that I do not have a cold coming on. In fact, I have a cold. My sinuses ache and are beginning to stream, my eyes are bleary and my throat is doing a reasonable impression of a cheese grater.

Sipping tea helps a bit, the steam clearing my nose a little. I glance at the clock again. Seven thirty. I am supposed to be at work in an hour or so.

I drink my tea, reflecting on what best to do, then decide that work is not a good idea today.

I will ring in and tell them not to expect me. No one is going to thank me for giving them a dose of cold anyway. Calling the office, I leave a message on the answer-phone.

I ponder on what to do next. The dogs have to have some kind of walk and I need to get tissues, lemons and other 'cold comfort' aids. Dressing as quickly as possible, with an extra pullover, and my long waxed jacket and hat, I am as waterproof as the day will allow. I put the dogs in the car, Duncan protesting all the way that he does not need to come and is entirely comfortable under the bedclothes.

I drive to Spring Woods and park up. The Four dash off into the woods through the horizontal sleet, while I make myself comfortable inside with the radio on and the heating turned up, then I wait for the dogs to return in their own time. After a moment, I turn the radio volume up so that I can hear it over the beating of sleetdrops on the roof.

Minnie and Duncan both return after only five minutes, almost launching themselves into the back of the car. Minnie expresses her profound disapproval of my weather making arrangements, her furry body speckled with semi-melted bits of snow, while Duncan wipes himself off against the back of the seats. Seamus and Shannon are not far behind them. Shannon arrives plastered with mud and dripping wet, whilst Seamus steps daintily between raindrops and appears only slightly damp. He steps lightly into the car and starts licking himself dry. Shannon leaps in, then shakes with gusto.

Concluding that walking duties are satisfied for the moment, I close up and drive to the corner shop. I am beginning to feel really, quite ill. I buy a box of man-sized tissues, a couple of tubes of throat sweets, a net of lemons and a jar of honey. As an afterthought I add a bottle of whiskey.

Back home, I put on the kettle to fill two hot water bottles then get a towel to dry off the dogs. Duncan and Minnie are all co-operation in this, Duncan enveloping himself in the fabric and Minnie rocking rhythmically against my movement to help with the towelling.

I go in search of Seamus and Shannon to find that Seamus is saving me the trouble of drying him by rubbing himself along the side of the settee and armchairs. Shannon has vanished. I find her upstairs, rolling on the be towelled bed-cover.

Once in bed, I prop myself upright, breathing stertorously through my mouth. My head aches and my muscles are catching up. A hot honey and lemon drink helps a little. It helps more when I drop in a generous slug of whiskey. This will not of course cure my cold, but it does stop me caring about it so much. The dogs have arrayed themselves about me on the bed and Duncan has taken up his customary position nestled against my stomach, arguing vigorously with me when I explain that he is wet and cold. "How..." he argues "...am I going to be warm and dry again if I cannot cuddle up?" I have no will to continue the discussion, so I lie listlessly against my pillows.

I google a Med site on the internet, checking my symptoms, learning that I have lassa virus, malaria and rhinosporidiosis. This is just too depressing. I feel like hanging an 'Out of Order' sign from my banging head and with no energy to watch TV or read, I tune in to Radio 4. One of my favourite programs is on. 'From Our Own Correspondent.' I let the dulcet tones of Kate Adie remind me that, however rotten I feel, there are those in the world a lot worse off than I am.

My streaming nose is red and sore. How is it that with my sinuses blocked, no air will travel one way and yet, pints of revolting mucus can flow the other? Not so much a blockage as a valve. Still, better out than in. One blow completely fills a hanky and I toss soggy tissues into the bin by the side of my bed.

The dogs notice this activity and there is a brief dispute over ownership of these delectable items, until the Four realise that there are enough tissues to provide plenty for all. Each dog selects one of the noisome delicacies and settles down with it on the bed for leisurely consumption. Seamus finishes his first tissue rather quickly and steps down again to choose another particularly succulent example.

Returning to his slot on the bedcovers, he nips small sections off it at a time, satisfaction writ over every hair of his face.

I drift off into an uncomfortable doze, propping a tissue under my nose. No one can see me and vanity is not at the top of my list of priorities right now.

The phone rings downstairs, rousing me. At first I think to ignore it, then wonder if I am being called from work. Prising Duncan off my stomach and levering my way out of the blankets and dog heap, I totter as I achieve perpendicularity.

The insistent phone blarts its summons at me as stiff muscles are bullied into action and I descend the stairs, staggering slightly as the Four barge past me.

I pick up the phone. "Hello." It hurts to speak. My throat is raw. An irritatingly bouncy and cheerful voice replies, dripping with fake charm.

"Hello, is that Miss Brooks?"

"Yes, who is this?"

"My name is Rhonda Fartworthy of Fartworthy, Piddleton and Snark Ltd UPVC Windows and Doors. How are you today?"

I am in no mood for cold calling salesmen. "I'm full of cold and I am not interesting in UPVC windows. Goodbye." I start to put the phone down but the voice cuts in again.

"Just one moment Miss Brooks. Our salesman happens to be in your area and you have been selected for a free survey and estimate for brand new…." I cut in.

"If your salesman really was in this area, you might know that I live in a seventeenth century cottage with stone mullioned windows. I am not interested in UPVC window frames." And this time I do slam the phone down.

Since I am out of bed anyway, I open the door to let the dogs out. The weather has now added freezing fog to its menu del dia.

Putting on the kettle to refresh my hot water bottles and make myself another drink, I intend to make a hot **lemon, honey** and whiskey, but end up with a lemon, honey and **whiskey.**

I return to my bed to find the dogs there ahead of me, soaking wet again and drying themselves briskly on the side of the bed. Sighing, I climb into the blankets to find a sleet ridden Duncan already there. How does he do it? Three-leggedly, he somehow lifts the blankets and sheets, then slides underneath faster than I can. I haul him out protesting, wrap him in a dry towel and then put him back. At least the towel is warm against me.

I resume my doze, the dogs continuing their feast of freshly issued, revolting tissues, all except for Minnie, who has located my packet of cough sweets and is now sucking Strepsils out of their wrappers. Wresting them from her, I settle down again to listen to the radio.

Five minutes.

There is a knock from the front door. The dogs launch from the bed like so many ICBMs, including Duncan from under the bedcovers, who takes my blankets with him as he departs, leaving me in the cold. The Four charge down the stairs, screaming the announcement of Doomsday while I lurch into my slippers, give my nose a good blow, then follow them.

Wrestling the dogs into the living room, I open the front door. Two immaculately groomed young men wearing long overcoats stand there, ribbons of rain running from the spokes of their huge black umbrellas. I have no idea who they are. They show no reaction to my wild and dishevelled appearance.

One of them speaks. "Good morning. I'm sorry if we picked an inconvenient moment, but we wondered if you might like to discuss your views on God and his Kingdom?"

For a moment I am speechless, trying to think of some suitably venomous epithet with which to puncture these two witless nerds, but my brain is only firing on three cylinders, and I feel too apathetic to tell them what I am actually thinking. "No." I say. "My religious views are a private matter. Thank you." and I close the door in their faces, just in time to be overcome with a fit of coughing.

Once again, in the kitchen anyway, I put a pan of milk on the stove to make another hot drink, then open the back door in case the dogs want to relieve themselves. Minnie and Shannon show no interest, whilst Duncan dashes upstairs at the suggestion that he should venture out again. The weather is appalling, with a thin layer of semi-melted hailstones over the lawn. Seamus is undeterred. He goes about his business outside and seems not to notice the battering deluge around him. I leave him to it while I go to make my drink. When I return, Seamus has dragged a large stick into the lounge and is cheerfully dismantling it on the carpet. As I head upstairs, he follows me with the stick, jamming it sideways several different ways, before getting the angle right to ascend the narrow staircase.

I draw the line at Seamus bringing his stick onto the bed, so with a hurt expression, he retires to the carpet to demolish his prize, spending a pleasant half hour or so, crunching wood and spitting out bark.

Minnie attempts a move on my hot milk but I beat her to it. I inform the dogs that I want a bit of peace and quiet, with threats of the wrath of Heaven if I don't get it. After a few minutes, the warmth of the milk soothes me into sleep.

I wake, feeling much better. Checking the clock, I have slept for hours. My cold is far from gone, but at least my head is no longer pounding. I sit up in bed to read, book in one hand, tissue poised for action beside me.

Seamus and Shannon are sitting on the floor beside me, playing the 'Bite my neck' game. I have never quite fathomed the rules of play, but they are enjoying themselves and at least now there is some spare room on the mattress. Duncan is keeping me company sat on the bed, above the covers for a change; alert and attentive as I idly scratch his ears with my free hand.

In front of the bed is my mirror, a beautifully carved pine stand mirror with candy twist legs, angled such that, just now, I cannot see my own reflection, but I can see Duncan's. He is looking my reflection in the eye.

Looking back at Duncan's reflection, I smile. His face lights up and he wags his tail. I put my book down and move my, now free, hand up and down. His eye and head follow the reflection of my hand in the reflection. Finally, I wave at him. He turns to face me, reaches forward and licks my face.

It is said sometimes that animals have no 'theory of mind'.

i.e. the ability to understand the mind of another being or the capacity to understand that another may see the world from a different point of view. In short, are they self-aware?

A standard test for this, is to put a drop of paint on the face of the animal, say a chimpanzee, then show him a mirror. If the animal reaches for the drop of paint in the reflection, he has failed the test. If he sees the reflection, but reaches for the paint on his own face, he has passed.

Typically, a human baby of less than about two years old will fail the test. An adult chimp will pass. A robin will fail, attacking its own reflection. Some say that dogs will fail, not understanding that what they see in a reflection is not real.

Duncan has just passed with flying colours, understanding perfectly that my reflection and I are not the same, and that what I see and what he sees are not necessarily the same.

Animal intelligence intrigues me. Beyond doubt, at some level, all living things are biological machines, crafted by nature and selection to survive in their given environments.

Some animals never get further than that. It is difficult to imagine the thought processes of say, an earthworm. How much 'mind' do you need to pass soil through the tube that is your body? Even for 'higher' animals, does an anteater need intelligence to dig out termites? Or just a good quality algorithm in the brain for the process of the demolition of a termite mound?

On the other hand, we are still exploring what 'intelligence' means when applied to the apes, whales and dolphins, octopuses, elephants and crows. My inclination is always to give credit to the beast. Just because we humans have not yet recognised the signs, does not mean that 'mind' is not there. There is a saying to the effect that absence of evidence is not the same as evidence of absence.

Dogs are a special case. Our companions for, who yet knows? Ten, twenty, thirty thousand years, they have co-evolved with us, to act as our eyes, ears and especially noses. They can read our body language and facial expressions in a way that their ancestors, the wolves, cannot. Indeed, I know plenty of humans who cannot read my moods in the way my dogs are able. Dogs are symbiotic with us in a way that no other animal is.

Shannon is undoubtedly the most intelligent dog I have ever known. When I say intelligent, I mean in the human sense, rather than the canine.

Paddy had been wily. Duncan is similarly canny. Minnie is not all that bright, much of her potential I think curtailed by her background. And Seamus, bless him, for all his sterling qualities, will never be swot of the school.

But Shannon is different. I talk with Shannon. She does not have speech, but she understands it. When I talk to Shannon, she reacts, she knows.

In the house, I call for Garry. Three dogs mill about. Shannon dashes upstairs to get him.

I am walking by the reservoirs, a pleasant stroll on easy paths right around the waters, or alternatively, straight up the hillside to the Pennine Fells and a much more strenuous hike for as far as you could wish to go. Today, we are sauntering along by the water's edge, taking a pleasant constitutional in the fresh air. I am here with The Four and we have arranged that we will meet with Garry when he arrives after work.

The sunlight sparkles on rippling water as we approach the far side of the reservoir from the car park. From here, I can see the gate and also, a speck in the distance, I see a figure pass through the gate, walking the same circular path as we are, but in the opposite direction.

When the speck is close enough that I am sure it is Garry, he is still on the far side of the reservoir. I can see him clearly but it is more difficult when your viewpoint is eighteen inches from the ground.

"Look!" I say, to The Four. "It's Garry." And I point. Of course The Four are all excited. Three leap around randomly, looking everywhere, barking enthusiastically but pointlessly.

However, Shannon looks at me, follows my pointing and *concentrates*. She hesitates for a moment, one forepaw slightly raised, and then with a yip, races off, over two stiles, through a kissing gate and across a small footbridge over a feeder stream to the reservoir, before flinging herself into the arms of her beloved, if slightly startled, Garry.

Garry and I finally meet five minutes or so later, both still laughing. "That was nice." he says, grinning.

I arrive home from work, unlocking the kitchen door with the usual howling doggy chaos coming through the door to greet me. Opening up and stepping inside, I am met by the dogs; correction, three of the dogs.

After a moment's confusion, I identify that I have Seamus, Shannon and Duncan greeting me. No Minnie. Where is Minnie?

"Where's Minnie?" I say out loud, this being one of my standard ways of calling for a specific dog. "Where's Minnie?"

Shannon stops and catches my eye. Certain she has my attention, she goes to the foot of the stairs, checks that I am following, and leads me to my bedroom, where, somehow, Minnie has managed to lock herself in.

Shannon does this sort of thing all the time. She understands a lot of what is said around her. It is almost unnerving sometimes, seeing her react to speech, often not even aimed at her. I do not doubt that her understanding is tied in with voice tone and body language, but for that matter, the same can be said of people. On the other hand, she does suffer from political deafness. How is it that a dog who cannot hear her name being shouted at her from ten feet away whilst out walking, can nonetheless hear, through two floors, three walls and a staircase, the sound of the foil lid of a yoghurt pot being quietly peeled back?

Bracken and More

The day I find 'Blackie' in the woods, I do not know what on earth I am going to do with him. I do not want to take him to the rescue centre. Having taken responsibility for him, I am reluctant to pass him along to someone else. However well-meaning they are at the centre, I want to know what Blackie's future is going to be, to be one hundred per cent sure that all goes well for him.

However, even on a temporary basis, I cannot keep him myself. I am simply out of space and facilities. However, Blackie is in luck, because Garry thinks he is wonderful. Blackie is a big strapping dog, and they do say that dogs and owners tend to resemble each other; I wonder what says about me? Blackie moves in with Garry, in his house at the far side of the village, and becomes 'Bracken'.

We share walks together, Bracken soon fitting in with the Gang of Four to become a kind of 'Fifth Beatle' to my canine tribe. He and Seamus strike up a particular friendship and oddly, Seamus does not object to Bracken being around Shannon. Instead, two boys together, they romp off as a pair to go exploring.

Bracken becomes Garry's best mate and pal, and they adore each other. However, Garry must go out to work and Bracken spends a lot of time by himself.

Garry and I both work during the day and we split the lunchtime load of coming home to look after the dogs. However, while we take turns to visit both homes, The Gang of Four all have each other during the day, but Bracken is by himself. He really needs a friend, not just Garry but a canine pal, someone who can be company for him during the long, lonely hours of work.

Garry visits the rescue centre to choose a friend for Bracken, asking me to go with him, to look and offer opinions. I am very happy to do this but point out that it is a very personal choice for him. I can hardly choose a dog for someone else. What I can do however, is offer my views on whether any particular dog might be unsuitable. For example, Bracken is a big energetic dog. He needs a robust companion. Any dog too delicately built, or of shy personality, might not do well living with him.

I need not have worried. Garry's choice is I think, an excellent one. He is not a large dog, but 'Harvey' is a rufty-tufty little charmer with a big personality and the most enormous tail and ears. He is a cracker and I am sure that he and Bracken will get on like a house on fire. Garry must go through the usual checking process, the required visits and walking before he can adopt Harvey and so there is a wait of a week or so before Harvey will be able to come to his new adoptive home.

A couple of days after the visit to the shelter, Garry and I are walking through the woods with The Four and Bracken. Or more precisely, Garry and I are walking with Shannon, Minnie and Duncan. Seamus and Bracken have already cleared off together, having fun. Neither of us is worried. The Boys don't go looking for trouble and they will return by the time we have done a circuit or two of the woods.

We encounter some of the regulars; Olivia with Maggie, Suzi from the farm; an ageing collie who will simply tag along with anyone walking up through the farm and then accompany them back again. The problem with Suzi arises if you do not plan to return to the farm, in which case Suzi must be sent back home. Everyone in the area knows the words "Go home Suzi. Go home." And good as gold, Suzi trots back over the fields to her own Mum.

There is another dog. A large greyhound is hanging around under the rhododendrons, looking aimless and lost. Mmmm…. No collar. Dumped; yet another.

Greyhounds are one of the most unfortunate breeds for being abandoned. A working dog who is too old, or does not measure up for racing or coursing, has no value to the low-lives who breed them to be no more than running machines. At that, the lucky ones are dumped. The unlucky ones are often hanged.

This dog is one of the fortunate ones; at least she has been abandoned where she will be discovered.

She is not shy or particularly nervous and it takes only a few minutes for me and Garry to get close enough to slip a lead around her neck. I start talking to her. "Lovely girl. What a good girl. Sheba's a good girl isn't she."

Garry looks at me askance. "Sheba? You think it's a good idea to give her a name? It's not as though either of us can keep her."

I shrug this off. "It's just a way of being able to talk to her. If she has a name, then she has something to respond to. We can at least tell the shelter a bit about her and how she has behaved. Do you think you can accommodate her overnight? It's a bit crowded in my place. I'll give the shelter a call in the morning and see if they can take her."

Garry agrees to this happily enough and we go our separate ways, he with Sheba and Bracken, me with The Four to contact the rescue shelter.

When I call the shelter, they are sympathetic, but unable to take Sheba for a day or so. Can they call me at the weekend when they have had a few adoptions and have room in their kennels? I tell them it is no problem for a few days, then drive to Garry's house to let him know, and to take him some extra dog blankets and towels.

I arrive to find Garry, Bracken and Sheba all settled on his settee watching TV. Sheba seems very comfortable with her new circumstances and Bracken is thrilled at this new development. Garry is unsettled however.

"I'd keep her, but I've already committed to taking Harvey. I'm supposed to be picking him up at the weekend."

I understand this completely. It goes against the grain to surrender an animal once you have any kind of link with them. As they say, if you pick up the baton, you run with it. I have a feeling that I know which way this is going to develop....

Sure enough, by the following week, Garry has become the unintentional owner of three dogs instead of one. Bracken, Sheba and Harvey form an instant pack with their 'Dad' and with each other. Certainly, any loneliness problem that Bracken had, has been solved at a stroke.

And now, when walking in the woods with my Gang of Four and Garry's Gang of Three, life becomes very exciting. The two groups quickly come to view each other as two branches of a single pack. They respond as one. Rabbits are flushed out. Squirrels are chased. All is fun and joy and excited barking as seven dogs run in silly circles playing 'Chase me-Catch me'.

Sheba quickly shows her colours; in her previous life, she has been used for either hunting or coursing. If a rabbit is spotted, six dogs will chase it hysterically into the undergrowth, but Sheba stands still, watching and calculating.

She lopes forward, swinging around the shrubbery and away from the rest of the pack, but in the line of the fleeing prey, appearing a minute or so later with a dead rabbit dangling from her mouth.

The first time this happens, Garry is horrified when I take the rabbit from her - she surrenders it easily enough - and then take it home to skin and turn into casserole. I point out to him that, firstly, I grew up eating rabbit because my father bred them for eating, and secondly, it is a waste of perfectly good food not to eat it. I give the skin back to Sheba as her prize but Garry never really settles to eating 'bunnies'.

This is not the end of Garry's dog acquisitions. A few months later, a friend of mine, Mary, an old lady who has become crippled and can no longer exercise her dog properly, is looking for a home for 'Murphy'.

Murphy is a lovely dog and I have walked him many times for Mary, but I cannot accept him myself. Five is simply too many dogs for me, but Garry finds room for him, and so the charming, black be-curled Murphy also joins Garry's pack.

※

Garry is away for a few days and I am looking after Bracken, Sheba and Harvey for him. Today on our walk, we are The Gang of Seven. Even in my large estate car, roomy for most purposes, space is tight as the canine septet mill around the back.

The day is bitter cold, with temperatures well below freezing. The canal is almost completely iced over and there is thick snow on the ground. The dogs love this. I take them to fields away from the side of the canal where they can play in the snow, Minnie and Harvey tunnelling through it, noses down like a snow ploughs, Seamus, Shannon and Bracken haring around in circles and Duncan playing snowballs with me, trying to catch them in his mouth then digging, single-leggedly, to find them again as they collapse in his mouth and he thinks he has dropped them. Sheba is watching eagle-eyed for the hares which live in this field.

Despite the fun, I keep it brief. What we call in the North a lazy wind, is whistling through me, not around me. Duncan and Sheba, thinly furred, are shivering. Minnie, thickly furred, is perfectly warm, but her low slung body is accumulating snow that grabs her fluffy tummy, freezing into icy balls which trail the ground. Even Shannon, Seamus and Harvey are beginning to worry at their toes, where snow is balling into their pads.

Bracken is unfazed by any of this. His thick fur and large bulk protect him against the weather. He is seemingly unaffected by ice and snow. Still good to go, he announces it loudly to Seamus, jumping at him, paws splayed in an invite to play Tag.

Seamus brushes him off. He is ready to go home and I lead the dogs down the small track past the canal towards the car park.

Most follow me, but Bracken, still excited, charges off the path, and as I, belatedly realising what he is doing, try to call him back, onto the canal and over the ice. He skids across the surface to the centre, and my heart in my mouth as I watch, the ice collapses under him and he falls through.

Oh my God!

Can he get out? "Bracken! Bracken!" I call to him wildly. As yet he does not realise his danger and is simply paddling in the ice water, looking wetly surprised at this unexpected development.

I call him again, and this time he tries to respond, firstly by swimming towards me and the safety of the bank, and then, when he realises that he cannot swim through the ice, by trying to climb onto the surface. The thin frozen shell simply cracks under his paws, stranding him in the freezing water. Bracken continues to try to reach me by climbing out.

I am really panicking now. Can he get out? Can he get out? Seamus is stood beside me, tail wagging. He never doubts me.

Bracken is actually making good headway. He has made an opening into the ice perhaps twenty feet from the bank. With his great size and strength, although he cannot climb out, by breaking the ice with his efforts, he is effectively digging himself a channel through. This ice breaker of a canine has cleared himself a passage first five and then ten feet through the ice and the bitter water.

Bracken understands his danger now, but I can see that the cold is beginning to take its toll. His thick underfur protects him against the cold of the water, but only so far. He is beginning to struggle.

"Come on Bracken." I shout, encouraging him. "Come on. Good boy. You can do it." Seamus joins in, yipping loudly, and Shannon too, cheering him on.

Bracken makes more, slower progress. The ice is thickening here towards the bank, making it harder for him to break, but not yet strong enough for him to climb out.

And as I see him slowing, I wonder if he will make it. How deep is the canal here? Should I get down into the water with him?

If it's a couple of feet deep I will have no worse than wet clothes and cold toes, but if it is deeper than that, I would probably drown with him if I tried.

Finally, Bracken is close enough for me to grab his collar. With his huge weight and dripping wet, there is no possibility that I can lift him out myself, but I try anyway, and it does the trick. The extra leverage my pulling gives, enables him to get a foothold on the ice, and then the bank, and he pulls himself out. Seamus barks and spins like a top. Shannon simply sits and looks at me, her gorgeous amber eyes thoughtful.

Bracken, for good measure, shakes himself all over me. I am now soaked to the skin from the thighs down. Counting my blessings, these being mainly that I will not have to tell Garry that I have drowned his dog, I head back for the car and a hot bath.

Seamus and Bracken are good pals. As the two senior males in their respective packs, they have formed an alliance, or more precisely, a 'Boys Night Out' club.

If Garry and I meet in the woods, the two packs merge, and then, while the rest of us; me, Garry, Shannon, Minnie, Duncan, Sheba and Harvey, promenade together through the woods, Seamus and Bracken pick their moment to vanish off, only reappearing half an hour later after Garry and I have yelled ourselves hoarse trying to call them in. When they deign to return, they are utterly unrepentant, panting and cheerful. 'Oh, were you looking for us?'

Neither of them behaves like this if the packs are separate. When I am walking alone with The Four, Seamus stays close by as outrider to the group. Garry assures me that Bracken behaves the same way if it is just his group on the walk.

But put the two packs together and suddenly, for Seamus and Bracken, it is 'We Boys Together.' It's time to dash off to the pub, drink lager and talk about girls and fast cars.

Needless to say, I blame this errant behaviour on the part of my otherwise immaculately behaved boy, on Garry's undisciplined rowdy. And of course, he says exactly the same.

Seamus is always a bit of a so-and-so for wandering off when it suits him. Neutering him has never really changed his inclinations and I am constantly having to go look for him. I never really worry about him as he has good traffic sense and is not looking for trouble. He just enjoys filling his day with an amble down the lanes and calling in on friends.

I am woken early by the phone ringing. "Hello." I answer. Who is ringing me at this hour? I check the clock; six thirty.

Garry is on the other end of the line. "Lost something?" He is laughing.

Still half asleep and befuddled, I have not yet had my intravenous coffee…. "Sorry, what? What?"

Garry is still laughing. "Have you done a head count yet?"

I sit up and look around the room. Three dogs and a cat, no Seamus.

2 + 2 = 4.

"Have you got Seamus there?"

"Yup. He called by, at around three this morning. Bracken told me he was outside asking to come in. Since you didn't phone to ask if I'd seen him, I reckoned you hadn't missed him, so I didn't see the point in waking you."

Oh God…. Isn't it supposed to be cats that have homes of convenience? "Garry, I'm really sorry…"

He is still laughing. "I'll call by on my way to the woods. If we go together then perhaps he'll come home with you."

Dog Days

I have discovered a new and beautiful walk, to the East of Clitheroe and on the edge of the Ribble Valley, but in the most unlikely of places. There is a small industrial estate, The Pimlico Estate, which houses a cattle auction market and a number of standard 'metal box' type industrial units. Sandwiched in between them is Salthill Quarry, set to the side of a road which could not look more ordinary. A modern throughway, flanked by commercial buildings and lined with very ordinary hedgerows gone a bit straggly, hawthorn, blackthorn and the like. Step behind the hedges and something wonderful lies there.

Having found this place by accident, it astonishes me. Designated an SSSI, it is not a large area and its glories are not immediately obvious. You have to look at what is around you.

Bounded by dry stone walls, narrow paths wind through grassland teeming with wild flowers, butterflies and every kind of insect life. The air is a-twitter with bird song and laden with fragrance from the meadowsweet growing freely here. On a warm day, with sunshine to open the flowers, there are cowslips, knapweed and wild strawberries. The local stone is limy, and harebells bloom in response. Common blue butterflies flit around me when the air is warm and still, and orange tips are not unusual.

But it is not for the flora and the fauna that this micro-Eden is designated SSSI. It is for the geology.

I am standing in an open meadow, grass clipped to lawn by rabbits. There is a sizable gouge in the ground exposing the limestone and I guess that this is part of the original quarry. Wandering over, I stand on the bare rock, gazing out at the sunny vista about me and glance down at what I am standing on.

Then I *look* down.

The naked rock is broken and cracked, with large numbers of shards scattered about in a rubbly mass, through every size from pebbles to boulders, raw and unpolished, broken or eroded from the bedrock. Each piece of stone; every piece of stone, has a structure to it. Everything about me is made up of fossilised creatures, tubular and segmented.

Later, at home, I identify these as crinoids, creatures resembling sea anemones on stalks. I am standing on a reef that was alive and growing some three hundred million years ago when these lands were under shallow seas and in warmer climes. In this simple spot, hiding behind a facade of modernism and industrial activity, I am looking straight down into Deep Time.

Wandering, I amble down tiny beaten paths by the dry stone walls and it dawns on me that the individual stones of the walls are also largely made up of a mass of the crinoids. Everything around me is either alive now, or has been alive, a very long time ago.

I choose a rock, a rough four-inch cube, bright with detail, as a souvenir. At home, I use it as a door stop to my back door for some time until my visiting mother spots it and somehow, if finds its way back to her house.

Dogs don't 'do' personal space. It's a human concept, not a canine one. If you are going to keep a dog, or several dogs, it is vitally important that you remember this, and more to the point, learn to live with it, and its consequences.

A strange man sits too close to me on a train or on a park bench. I do not like this. At best it is uncomfortable, ill-mannered on his part. At worst, I feel threatened by it.

I stand in a lift with a small group of people. It is not too crowded and there is plenty of space for everyone. But the woman standing next to me is too close. I shuffle away a little and she follows. This feels entirely wrong. Is she a pick-pocket? Or just weird?

I am on a date with a guy I met on the internet and this is the first time we have met. His profile looked promising and he sounded good on the phone, but here, meeting him for the first time, I have followed the rules. He knows only my first name and he does not know where I live. We are in a public place and I have seated myself at the opposite side of the table from him. Now that I meet him, I am not keen. His body language feels wrong and I lean back in my chair, away from him.

He leans forward, trying to get closer, despite my clear physical hints that I do not wish to be closer. I will have a polite two drinks, soft, not alcoholic, and then leave. We will not be having a second date.

These are 'people rules'. Dogs do not obey them.

I am lying on the settee. There is a dog sandwiched between me and the back of the settee. Another is laid over my feet and one is in my arms being cuddled. The fourth is wearing a trail in the carpet, pacing up and down trying to figure out how to crowbar his way into this canine-human jigsaw. I am hot, pinned down and uncomfortable, but if I get off the settee for my drink, I will spend the next half hour trying to regain my place.

I am lying in the bath. The theory is that, it having been a tough day at work and having fulfilled my dog-walking duties with a three-mile stretch around the fields, I am to lie here, luxuriating in hot sudsy water with a glass of red, an apple and a good book.

The reality is that, I have two canines leaning over the bath looking down at me and panting 'dog breath' in my face.

Periodically they lean further in to lap at the water, then, having coated their noses in foam, snort it off into my face.

As I try to lie low in the water, I hear the noise of lapping coming from the toilet bowl.

⁂

It is early. I am still half asleep and I do not have nearly enough coffee inside me. Wearing only the long tee-shirt that does me for a nightie, I lean over the bathroom sink to brush my teeth. Moments later, I stand up with a startled "Yow!" as the long, icy wet end of a dog's nose goes under my tee-shirt and up….

⁂

I would like a little privacy. It is only for a few short minutes in the bathroom and I have carefully closed the door, ensuring that the latch clicks into place. I sit, peacefully staring into space to commune with nature. There is a bang on the door. The door bounces against the weight of a medium large dog rebounding from the timbers and the latch clicks off. Four dogs jointly shoulder their way through the door and into the tiny space, then cluster about me. I wave the nose of one away from probing me too deeply, whilst fighting another for possession of my underwear. I find that I have lost the impulse which brought me in here in the first place and wearily know that I will have to repeat this performance in half an hour's time.

⁂

Seamus is looking up at me, catching my eye. "Can I have that?"

I am sat on the toilet, still trying to have a few quiet moments. I look around. "What?"

He looks at me first, until he sure he has my attention, and then transfers his gaze to the empty toilet roll middle on the laundry basket next to me.

Just to be clear, the nose and droopy ear tips also point to indicate this delectable object.

"That. That there. Can I have that? Please."

With a sigh, I hold out the cardboard tube. Seamus takes it politely from my hand and vanishes downstairs. By the time I find him again, he is laid on the lawn with his booty, blissfully nibbling off quarter inch squares and eating them. Doubtless I will be cleaning them up again, suitably processed, in a few hours' time.

New Times

After nearly twelve years of living single, I meet John. It comes as a great surprise to me that I have met someone with whom I am willing to share my space again. Twelve years has made me very independent and a bit set in my ways. I have my house and my routine and I know how to run my life. There have been boyfriends, Garry having being the main, but I am far too fond of having my own way to be willing to consider myself, I had thought, anything but young(ish), free and single. Nonetheless, John and I meet and instantly click. It happens that way sometimes.

The first time I invite him back to my house, it is latish one evening after we have had a meal together in a local pub, discussing everything from politics to physics, economics to cosmology. John follows me as I drive through the mess of tiny lanes and roads that track through to my cottage.

It is very dark. He tells me later that a report on the radio of a woman who had gone bonkers and attacked a man with an axe; combined with the dark roads and the hooting of the owls, made quite an impression on him. And then, arriving at the cottage, he is met with the welcome of The Gang of Four, with the howls and gnashing of teeth that is their response to a stranger at the door.

I have of course mentioned that I have dogs, but have been unspecific about how many I have in my little house. Over time John and the dogs grow to love each other. He and Seamus come to have a bit of a 'man-to-man' relationship, Minnie and Shannon like to go through the 'tickle my tummy' routine and Duncan plays up his role of the eternal puppy.

Although living in Manchester, John spends more and more time with me in Whinshill Cottage. This begins to lead to difficulties. Buying Whinshill Cottage all those years ago, it was a home for me, a dog and my books.

The cottage, a 'two-up-two-down', was fine for my purposes then. Over the years I have cleaned up the loft space and turned it into a usable room; my office, home for my text books, lecture notes and other paraphernalia, and I have converted the small child's bedroom into my library.

I love the feel of my books around me, the world at my beck and call, with volumes on every subject from geology to art, physics to poetry. Richard Dawkins rubs shoulders with Tolkien, Asimov with Machiavelli, and the brothers Grimm with James Lovelock. It all works well for me.

Now however, my little cottage is housing me, John, four dogs, Polly the Cat (acquired when Garry's sister rescues a stray who promptly 'produces'. I am more or less informed that I am having a kitten.) and offices for his business and my work. Whinshill Cottage is simply not viable as 'Home' any longer.

John's business is property renovation; buy a wreck, do it up and sell it on. I have done some house restoration myself. My first home was an old cottage, purchased almost as a write off, which I and my, then, husband renovated. So it is now a natural thought that together, John and I should find a house, of a more sensible size, suitable for renovation and which we could make our home and perhaps make a little money on. I start looking around.

Pendon Edge

⥬

The remit is: a house of generous size, a character property, an enclosed garden for the dogs, access to walkies, easy access to Manchester for work purposes for both John and I, and 'potential'.

I find what seems to be the perfect property about ten miles away towards the Yorkshire/Lancashire border. It is a Georgian semi-detached house and has been a library in the past. The other half of the same building was originally the school master's house. Although fronting onto a main road, there is a decent sized back garden, albeit badly overgrown, and the views to the rear are wonderful.

This backdrop is spectacular. The village name 'Pendon Edge', refers to an escarpment running all along the valley. Pendon Edge village itself is a single road running along the bottom of the valley. To one side, the hillside rises towards Burnley and the Pennine moors and to the other, spectacular cliffs strike skywards, culminating in a high, harsh plateau. After rain, water cascades from the plateau in astonishing falls, carving the rock into shapes uncannily like Easter Island statues, giving the impression of sharp faces gazing down into the valley. It is certainly one of the most arresting views in Lancashire. The house looks towards these cliffs and a track down the side of the house leads to perfect doggy walking territory, so The Gang of Four will be just fine.

The inside of the house is a mess. Built over four stories, it is a tall thin building with a garden flat at the bottom, a huge attic space at the top and bedrooms in between. The whole house is packed with 'stuff'. The first time John and I visit to view the property, there are a couple of bedrooms where it is actually impossible to open the door against the clutter inside. Easing the door open as far as we can, we crane our necks around the corner to see inside.

Viewing the house from the outside, most of the windows are blocked by piles of books, boxes and god-knows-what stacked up against the panes.

It hardly matters. The house is potentially very beautiful and is an ideal renovation project. There are no real building works. It is all cosmetic work and elbow grease. This is at a time of climbing property prices and the house will make us a lovely home. After some negotiations our offer is accepted and a contract drawn up. What could be more straightforward?

A few days later John and I decide to take the dogs for a walk along the track of their soon-to-be-new-home. The Four have lived in Whinshill Cottage for many years and so it seems sensible to give them a taste of what is coming, to take some of the trauma out of the move. We park up and the dogs all tumble out, barking excitedly to find themselves in this new and unknown area. They love the walk. The track is full of fascinating doggy smells. There is a little stream for them to play in. The tunnel under the railway line is cause for great sniffing and widdling. It is a great success.

Walking back along the track, there is a couple coming towards us with a couple of dogs. We say 'Hello.' as we pass. Their dogs and ours exchange sniffs and news and we chat with them for a few minutes.

"Yes, we're buying a house nearby. So we'll be moving here in a few weeks."

"Oh yes? Whereabouts?"

"The big Georgian place at the end of the track here."

The couple exchange 'looks' and smile. "Good luck." he says. "My brother tried to buy that place off her. She led him a complete dance before he gave up on it. Cost him hundreds it did, with surveys and everything."

John and I are baffled but unmoved. "We've signed a contract. The sale's going through in a few weeks."

The couple exchange glances again. "Well as I said, good luck. I'll look forward to meeting up with you again." They walk on.

"What d'you think that was all about?" I ask John.

"It hardly matters does it." he replies. "The contract is signed now." As it turns out, this is not prophetic.

The owner of the house is 'Amanda'. It transpires that she does not actually want to sell the house at all, but is having to do so because her parents, having helped to buy out her husband when she divorced, now need their money back. They are elderly, whereas their daughter is working in a good job, and it is time for her to downsize.

Amanda's modus operandi has been, to have the house up for sale, allow viewings, accept an offer and then put every possible obstacle in the way of the actual sale. In addition to the couple we have met on the walk, over the next few weeks, bizarrely, John and I meet three other people who have tried to buy the house and eventually backed out, having first wasted a lot of money on their attempted purchase.

We make arrangements for a surveyor to visit the property to make a valuation for the bank. Amanda refuses to let him view. Three times she blocks his efforts before he is able produce his report. The bank requests an electrical report on the house. Amanda refuses to let the electrician in, claiming illness.

Part of the contract we have agreed with Amanda, is that the purchase deposit will be paid by a given date. The bank makes a small error and pays the deposit one day late. We then receive a letter from Amanda's solicitor stating that, because of this, his client is cancelling the contract but will be retaining the deposit.

We arrange a meeting with both Amanda and her parents. Her mother and father clearly have little idea what their daughter has been doing and are shocked at what we tell them. To their dismay, Amanda says that she does not want to sell the house.

However, we make it clear that any detail of the contract can be discussed and is open to negotiation; timing, items to be left in the property, anything, except that the sale will go through. Amanda is not happy and at this point we leave. Her parents must apply the necessary pressure.

Eventually it is confirmed that all is in place for the sale to proceed. A week before the set date for completion, I drive past the house, expecting to see signs of packing. Looking from the car, nothing has changed. Items that were stacked up against windows previously, are still there. Furtively, I peer through some downstairs windows, not expecting to see furniture moved, but perhaps cardboard boxes being filled, or rubbish cleared from the house. Nothing has changed. Nothing. Inspecting the garage, it is the same.

Telling John what I have seen, he is as disturbed as I. We make a point of calling by the next day, at a time when we can reasonably expect Amanda to be in. Knocking on the door, there is no reply. We are about to leave, when the door opens in the next house. A pleasant faced lady says "She's in there y'know. I saw her arrive from work." We chat for a minute with our soon-we-hope-neighbour and then bang on the door again, more loudly this time.

Eventually, Amanda answers, barely holding the door open, peering around a crack at us. She looks sour and unhealthy. John speaks in his most jovial voice.

"Hello, we just thought we would drop by to check that everything is ready for next week? Packing and everything okay?" She mutters something at us and then closes the door. John and I exchange glances. We have a bad feeling about this.

I drive past every day. There is no sign of any activity whatsoever. We are baffled. Has she booked a lot of last minute help to pack up the house? Four storeys of furniture and a lifetime's worth of goods and junk. Why is she not packing?

The day of the sale arrives. Having received confirmation of completion from our own solicitor, John and I meet with Amanda's solicitor to collect the keys. Passing the keys to John, he says "It's not over yet. She's still in there." We feel sorry for the man. He thinks his client is a fruitcake. So do we.

John and I drive to the house, now legally ours. We arrive to find a small van parked at the front with Amanda's elderly mother and father trying to lift an armchair into the back. They look stressed, but nod courteously when we wish them good morning. Stepping into the house, a quick glance shows that almost nothing has changed from the last time we were inside. Furniture, ornaments, piles of newspapers and magazines, everything, is where we last saw it. We walk along the hall to the kitchen; the same. Standing in the kitchen, we quietly discuss what to do. The mother and father come in and then, just behind them, comes Amanda. She sees John and I stood in the kitchen, and without even acknowledging us, turns to her father and mother and asks "Did you let them in?"

The mother turns to us, flushed with embarrassment. John waves a calming hand at her. "We'll be in the garden. Why don't you talk to your daughter?"

John and I leave the three talking, and go outside to discuss what we can most usefully do next. Working inside the house is out of the question and we agree to start clearing the vastly overgrown back garden. Popping back into the house to have a chat with the mother and father, Amanda is nowhere in sight.

The parents are very apologetic, and John and I feel a lot of sympathy for them. They have the most colossal job ahead of them. Fortunately, we do not need to move in since we still have Whinshill Cottage available, the new tenant not being due to arrive for a few days, and so the situation is not the disaster it might have been for most other purchasers. John tells the parents that they can have the weekend to clear the house; we will work in the garden.

I explain to them that we will return the following day to work out in the back garden, and that I will be bringing my dogs with me. I have noticed that Amanda's cat is still in the house and point out that it would be wise to get the cat away. If The Four encounter her, who knows what will happen?

The following day we arrive, tooled up for work in the garden. We park at the rear and unload spades, shovels, shears, secateurs, pick-axe, crowbar and bonfire kit. The Four howl protest at enforced imprisonment in the car until I open up and let them though the rear gate into the garden.

A scene flashes before my eyes. As I open the gate, Amanda's cat is in the middle of the path. In the same instant, it sees the dogs and they see the cat. Regardless of my yelling, the dogs set off in hot pursuit and the cat vanishes over the fence.

The back door flies open, slammed back on its hinges, and Amanda bursts out of the house, screaming like a fishwife. "If anything happens to my cat I'll…."

I never find out what she would have done because I interrupt her. "Amanda. I told your mother and father last night, that we would be coming with the dogs today and that you should get the cat out of here."

Amanda's normally pasty complexion is flushed almost purple in rage. "I haven't spoken to them. They've not said anything to me."

I am trying to keep a lid on my temper, but it is fraying at the edges. "It's not our fault if you and your parents haven't spoken. We were quite clear that we were coming here to work today and that I would be bringing my dogs."

Her face churns like a five-year-old with a tantrum. "This is all your fault. If you hadn't turned up yesterday, we could have had the house packed up by now."

The sheer audacity, let alone the duplicity, of what she is saying takes my breath away.

"Amanda. This is not your house any more. You should have been out, with all your goods, and your cat, yesterday. You should have been packing weeks ago."

"The only reason you are still here, is that John gave your parents an extra couple of days to get the house emptied. If it wasn't for that, you would have been facing a large legal bill for compensation and costs."

Her face twists, and if it is possible, becomes even more highly coloured. Amanda stands poised as though she is going to attack me. For one moment I think she is going to launch herself at me, to punch me.

Make my day....

John intervenes. "Go and find your cat and get it out of here. We are working here in the back garden, and the dogs are staying."

She turns on her heel and marches inside the house. This is the last time we see Amanda. A little later we encounter her parents again, still heroically trying to empty their selfish daughter's enormous house into the tiny van. The day after we learn that Amanda has gone on holiday to Italy.

The following Monday, the house is emptier, but by no means empty. Amanda's father passes us a key, looking ill with exhaustion. "We've had enough. Anything that's left is yours." Technically John and I could make something of this. A seller is legally required to leave a house properly emptied. However, we do not have the heart to insist, and who knows, some of the remaining furniture might come in handy.

Working our way through the house, we discover that some things have been removed which should not have been. A rather attractive cast iron fireplace from one of the bedrooms has vanished.

On the other hand, in the garage is a monstrous safe, eight feet high and weighing probably a couple of tons. We contact the parents and are assured that the safe will be removed and the fireplace returned, but nothing ever comes of either.

Giving up on it as a bad job, we take the house as we have it and move on. It is still full of junk and rubbish of all kinds. It has been my intention that the basement floor, with its back door onto the garden, should be the 'dog flat'. However, it is stuffed of old furniture, broken fridges and boxes of miscellaneous bits and pieces that I want to sort through, on the off chance that there is something useful in there. Much of it is however, outright trash, and I cannot in conscience leave the dogs down there. I don't give a damn if they entertain themselves with the 'toys' down there or piddle on the stinking carpets, but I do not want them hurting themselves on anything. So for the moment, if John and I go out, The Four stay up on the first floor in the kitchen.

The kitchen has a rather old fashioned connection to the outside world, with a set of stone steps leading from the kitchen door down to the garden. The steps are rather attractive and I am looking forward to planting clematis or rambling roses to scramble over them.

Right now, I settle for sitting at the top with my back against the kitchen door, a cup of coffee in hand, enjoying the outstanding views of the cliffs. This is not truly comfortable though. The stone is cold and hard under me and the door jabs into me with the sharp edges of a battered cat-flap.

It is a few days after we have moved in and the house is in complete chaos. John and I return home after being out for a couple of hours, buying paint and other materials.

Before leaving, we carefully ensured that the dogs were locked in the kitchen, so on our return, we are surprised to find that they are all out in the back garden, basking in warm August sunshine. How have they gotten out? We can see from the gate that the kitchen door is still closed.

The mystery is solved when Shannon jumps up to greet us, wearing the remains of the cat-flap around her neck. I would not have believed that such a large dog could have exited via what is left of the hole in the door. Removing Shannon's stylish necklace, I go in search of a bit of board to block up the hole.

Our new home is a mess, long neglected, abused and ill-maintained. We work our way through a confusion of abandoned furniture, broken fridges, 1960's crockery and cutlery, dead plants and junk of all kinds.

Under the eaves we find that, not only has the roof been leaking, but it has been leaking into ancient carpets, rolled up and stored there since God knows when.

Confined in their narrow, ill ventilated spaces, they stink. Moving them is problematic. They weigh a ton with all the water they have absorbed, and are in an advanced stage of rot, so when we try to pull them out, they simply rip. They are deeply, deeply unpleasant; slimy, black and spraying filth and spores whenever they are moved. In addition, we are four floors up. How will we get them down?

There is a small window, broken, to the attic space. Fortunately, it looks down over the side garden, not the road. Wearing face masks and rubber gloves, between us, John and I slice the carpets into pieces small enough to handle, haul the unsavoury items to the window, and checking briefly that no dogs are below us in the garden, chuck them bodily to the ground. We actually hear a 'splat' as they land.

Clearing the back garden is instructive. There is a narrow path leading from gate to door, with a tiny lawn to one side and beyond that, a number of vastly overgrown leylandii, thirty or forty feet high. I loathe leylandii at the best of times, but these have been allowed to run completely rampant.

We start to cut them back, not too difficult a task as the wood is soft. Tackling them one by one, we think there are perhaps a dozen trees to get down. By the time we finish, John and I have felled thirty-eight of the monsters, so intergrown and woven together, that it was previously impossible to separate them.

Suddenly the garden opens up. Sunlight reaches the lawn and the tired flower borders.

At the far side of the garden, what has appeared to be just a tumbledown shed in the corner, is revealed as a tumbledown shed set in a large area, six feet deep in further junk. Rotten timbers, old fencing panels, ancient gas bottles, five-gallon plastic containers full of unidentifiable liquids, all vie for space with nettles and brambles. With axe, saw and crowbar, we start at the outside, working inwards to clear the space.

By the time we are done, the garden has expanded from an apparent twenty feet by ten strip of turf, to a walled space of perhaps fifty feet by fifty. People walking past on the side track stop and stare, commenting in astonishment that they had no idea the garden was so large. We are fairly astonished ourselves. Another few days' work has the ground cleaned, levelled and raked for grass seed. It is October and a warm Autumn. By the end of November, we have a large and lovely lawn.

Meanwhile, the work in the kitchen has come on beautifully. Simply ripping out all the old units and stripping back the walls to the bones, we now have the joiner in to put it all back together again; Jeff, my old friend of years ago. His last work for me was fitting my wardrobes at Whinshill Cottage.

Jeff is fitting new units, replacing the ceiling, boarding up some strange gaps in the walls, making a useful cupboard out of a weirdly shaped space in one corner and refitting the external door so that Shannon can exit without taking the cat-flap with her.

The dogs and Polly the cat naturally find all this most interesting, and have been helping at every opportunity. Seamus has been breathing in sawdust and sneezing it back again over Jeff's lunch. Minnie is picking up odd 'toys' such as polishing rags, bits of architrave and stray ham sandwiches.

Polly is her own way very dog-like. She joins us for walks, and is a fully-fledged member of the pack, albeit right at the bottom of the pecking order so far as the dogs are concerned. Her contribution to the renovation is to help count screws, nails and drill bits, batting them over the floor tiles to 'make them go'.

Fortunately, Jeff knows my Gang from years back and rather likes them, otherwise the day might have become quite fraught.

The work done, it is looking good. I congratulate Jeff on what he has done and agree that he will return in a week of so once we have had the electrician and plumber in. After he has left, I clean up a bit and start to cook a meal, an ambitious enterprise right now. Cooking facilities are limited and I must wash dishes using a hosepipe into the sink.

I feed the dogs. This is done with a routine I have long established. Each dish is filled with an appropriate amount of food. The dogs do not huddle around my feet. They know the drill and the dishes go down in order of seniority. "Seamus." I say, putting his dish on the floor. Shannon, Minnie, Duncan, Polly all follow in that order. Each dish goes down and is immediately adopted by its owner, except Polly.

Where is Polly? No sign of her. I shout out into the back garden for her. Still nothing. In the hall, I shout upstairs. Still, no Polly. I ask Shannon "Where's Polly?" She gazes at me with liquid eyes but does not respond. Ah well. She's probably out mousing. Polly loves this garden with its nooks and crannies in the dry stone walls.

When Polly has still not returned two hours later, I am beginning to worry for her. She loves her food and it is not like her to miss a mealtime for so long. I call again around the house and then, finally, realise that I can hear her from the kitchen. At last! I go to the kitchen to put her food out and… no Polly. I check behind blinds and under the table.

I can hear her, mewing. She can't be locked in a cupboard, none of them have doors yet.

I can still hear her, quite loudly in fact. She is close by somewhere…. I look up, and there, peering down through a hole cut into the ceiling for one of the flush-fitted lights, is my cat. Her face fills the small circular opening as she inspects me from above. She shows no sign of alarm, simply fascination at this novel situation.

I inspect her possible exits. There are none. Jeff, an excellent joiner, has left the work fully stage-completed and all gaps, spaces, apertures and cracks have been professionally sealed.

I sigh and pick up my phone. "Hello. Is that you Jeff? Ermm…. Look I'm sorry to disturb you on a Friday night, but I've got a bit of a situation here…."

Finished, the kitchen cum dining room looks fabulous. The kitchen itself is clean lined and elegant in a shaker style, all long lines and verticality. Jeff, having installed the kitchen units has, with considerable flair, reamed out the woodwork of the door of the new under-stairs cupboard to match the factory made cupboards.

There is a good quality laminate flooring laid, ideal for kitchen splashes and dog paddles alike. The, previously dismal, nineteen fifties style gas fire has gone. The chimney opened, a real fire is in place and a beautiful marble surround sets it all off.

With fresh paint on walls and windows, long, chic linen curtains and fresh flowers from the garden, it looks simply splendid. We are delighted with the result. A previously dull, dark and dingy room is now light, airy and appealing.

The only blight on the room is the result of lack of forethought on my part. A dining room needs a dining table, and for this I chose a very attractive, glass topped table on a chrome steel frame.

This would not be my normal choice as I tend towards traditional furniture rather than modern, but in this case, the table was chosen to help maximise the feel of light and space in the room. It does this very well.

The problem is the glass top. I expect to have to dust it down every day. The polished surface does show up every mark or speck of dust, but I can take that in my stride.

However, sitting down to a meal means that, with four dogs underneath, watching every mouthful from fork to lips, and with noses pressed up against the glass, the underside of the table top is constantly coated in, let's call it mucus. And it is impossible to avoid looking at it either; not ideal when you are eating.

Cleaning this off is problematic. It is under the glass, so I must get onto hands and knees, then twist up to clean the marks.

A supermarket search for some kind of specialist cleaner is fruitless. Ink, yes. Coffee stains, yes. Red wine, tomato sauce, curry sauce; they are all out there on the supermarket shelves. Dog snot, no. And it sets like concrete.

And then, having cleaned it off, at the risk of a twisted back and housemaids knee, the little buggers go straight back and give it a fresh coating.

All this aside, eating with The Four under a glass table is an unnerving experience. As all dogs know, any food can be potentially claimed that has not actually entered the mouth of their human, so food is to be watched at all times. Passing egg and chips from plate to mouth with four snouts and four pairs of eyes under the glass, following the fork like the ball at a tennis match is off-putting. Slobber, drooling down gelatinously, from jaws to the floor, also dims the appetite. After a while, I find that I am really not that hungry and wander off to do a bit of painting upstairs instead.

༺༻

We have a carpet fitter, Jack, working in the lounge, measuring up for new carpets. Meanwhile, John and I are working upstairs, ripping out an ancient bathroom.

In the midst of levering apart an old cupboard, we are stopped in our tracks by a blood-curdling scream from downstairs and the sound of crashing movement. Dropping everything, we race downstairs, thinking that Jack has had some dreadful accident. Bursting into the lounge we find him running dementedly around the room, hurling himself backwards against walls. Polly is clinging to his back for dear life.

"Get it off me Get it off me." shrieks Jack. "Get the rat off me." Then he reverses into the wall again, trying to reach around his back to knock off the 'rat'.

John and I are helpless with laughter. "It's alright. It's only the cat." We try to tell him, but have trouble getting the words out.

On his hands and knees, Jack has been measuring up the lounge. Polly has wandered in to help with the job, decided that her best contribution would be to sit on his back, and jumped aboard. Jack, feeling 'a rat' attack him, has gone nearly hysterical trying to shake it off. Naturally, Polly's reaction is to cling on tighter, digging her claws into his skin and doing nothing to help Jack's state of mind.

Jack is deeply offended. John and I are crying with laughter and all but unable to speak. He decides not to quote for the work and we have to find another carpet fitter.

The Pennine moors above Pendon Edge are high and unforgiving but grimly beautiful. For much of the outside world, the area is famous for Howarth Moors, home of the Bronte sisters and for Holmfirth, of 'Last of the Summer Wine.' fame.

In Summer, tough grasses, sedges and gorse stretch as far as the eye can see, any trees being small, stunted by the winds that wail down from the heights. In Winter, you walk with hat, coat and gloves and be sure to carry a blanket in your car, 'just in case'. But there is some marvellous walking there if you are sensible and dress properly; something solid on your feet to deal with the uneven ground and a windproof jacket to handle the breeze which blows on all but the very stillest days, and which can, even when you think it calm, suddenly gust up, whipping your breath away.

And now, you can step out briskly, get the heart pumping and the limbs stretching. You will not overheat easily. Instead, air laced with the fragrance of hawthorn blossom in Spring, or the tang of snow in Winter washes over your face, as fine to the taste as chilled water on a hot day.

In places, deep gullies cut through the steep-sided hills, sculpted by the wash of a million rain drops biting through peat and stone to produce clefts that, even when small, will snatch at the ankles of the unwary. You must watch your step.

Some of these gullies have grown into gorges, and footpaths, often made by the tough moorland sheep, can be wayward. A route that looks trivial on the map, may wander far from the line of sight, as walkers pick out the safest way to cross, or more likely, go around, these chasms.

I have discovered this place by my usual method of driving around and getting 'creatively lost'. This is a favourite technique of mine and I have found some wonderful walks, and drives, by this method. In this case, I have followed roads up, up, up.... On the heights I see a car park by the roadside, close by a dozen or so wind turbines.

The wind turbines fascinate me. There are those who scream loud objections to them, saying they blight the landscape. I am not one of them. For me, these structures, harnessing the wind, providing electricity in a clean sustainable manner, are part of our future. Arguments fly back and forth as to efficiency and cost effectiveness of producing the energy, but these are details, solvable by technology and the long-term economics of energy. The principle is there and I find them beautiful. Soaring structures, higher than most steeples, and with a graceful sweeping of the blades that means they are earning their keep both aesthetically and economically.

But today, I shall walk in the opposite direction. I am unsure as to how The Four will react to these huge structures churning over them, and decide that we will familiarise ourselves with the area before I take the tracks by the turbines themselves.

The Four disgorge from the back of the car, identify a kissing gate out from the car park and are there ahead of me, clustering around, waiting for me to open up. I let them through. Shannon races away down the narrow track marked in the tough grasses, Duncan tripodding right at her heels. Minnie trails behind, puffing as she tries to keep up.

Seamus lags behind, carefully sniffing at and analysing the posts of the gate and fence. He has important land claims to make before he joins the rest of us.

The winding path leads through tussocky grass, gradually downhill in the general direction of a distant reservoir. In this area many of the valleys have been dammed for water catchment. Without exception, they make wonderful walking areas.

I follow the path, alternating between striding out and placing my feet with care. This is not a good place for a strained ankle. Descending, the landscape takes on strange forms, moonscape-like; not a natural environment. In places there are large hummocks, five, ten, twenty feet high, green with turf. In others, the hummocks are simply piles of stones, heaped high. I cannot imagine what the reason for all this is.

I wander off the path, exploring the hillocks. The mystery is partially solved when I encounter the remains of old kilns. Something has been processed here; the hillocks are spoil heaps. Following the paths downhill once more, there is a rushing streamlet, rocky bottomed. I do not doubt that in winter storms, this rill from the moors can be a raging torrent. The boulders carried down will be considerable. Someone has been picking and choosing amongst the boulders for the kilns.

Later, back at home, I look up information on the area. It transpires that my hillocks and kilns were once, between the sixteenth and nineteenth centuries, a major source of lime. Limestone, washed down from the high moors, was heated in the kilns and the end product, lime, transported out by mule. The industry was killed, at least in this form, by the building of the canals, which allowed limestone to be gathered from more convenient areas. My glorious, wild walk is a once-industrial landscape. In the end, Nature always reclaims her own.

The Gang of Four is thrilled with the discovery of the stream, splashing and frolicking through the water, lapping it up. I join them, quenching my thirst with water fresh from the peat moors and clear as it comes, tasting better than any that comes from a tap

Loafing around on the banks, we play together for a while, me throwing stones into the water and the dogs trying to catch them. Seamus, Minnie and Duncan are confused by the sinking pebbles.

Only Shannon has mastered holding her breath to retrieve from below the surface, although the rock she produces is not generally the same one I threw in the water.

On another day, I decide that it is time to explore the other side of the road and the area by the wind turbines. The footpath will take me directly under the windmills. Unsure how the dogs will react to this, before decanting The Four from the car, I carefully check that I have a full set of four leads in my pockets.

The turbines are huge. I find them majestic, with the blades sweeping down, whooshing past, twenty feet over my head. Strangely the dogs do not seem even to notice them, trotting along completely unconcerned at the monstrous blades passing above. I have often thought that dogs live in a more or less two dimensional landscape. Looking up is not in their remit....

….. unless you are Seamus and have a suspicion of all things airborne.

Seamus wanders a seemingly random course to and fro across the path, checking out sniffs and smells, and ensuring that any particularly outstanding tussock of grass has been peed on and marked as his. As a blade passes overhead, the rush of noise attracts his attention and he looks up....

"What the fuck is that?" Momentarily, he hits the ground, then, no Don Quixote he, Seamus is gone. No tilting at windmills here. Wilting under windmills more like. In fairness to him, H. G. Wells' Martian war machines would have looked not dissimilar.

Swearing under my breath, I give chase. Shannon, Minnie and Duncan are completely unfazed by the turbines and enjoy this new game of 'Chase Seamus' that he and Mum have cooked up. Fortunately, Seamus has run away from the road. Not so fortunately, he is about the same colour as the brown and tan tussock grass growing all around. I have trouble spotting him for a while.

Eventually Shannon catches up with him and her chase-me-catch-me message brings him to a halt. He is all manful insouciance now that Shannon is there. I arrive a couple of minutes later with Seamus running through his 'What, scared? Me?' routine with Shannon. I slip a lead on him but, no matter how I try to persuade him, nothing is dragging Seamus back in the direction of the turbines. I pick out a long looping path that takes us away from the turbines and back to the car from another direction entirely.

Apple Tree Farm

John and I need to move again. Although he moved to the North to attend the University in Manchester, his business is in the South and he needs to be closer to his work. The long hours of travelling, trying to run both halves of his life are taking their toll, and so we are looking again for a new home. This will not be our 'Forever Home' but a stepping stone towards it. I am finding this difficult and longing for the home I can really call my own. I do not mind, much, living in a building site all the time, but the lack of permanence is hard for me. Knowing that whatever I do and however well I work to make a house 'right', it will not be mine to enjoy, is hard and feels unnatural.

Still, that is how it is and I am searching for our next project. John would like to be based near Oxford as he has links to the area. He takes me there to see the small Oxfordshire villages, The Oxford Boat Week, his favourite pubs. It is all very attractive and I can see why he likes the area. I have no strong feelings about this. I have been a Northerner all my life and so anything much south of Manchester is foreign territory to me. I search the internet, signing up to a number of property search, renovation and restoration sites, and my e-mail daily overflows with offerings. We visit several, but so far, none have inspired either of us.

A new ad pings into my inbox. The property looks good, very good, but my knowledge of southern geography is vague. I shout through from my office "Where's Tewkesbury?"

John appears at my door. "Not exactly sure. Why?"

"Take a look." I gesture at the screen.

He leans forward and briefly scans the screen, then pulls up a chair to sit and read properly.

The ad is for an old farm in Gloucestershire; farmhouse and cottage, barns, a few acres, all in need of TLC. It looks good. We make an appointment to view.

Our visit is in March, but Spring is late and it feels like Winter. A sharp wind bites us and the land is drear under grey skies. Mud sucks at the wellies I have brought along for the occasion, but the property is wonderful and just what we are looking for. Old and full of character, timber beamed and traditional, resplendent with the possibilities left by a farming family who are retiring, want to down-size and who do not have the energy to bring it to its potential. And, despite the grim weather today, the outlook is glorious, with Gloucestershire countryside spreading in all directions.

John and I both love the house and everything about it. We go through the usual motions of surveys, mortgage etc, arrange tenants for the Pendon Edge House and, at the beginning of August, are ready to move to Apple Tree Farm.

On the day of the move, having already taken our furniture down in a self-hire van, storing it in a barn, John and I travel in convoy in our separate cars; John's sports car in front, me following behind with The Four in the back, and Polly in a cat basket. Polly is very unhappy, crying constantly.

We are well down the M5 when, ahead of me, in a slightly Pythonesque moment, the rear half of John's car suddenly expands outwards and then collapses back on itself. I have just watched a car engine explode.

Hitting my hazard lights, I follow close behind as John freewheels to the hard shoulder. A brief investigation reveals a failed gasket. His car is not travelling any further today and this leaves me in a quandary. While John phones for roadside assistance, I am conscious that in my own car are four dogs and a very unhappy cat. All of them have already been locked in for some time and cannot stay in there too much longer. Letting the dogs out to pee here on the motorway hard shoulder is unthinkable.

We agree that once we know for sure that John has help on the way, I will continue the journey and wait for him at the farm.

Arriving in Gloucestershire an hour later, I release the dogs to their new home. They are ecstatic and race around the garden, madly exploring. Polly is not so well off and I am careful to ensure that all the doors are closed before I let her out of her basket inside the farmhouse. She is frightened; her fur and blankets soaked in urine.

I let her loose and start trying to clean her up, but she rejects my efforts and starts cleaning herself. I decide that if she feels happy enough to groom, then she is basically okay, so I chop up a chicken breast for her, brought for the purpose. This settles her and I feel confident that I can leave her to herself.

Also in my car are those day-of-moving-essentials, a kettle, tea and coffee, mugs, a toaster, bread, butter and jam. I set up in the kitchen, make myself a brew and pour a little milk for Polly. She now seems entirely happy again and, despite my good intentions to keep her in the house for a day or so, dashes outside between my legs the first time I open the door for the dogs. I spy her exploring a hay barn, occasionally pouncing, and decide that if she is mousing, then all is well.

John arrives hours later, in the cab of a pick-up truck, his car loaded on the back, and bone-tired. I have lit a fire in the stove of the more liveable of the lounges and located the switch for the immersion heater to give us some hot water. As he soaks weary bones in a steaming bath, we share a bottle of cava to toast our new home.

And so we start on our next renovation project. Apple Tree Farm consists of a farmhouse and cottage joined. Research tells us that over a period of some centuries, the two buildings have been two dwellings, then one, then two again and so on.

As we buy the house, the status is a little hazy as it is being treated by the local authority as one dwelling for some purposes, but two for others. In practice it is two homes, with the younger half of the family having lived in the house, and the older half in the cottage. Our plan is, first to renovate the cottage and sell it off. The mortgage is significant and we badly need to reduce it.

Apple Tree Cottage is, frankly, a mess. Badly treated and under-appreciated, it has last seen significant work inside sometime in the 1950's and then, it was a botch-job. The building is several centuries old, but the work done in recent times is awful.

Partitions that appear to be solid walls turn out to be fibre board, or even card board, damp and riddled with spores. We pull these down, coughing as we do so, despite the masks we are wearing. Ceilings are the same abominable material and are already hanging down. The walls, which appear to be timber framed oak, their beams painted, turn out to have been plastered over and the beams painted back in with black gloss paint. Given the age of the work, the paint is certainly lead based. The 'kitchen' is a sink and not much more. The plumbing is suspect and the electrics are extraordinary.

So the innards of the cottage need to be stripped back to basics and re built from the bottom up. Our team of workmen work hard and long to remove the detritus of several decades and reveal the true beauty of this lovely old timber framed cottage.

Meanwhile, I am having second thoughts about selling the cottage. John and I are living in the farmhouse. Selling the cottage will reduce the mortgage, but there still needs to be income to support the remaining debt to the bank. I have no earnings right now, having left all I knew a hundred miles to the North. I approach John.

"You know; the Cotswolds are a ten-minute drive from here."

"Okay......?"

"And Tewkesbury is a historic centre..."

"Go on...."

"I've been looking at holiday rentals within about a half hour drive of here and what people pay to stay in the area...."

I outline my thoughts. It seems to me, from the 'back of an envelope' level of research I have done, that on any reasonable occupancy, our renovated cottage should be able to earn enough to support its own share of the mortgage and make a reasonable bite into the rest. John is hugely enthusiastic and tells me to get on with it; to locate a suitable rentals agency to find us some bookings. We will aim, he says, at having our first booking in for Christmas.

So, as work on the cottage continues, I search for a specialist agency who can fill it with eager holiday makers. My *curriculum vitae* is wide and varied, including everything from teaching and lecturing, through retail, wholesale and running my own business.

I pride myself that I can turn my hands to most things, but I have never done this kind of work before and I am keen to take advice from the experts. After some dredging of the internet, the company I choose, a purported specialist in holiday cottage rentals, sends an agent to visit us, touring the cottage and its gardens.

We ask him to look beyond the works going on; the new water tank sat out on the lawn, the kitchen units piled higgledy-piggledy in what will be the lounge. He agrees happily that it will be a wonderful holiday let, but if his company starts to take bookings, will it be ready for Christmas? We assure him that it will.

The agent is doubtful, but he discusses expected rental prices, their own charges for services and glibly assures us that they can easily have the cottage seventy per cent occupied. I am impressed by this.

I have worked my own calculations assuming only fifty per cent occupancy. i.e. that we will have guests occupying the cottage for fifty per cent of the time; Summer season, Easter, Christmas and New Year, and perhaps a few more 'bonus' bookings. At other times, the cottage will probably stand empty.

We agree contract terms, our pay back, their charges; they will be exclusive agents, such-and-such a set of facilities will be available for in-coming guests. The agent produces a long catalogue of necessities for the guests; it is a staggeringly long list.

I have always stayed anywhere that would accept me with a dog, and have never considered that tea and coffee facilities, a hair drier in the room, brand new furniture and fittings, and a heated towel rail, are requirements for a short rental. I am assured that all these and much else besides, must be there and available in the cottage if the guests are to be happy with their visit and give satisfactory feedback. Running an eye over the list, it tots up to several thousand pounds on top of the, already elastic, build budget. John scans it and clearly has similar views.

The work continues and only a few days later, I receive a call from the agency. Do they have my absolute promise that, if they accept a Christmas booking, the cottage will be ready? I swear on the graves of my ten most recent ancestors that any guests they send will walk into a holiday cottage, not a building site. The agent outlines an agreed price, a set of dates to mark on my calendar and informs me that there will be ten in the party. They will arrive sometime after three pm on Christmas Eve. Elated, I rush to tell John. We are officially open for business.

He is equally delighted. "I'd better tell the workmen then."

The foreman is horrified. How could we have accepted a booking when the work is not completed? We point out that our budget is not going to take us much past Christmas. If they haven't finished the work by then, his team might as well go home anyway.

I leave John and the foreman discussing the work program to separate Absolutes, from 'Really Should Haves', 'Would Be Nice to Haves' and 'It'll Wait 'til Laters.'

The first casualty of the timescale is the bathroom. John and I had intended to refit it, but a fresh coat of paint, new curtains and some nice accessories will have to do. Works in the garden such as a barbecue can easily wait until Spring. Essentials are a decent kitchen, toilets that do not have to be condemned by Health and Safety, painting and carpeting throughout. I cannot start any decorative work until the builders have finished. All else aside, there are six of them, all sleeping in one of the bedrooms. The guys look after the place well enough, but with so many in there, the air in there is smelling a bit second-hand.

I settle for working on the gardens to front and rear, clearing brambles, trimming hedges, planting spring bulbs and cleaning out a goldfish pond which I did not even realise was there until the weeds were cleared.

The builders work well together. The plumber who cannot work in the kitchen until the electrics are finished, is happy to labour for the joiner who is installing the units. The electrician who is being held up because he must wait for parts, helps out the carpet fitter. Despite seeming chaos, the cottage begins to look more like a holiday home and less like a demolition site.

It is December twenty third. The builders are leaving and we will not be seeing them here again; the works are completed. There is a brand new kitchen. The revolting toilets have been replaced, along with all the plumbing that went with them. The electrics have been replaced en masse. There are fire detectors and a new water boiler. The beautiful oak beams, centuries old, are breathing air again, polished and honey golden. There are new carpets and flooring throughout, chosen for practical, hard wearing qualities. Where plaster and ceilings were damaged or missing, they have been replaced or repaired.

Nine p.m. Our first guests will be arriving in eighteen hours' time. Since the builders started packing up at lunchtime, I have been painting walls, ceilings and woodwork. John is assembling beds, wardrobes and tables; IKEA has done well out of our business in the last few weeks. Together, we move in the armchairs and the enormous sofa-bed that will provide extra sleeping space. There is a tottering pile of packing and wrapping from the new sheets, pillows, towels, rugs, curtains, plates and crockery, cutlery, kitchenware and more, that is needed for ten guests expecting a luxury Christmas stay. I set up the TV, dvd player, cd player and slot dvd's and cd's onto shelves. As John completes each bed, I make it up with the new linen and blankets, folding spare bedding into wardrobes. As we approach midnight, I am stacking plates and dishes into kitchen cupboards and John carries spare camp-beds up into storage. We must sleep, so we go to bed and set the alarm for an early start.

At six a.m. I am making coffee and porridge. The cottage smells of damp wood and new paint, but lighting the wood-burner starts to drive off the stale air. I give priority to setting out scented pot-pourri, candles, and for good measure, splash drops of citronella and peppermint oil over carpets and curtains. John stacks logs by the back door.

As an afterthought, I grab half a dozen oranges from my own kitchen in the farmhouse - so much less appealing than the warm and welcoming one in the cottage - and jab cloves into them. Stacking them in a bowl by the wood-burner, the warming fruits start to give off their oil, making the room smell beautifully Christmassy.

I stack towels in the bathroom and set out a basket with shampoos, toothpaste and micro-bottles of splash-on and perfume.

At the last moment I realise that none of the new bedside lights have bulbs in them. I dash round looking for the new bulbs, panic when I find the wrong sizes, and then calm down as John thrusts the correct bag into my hand.

Fortunately, it being December, we do not need to cut the lawns, but there is the Christmas tree to set up and decorate, trimmings for hearth and ceilings, and for good measure, holly and mistletoe brought in from our own fields. These last hang gracefully from the oak beams, exquisite and shapely, that make up the ceiling.

I pile a selection of magazines, picked up cheap from local second-hand and junk shops, under the coffee table and add the folder that contains house rules, phone numbers for emergency services, leaflets for local restaurants, taxi firms and tourist attractions.

I check the time: two o'clock. Our first guests could be here in an hour. Reviewing my dishevelled condition, I reflect that I do not look, or for that matter smell, good. Finally, I realise why I have felt uncomfortable for the last few hours. Running my tongue through my mouth I realise that I did not clean my teeth this morning....

Not daring not use the cottage bathroom - I would have to clean it again - I have a lukewarm shower in one of the freezing farmhouse bathrooms and throw on some clean clothes. As I pat some make-up into place, I see John almost walk through the shower, dry himself briefly, wave the hair drier at his head and throw on the first clothes his hands touch in the wardrobe. Irritatingly, he looks instantly elegant, urbane and relaxed. John has that annoying quality of being able to look good dressed in a bin bag. Some of us have to try hard to get the same effect.

It is ten to three. We have agreed that we will be calm and demure as our guests arrive. Of course, they may not be arriving immediately. Three o'clock is simply the earliest time at which they are entitled to arrive. It could be several hours yet before we see them.

It does not matter. We are both exhausted. John pops a couple more logs on the stove and I pour a glass of wine apiece. There is a second bottle of red, carefully arranged in a holder on the kitchen table, along with some glasses, and a bottle of white in the fridge.

We sit, kiss, touch glasses and enjoy the moment. Twenty minutes later, our party of guests pulls up outside.

John and I meet them; parents, grandparents and children of assorted ages, at the gate. We are all grace and casual welcome. We help them unload and carry their cases into the cottage. Beneath our smooth facade we are anxious. Will our guests like what they find?

"Oh it's beautiful!" says the mother, holding up her hands. "Look at those gorgeous old beams."

"What a wonderful place!" says a teenage girl. "I love the real fire. And doesn't it smell great."

From upstairs a boy's voice shouts down "Bagsy this bedroom!"

John's and my eyes meet and we smile at each other. We explain to the parents that they are our very first guests. We hope they will be comfortable, but if we have missed or forgotten anything, if something does not work or if they need help lighting the stove, if they would like to know where to find a good pub, or a pleasant walk; we are right next door.

And could they also please make a note of anything they feel should be added or changed to the cottage. We would like to know.

John and I leave our delighted guests, who are decanting bags of brightly wrapped Christmas presents from the boot of the car whilst Grandma and Grandad distract two toddlers. In the farmhouse kitchen we share a high five and a hug.

"We did it Love!" I say.

"Yes we did." John is grinning. It looks as though we have a success on our hands.

We settle in to enjoy our own Christmas in Apple Tree Farm. The weather is freezing and so is the farmhouse.

The ancient and alleged central heating system is utterly inadequate, powered by a geriatric range in the kitchen pile wood into the burner waiting for a little heat to exude. No matter what I do, the pipes are warm no further than the end of the kitchen. John has no better luck than I. We phone the old owner of the house to ask if there is some trick to making the decrepit heating system work. He assures us that it works perfectly, but thinking back, we remember that whenever we visited, the family were all sitting in the kitchen near the range.

There are however, two huge stoves in other rooms and we have set up home in one of them. The other is not suitable as it has a problem with damp. Not merely damp in fact. There is water running down the walls, and these are internal walls.

No matter, we will deal with this later. For now, we are making ourselves comfortable elsewhere.

Having spent so much time working in the cottage, our own accommodation is sparse. One day it will be beautiful, but just now it is very basic. The first item to go was the rattan rug which lay on the stone flag floor the day we arrived. As John and I lifted it, cautiously peering underneath, we were greeted by a cloud of dust, spores and fleeing silverfish. The rug was on the Guy Fawkes night bonfire, along with much else. We now have a couple of different, thick and woolly rugs down on the cold flags. Old newspapers separate the rugs from the flags and every couple of weeks we lift the rug to change the newspapers and give the rug itself an airing outside.

The dogs all have baskets and cushions scattered near the stove. Seamus in particular, growing older, is feeling the cold more. He is stiff when he first wakes on a morning and I make sure he is well insulated from the stone floor. If the sun is shining and he wants to sit outdoors, I try to persuade him to curl up in a basket but he will have none of it. Seamus has taken possession of an old door which was leaning up in one of the barns.

He simply asks for his door to be laid on the ground in the sunshine and then sits out there, very happily, for hours, lord of all he surveys. The other dogs have occasional squabbles over ownership of the cushion or basket closest to the fire, but priority is usually settled by the old rule of possession being nine tenths of the law.

It is a fact that the farmhouse is biting cold. I enjoy cooking, but making Christmas dinner in the freezing kitchen is hard. I take to keeping a sinkful of hot water constantly filled so that as my hands seize up with the cold, I can thaw them in the warm water enough to move my fingers. Nonetheless we are celebrating. Sitting close to the stove, the ceiling beams and enormous oak lintel of the fireplace bedecked with holly and mistletoe from our hedgerows, we pull crackers and drink hot spiced wine to toast our new project.

The day after Boxing Day the guests are due to leave. John and I walk out to meet them as we see them packing the car. John is immediately involved with Dad, giving him directions to the motorway.

"Have you had a good time?" I ask. "Has everything been okay for you?"

"Oh yes, it's been lovely." smiles Mum. "Almost perfect. We've had a super Christmas and the kids loved it."

Almost perfect? What have we missed?

"Don't worry." she laughs, seeing my expression. "For the Christmas dinner we wanted mashed potatoes. The only thing you missed was a potato masher."

We wave the party on their way and check out the cottage. We now must completely clean and prepare it for the next guests. The agents have brought us in a second party for the New Year.

They will not arrive until December 30th, so there is no hurry to the cleaning, but I must strip down beds, wash, iron and replace bedding for ten.

Part of this work has been done for me; some bedding is already piled up by the door, but as I strip duvet covers, pillow cases and sheets, it begins to dawn on me just how much work is involved in the cottage change-over.

By the time the New Year's party arrives, the cottage is spick and span again. It has taken me two days of constant washing, drying and ironing to deal with the bedding and I conclude that I am going to need to upgrade my current, domestic grade, iron, tumble drier and washing machine.

The New Year guests are also very happy with their stay. We join them at midnight on New Year's Eve to share champagne and Auld Lang Syne. Come January second, we wave them on their way.

We have no more bookings just now, but I am unsurprised by this. Who books a holiday cottage in January? I ring the agents to enquire as to the expected booking pattern for holiday cottages.

"Oh we'll start seeing enquiries around mid-February." she says. "By then everyone's well over Christmas, they've paid off their Christmas credit cards and they are thinking about Spring."

This makes perfect sense to me as I have previously worked in, among others, both retail and wholesale and have run market stalls and craft fairs.

This same spending pattern applies to 'punters' no matter what the trade.

Mid-January. Before we moved here, John and I chatted with some of our prospective neighbours about the local climate. I am quite excited by the gardening prospects of Gloucestershire, so much further South than my native northern climate. "Oh, it never snows here." they say. "Not ever. If you get snow here, the rest of the country is in lock-down."

Two feet of snow dumps on us towards the end of the month. The muddy and miserable yard, garden and land transform into a glistening Winter Wonderland, sparkling white in the mornings, glinting rouge in the evenings in reflected sunset.

We buy in more logs for the stove, but they are damp and do not dry out easily, even when stacked by the hearth overnight.

The snow stretches into February and the temperatures plunge further. I stop even trying to cook in the freezing kitchen. Anything more complicated than a baked potato leaves me with fingers painful with cold.

At last, March arrives, the sun puts in an appearance and the daffodils come into bloom. I contact the agents again. "How's business? Enquiries coming in yet?"

"It's a bit slow." she admits. "It's been such a chilly start to the year, but I'm sure it will pick up again now that the sun's shining."

March goes by, as does April and the agent obtains a two day Easter booking for us. I am becoming seriously concerned. We have put a lot of money into setting up our holiday business. It is not a viable concern on the basis of bookings for only bank holidays and festivals.

By the end of May, the agents have obtained no more bookings. At this stage, I have expected to be at least half full for July and August, but there is nothing. I write the agent a formal letter. They have agreed a contact on the basis that they are our exclusive agents and will produce seventy per cent occupancy. Thus far, we have ten per cent occupancy and that only on the easy-sell dates. I inform them that I will welcome any bookings they offer, but that I am now looking elsewhere to bring in business.

John by now, is also seriously worried. Our funds are limited and the mortgage must be paid. I am concerned that if I tie us to another agent, we will have a repeat of the same useless pattern, and so I choose a different approach.

To be a viable business, it is not necessary to charge sky high prices. This limits the clientele and also places far higher demands on what is expected for the money. I decide to follow the 'Stack 'em high, Sell 'em cheap' philosophy of business. I want the cottage occupied.

I set up a web-site. I advertise on EBay, Craig's list and Preloved. I target walkers, nature lovers and dog owners. I advertise 'dog-friendly' and 'pets-welcome'.

Knowing from experience how hard it can be to go on holiday with dogs, I am sure this will have appeal.

I link to the local racecourse to bring in the punters from the big races. I offer long weekends, single nights and discounts for long bookings. I arrange Romantic Weekends to fill long dark days in Winter; the firelight and the candles make for a most beautiful and romantic setting. I offer Bed and Breakfast.

The cottage is a hit. Within weeks, I am waving off one set of guests at ten in the morning and welcoming the next guests at three in the afternoon. It is hard work. I seem to spend my entire life cleaning, washing and ironing, but the money is coming in and, miraculously, the holiday business is paying almost the full mortgage on the farm.

John and I are both astounded, but delighted. We make new friends among our guests. Many return over and again. Couples as they leave are saying "See you next time."

I receive e-mails asking that, if I have empty nights or cancellations, can I give first refusal for a bargain break? Yes, of course I can. I would like to have three hundred pounds for a weekend, but I'll take ninety-nine pounds over nothing. And because I am willing to take lower prices, the downturn in the economy actually works for us rather than against us. People who cannot afford a fortnight in the Canary Islands can, nonetheless, afford a weekend in the Cotswolds.

I take bookings well in advance for July and August, Christmas, New Year and Easter, getting full price. For the rest, I accept whatever I can get and the cottage is fully occupied.

The work in the farmhouse continues apace. There is no particular timescale for it other than doing the works our funds allow. We have lots of space as the farmhouse is large and six bedroomed.

John and I choose a bedroom to be 'ours', plus a room apiece to use as offices, leaving the others free for the work of repair and redecoration. As with the cottage, the electrics and plumbing have to be replaced wholesale.

My sister Carol visits, this time arriving to find that, due to a last minute hitch, we have neither working toilets or hot water. One day she will visit me, and I will offer her decent hospitality.

Old buildings always have an element of adventure about them. When they have been worked, reworked, rebuilt, 'improved' or abused over the centuries, it can be anyone's guess what might be found under old plaster, behind woodwork or hidden below floorboards. There are always surprises.

My very first renovation, in a two centuries old, ex-tied cottage in Lancashire, produced a glorious inglenook fireplace blocked in behind a nineteen fifties' gas fire, a door into nowhere on the first floor where a set of stairs had, at some point in the past, been turned around, a wonderful beech hardwood floor, recycled from the ballroom of the derelict country house just up the road, and a ceiling space packed with oat husks which had been used, we assumed, as a kind of primitive insulation. This is a precis you understand, certainly nothing like an exhaustive list.

Over time, John and I learn of the idiosyncrasies of our ancient and dilapidated building. In August I am intrigued by the arrival of the flying ants season.

This entertains me at first, watching the hundreds, and then thousands of virgin ant 'princesses' launching themselves off into the sky to find their beau, mate, and then set up new nests as queens.

It ceases to be entertaining when we realise that some of the nests have penetrated into the oak timbers forming the framework of the house and cottage and that the ants are taking flight indoors.

This catches me by surprise the first year and I have some difficult moments with cottage guests until I get on top of the problem. The years following, I am expecting the 'festival of ants' and am prepared. I do not like doing it, but I set insecticide for the nests within the timbers.

The close to useless range which is supposed to power the central heating system is one of the first things to go.

It leaves behind an ugly chimney flue which has clearly been added to the farmhouse as an afterthought, but when we see jackdaws nesting up inside it in Spring, we do not have the heart to remove it, at least for now.

We replace the kitchen and bathrooms, install a new water boiler and new toilets. The main painting work is to the squarish, plastered panels between the beams of timbered walls. Cleaned, oiled and polished, the timbers glow amber, gold and ochre.

Painstakingly, I paint the plasterwork within each section, taking every effort not to splash paint. If paint gets into the timbers, it takes forever to get it out of the deeply grained oak.

Apple Tree farmhouse begins to look beautiful and to feel like Home.

Wayside Cottage

We have lived in Apple Tree Farmhouse for four years. It is March and Spring is in full swing. The sun is shining and the holiday cottage has been such a success that John and I conclude that we should look for another property to extend the holiday business. If we choose well, the income should pay the mortgage and the property will buy itself.

I trawl all the big property websites and estate agents' windows but cannot find anything that seems quite right. My criteria are simply 'Would I want to stay there for a holiday?' and 'Do I think it can pay for itself?'

I view a couple of likely contenders. One pretty house with river views is promising, but the River Severn is fickle and rises alarmingly sometimes. Flooding is a real risk. Then too, there is always going to be someone who will blame me because their three-year-old decides to go swimming. I shudder at the thought and walk away from that prospect.

Another property is perfect in almost every way; the setting, the large fenced garden, the views, but as we pace through the rooms, John and I conclude that it is simply not big enough. We know from experience that holiday makers are more than happy to cram themselves into a much smaller place than they would be content to live in.

Along with the bedrooms, every room should have the opportunity for sofa-beds and camp-beds. The rooms in this property are simply too small and the potential is not there.

I make a suggestion. "Let's just drive round the likely areas. If we search the back lanes and country roads, we might come across places that are only advertised with the small local agents."

John agrees that this is a good idea. Also, it is Sunday. There is bound to be a good pub along the way that will offer a decent pint, a pork pie and a pickle to go with his newspaper.

The Gloucestershire-Worcestershire border weaves and wanders. In this area, I am seldom certain which county I am in, but nestled here between the Cotswolds to the East and the Malvern Hills to the West is a broad plane, The Vale of Evesham, which contains some of the most stunning countryside in England. These are not the majestic, but often harsh lands of my northern hills, beautiful but austere.

These are rolling vales and meadows, the grass lush and green. Hedgerows abound with brambles, wild roses, sloes and apples; not just crab-apples, small and sour, but cultivated apples that have escaped garden bondage and are making a free life for themselves. Now, in Spring, there is little fruit in the hedgerows; we must wait until September for that, but as blossoms abound; haw, eglantine and blackthorn, bees and other insects bring the air alive with their fizzling tunes, and the birds twitter a counterpoint close by.

The land is extravagantly fertile, arable crops and fruit trees alike bearing bumper produce; apples, plums, asparagus. Traditionally, Kent is named "The Garden of England", but I think that award rightly belongs to Gloucestershire and Worcestershire.

John draws up on the verge, pointing at a property set back from the road; a large and stately house, almost a mansion, with the black and white timber frame common in the area. There is a 'For Sale' board by the gate.

I laugh. "C'mon Love, it's huge. Even if we could get it, you'd need a party of fifty to fill that place and make it pay for itself. And if it could be done, I don't want to run a place like that. It would make a great hotel, but it's no good as a rental." John purses his lips but reluctantly agrees. John likes grand houses.

I point to the other side of the road. There is another 'For Sale' board at the end of a small farm track. Well back from the road, down the track, is a second house. From here it looks ideal; a sensible size, set amidst fields and paddocks and a good distance from the traffic.

John agrees that it looks pretty good. "Let's ring the agent." he says. "Find out what they're asking for it before we go any further."

I ring the number on the board. It belongs, as I had anticipated, to a small local agent. I would not have easily found this on the internet. Certainly, it does not look familiar to me from my internet searches.

A female voice with a broad Gloucestershire accent replies. This accent does not have quite the rolling *'oohh aarrs'* of a Somerset accent, but it is not so very different, and we are certainly dealing with a local. I explain where we are and enquire the asking price of the house.

"Oh it's not the house you can see down the track." she says to my startlement. There is nothing else in sight. What other property could it be?

As I relay the message along to John, driving, the voice guides us down the track, past the house we can see and through a gate beyond, onto a vast open Common. The track continues out of sight through acres of open meadowland, dotted here and there by the odd horse. On the edge of sight, I can see a small herd of what look like Jersey cows. As we continue down the track I ask the agent if the owner is likely to mind our turning up on his doorstep.

"I'll give them a call." She says. "Perhaps they'll be happy to show you round."

By the time she calls us back, we have reached the end of the track. A gate bars our way, leading to a garden and a cottage out of dreams. It is not the thatched, painted on a chocolate box, variety of cottage, but a brick built, slate roofed and very practical looking home.

It nestles in an acre or so of garden and this in its turn, is set into the vast grassland we have just driven through.

There is no other house in sight and even the M5, the busiest motorway in the area, is a muted hum on the wind. It is jaw-droppingly beautiful.

I am staggered, and I can see that John is thinking the same as I am. The agent says that the owners are happy to show us around so long as we do not mind 'taking them as they are.' Quickly I enquire the asking price. It is steep, but not unreachable. Anyone with a love of the country would want to holiday here.

I am excited and I grin at John, who grins back. Then, as the door opens and a man steps out, we both school our features back to a carefully crafted 'sceptical buyer' expression.

'Alex' introduces himself and invites us in. A small cocker spaniel wraps himself around our feet, desperately wanting to be 'in on it'. Alex apologies for the terrible mess in his house; we have caught him by surprise and he has not had the opportunity to tidy up.

We step inside to find an immaculately neat and orderly kitchen-diner. A couple more large dogs amble across, sniff us over and amble off again, depositing themselves on a large settee at the end of the kitchen. Noting the radiator directly next to the settee, I already know most of what I need to about their owners. These are nice people.

Alex shows us around the house. It is ideal. The large kitchen diner, several small rooms downstairs, perfect for large parties who would like a choice of quiet sitting, TV lounge, another room good to let the kids hangout or even as an extra downstairs bedroom.

There is a shower room on the ground floor, with an extra loo. Upstairs there are three bedrooms, all a good size and another bathroom. Outside there is a huge prefab outbuilding, rather dilapidated, and a small brick shed which, although full of garden clutter now, says 'outdoor privy' to me.

The garden is a long expanse of lawn, with a high hedge to one long side, ending in wild tangle of hawthorn and blackthorn thicket. Standing with the house behind, the view is astounding, over acres of waving grassland and beyond that, across fields and pastures, leading the eye to the horizon and the Cotswolds hills. Alex points out that looking the other way, over the high hedge, is the view of the Malvern Hills.

As we drive away, John and I discuss tactics, how to raise a mortgage, where to find the cash to put down a deposit. Can we get this off the ground in time to catch the Summer holidays? We have told Alex that we need to go away and discuss things, that we are interested, but that the cottage is very isolated. We must consider whether it is right for our purposes. John and I both know we are bluffing. If I had written the remit for the perfect house for our new project, this would have been it. Wayside Cottage is sublime.

We move fast, arranging a mortgage, assembling a deposit, agreeing a sales contract. I am already working on my holiday advertising; July is approaching fast and whereas when setting up Apple Tree Cottage, I was a novice, now I know what I am doing.

Alex is all co-operation and is intrigued by our plans and how we intend to market his former home.

The bank takes longer than expected to agree the mortgage. The cottage does not tick the standard boxes. It is isolated. It has its own water supply. It has, astonishingly enough, three different postcodes because three different nearby residential areas all try to encompass it within their boundaries.

I begin to worry. I have accepted bookings, and more to the point, money, from holiday makers expecting to stay in Wayside. The first holiday is booked for early July and it is now June. I had expected to complete the purchase by now and to be in the property, freshening paint and getting furniture into place.

When asking permission of Alex to start decorating before completion, he agrees without hesitation. He is no longer living there and as he points out, if the sale falls through, at least his house is freshly redecorated for the next buyer.

Two weeks before my booking deadline, the sale completes. We are the owners of Wayside Cottage and can work freely. My mother comes to visit, thinking that she will be staying at Apple Tree House. I am tied up with another appointment and so a friend picks her up from the railway station, dropping her off at Apple Tree.

"Don't unpack your bags." I laugh. "We're not staying." And Mum has her holiday with us, painting and decorating to get Wayside ready for the first guests.

Again, the project is a huge success. I fill Wayside Cottage easily and the guests love it.

The flexibility of the large number of rooms makes it perfect for large parties and sixteen people are as comfortable in the house as two. It is easy to clean and has everything on site. Between Wayside and Apple Tree, I am kept very busy.

We lock up the outbuilding. With a dilapidated roof, it does not look very safe, and we do not want small children wandering in there. However, we do want to be able to work on the building to provide extra accommodation.

Both John and I have ideas on how it should be done, but the first task is to make the roof safe and watertight. I order building materials to be delivered, first clearing it with the current guests, a family of four.

They are unconcerned about the delivery, the mother telling me she is too busy pretending to be a farmer's wife, picking blackberries from the hedgerows on the Common and making bramble and apple pies.

There some hundreds of pounds' worth of materials in the delivery and so I want to check what has arrived. John and I drive to the cottage, having agreed that we will not disturb the guests. We will simply park out on the track, pop into the garden to check the delivery and leave.

It is a glorious Autumn day, the sky that shade of opalescent blue that is special to an English September, and the sun is hot.

John and I drive slowly up the track, the tall grass of the Common dried now to standing hay. The air is still, fragrant with the scent of warm herbage, and there is little to hear but bird song and bees.

As we pull up to the gate, discussing whether to get out, we can see our delivery on the drive and can almost count the goods from here. There is a car parked to the side, and we do not wish to disturb our guests.

Suddenly, the front door of the cottage bursts open and two teenage boys, perhaps fourteen or fifteen years old, tumble outside towards the blow-up swimming pool we now notice on the lawn.

The boys are stark naked and have not seen us. Mum and Dad also appear at the door, more modestly dressed, to the relief of John and I, waving at the boys and telling them to get into the water. One of the boys notices us, shrieks and points, then dashes back inside, closely followed by his brother.

Mum and Dad walk over and so of course we get out of the car. They are concerned that we are upset. We are concerned that they are upset. Then the tension shatters as we all realise that, in fact, we all want to burst out laughing.

As we drive home, John and I agree that we will make no more off the cuff visits to our guests.

It is October and Wayside Cottage has as many bookings as I could wish, more than fulfilling hopes and expectations and easily paying for itself. An hour previously, I have waved the previous party of guests off down the track and in four hours' time I have another party due to arrive.

By then I must clean the cottage, strip and remake beds, check drawers and wardrobes for any of the interesting variety of items which guests leave behind (toys, dvd's and cd's, underclothes, overclothes, romantic left overs that need cleaning up from under the beds; I must keep a constant watch for contraceptives).

Just having mopped the kitchen floor, I am having a coffee, leaning on my mop and bucket and gazing out at the matchless view, this place of my dreams. The dogs are with me. They always come with me 'to help'. Seamus and Shannon are gambolling on the lawn while Minnie is sitting in the shade, panting. Duncan is, as ever, by my feet.

Although it is late Autumn, the sun is shining over the Common, hay cut short now to stubble; hedgerows bright with haws, hips and brilliantly scarlet, grape sized crab apples, sour enough to melt your teeth but wonderful for jams and jellies. Red admirals sip juice from windfall apples, half rotted and smelling sweetly of wild cider.

Random thoughts occur to me. "Bathrooms next. - Look at those butterflies. – I wonder if butterflies get drunk? - Where have I put the bath cleaner and the toilet ducks? - Ye gods but it's gorgeous here. - Was it bedding for six or eight they asked for? - Why am I doing this? - I should plant more fruit trees over there, plums and apples would do well, might get away with peaches. - Did I put those fresh towels in the car?"

"Chickens would be good down there at the bottom, they could eat all the windfalls from the Victorias and that old Bramley. - I could open up the old well for the chickens. - Veg beds too. - Why am doing this?"

Why *am* I doing this?

Here I am, in a place which, should I ever go to Heaven, I expect it to look much like this. I'm renting it out to other people all the time and all I get to see of it, is to visit here twice a week to stick my arm down the toilet.

Why am I doing this?

I must be bloody mad. I don't want to rent out Wayside Cottage. I want to live here.

What will John say?

It transpires that John has already been thinking the same thing. Discussing it, we agree completely that we should move again, to live in Wayside Cottage. We will rent out Apple Tree Cottage and Farmhouse to tenants and live at Wayside. In October we move house again.

Egg-Citing Times

We have lived in Wayside Cottage for just a few weeks and Winter has arrived. One of the coldest winters in many years, it takes the land in an icy grip. While there has not yet been snow, it is only a matter of time. Temperatures plunge, puddles ice over and freezing fog hangs low and threatening.

In Apple Tree Farm, we have a tenant. Bringing in a mass of farm cats and chickens, she says that she loves living there, that she is setting up a chicken breeding business with a partner, that she will run the farmhouse for Bed and Breakfast. She has lots of plans. It all sounds very good.

It is a disaster. She has no understanding of costs and neither does she understand what it means to 'break even'. She leaves more and more of her work with the poultry to her business partner and then, after only a few weeks, I receive a message saying that she has vacated and that the farmhouse is standing empty.

Immediately, I drive to Apple Tree with the dogs, to assess the situation. I can handle any remaining bookings on the Bed and Breakfast. That will avoid fall-out with and guests. But what of the cats and the chickens?

Most of the cats were feral and have done what feral cats do, vanishing into the landscape, but a few of them at least, are partly domesticated and have been simply abandoned. They hang around the farm, hoping to be fed. I call a local rescue service and they agree that the cats can probably be rehomed. A couple of days later they call by and collect them.

The chickens are a different matter. I am unsure of how many there are and of what is happening with the 'business partner'. Checking the coops, the chucks seem to be well enough, but when I speak with the partner, he is unenthusiastic.

He says he is having difficulty finding time to look after all the chickens and is selling them. I am wary of what is happening, noticing that he visits the farm less and less over the next few days. When he does come by, it is only to sell a few of the birds.

Things come to a head quickly. Only a week or so later, I pull into the farmyard one day, The Four racing off into the back garden and fields, enjoying a visit to their old home. A couple of minutes later, to my horror, Minnie returns with a chicken dangling from her jaws. I am about to take her severely to task for her crime, when I see the other bodies. Minnie has not murdered the chicken but has simply picked up a carcass.

There are feathers everywhere. I see limp bodies strewed over the ground, so many of them, most of them hens, but the bulk of the feathers I can see scattered, are from roosters.

When the vixen from up the hill came calling, at least one rooster put up a grand fight. He has died valiantly but in vain. Later I find two more dead roosters. Another returns the following day, horribly injured and I put him out of his misery. Any others have been taken.

Scanning out over the field I can see more of the chickens here and there, all hens, still alive and scattered widely, foraging through grass and horse droppings. If it were not for the foxes, this would be chicken heaven.

The coop stands open, its door wide, slack in the wind, and more corpses scatter the floor inside. A couple of the girls are on the racks, laying, while others cower under the eaves, traumatised.

The chickens have been simply abandoned to the foxes, the coop left unprotected.

How many hens are there? They cannot be left here. If I take them to Wayside, where can I keep them? With the freezing temperatures, I am not able to start building coops and runs.

Making my plans on the move, I ring ahead to John, who agrees that we must immediately launch 'Operation Chicken Rescue'.

While I drive back to Wayside with The Four, he assembles crates, cardboard boxes, a big fishing net and other paraphernalia that might help us to capture the skittish, frightened birds.

Possibly the easiest way to retrieve the birds, would be to wait until dark and simply pick the hens from their perches in the coop, but of course, the fox will be thinking exactly the same.

We must get them out of there, as many as we can, before dark.

I call by an equestrian supplier for a bag of grain. My knowledge of chickens is limited, but I do know that they like grain. By the time I arrive at Wayside Cottage, John is waiting and he has already started clearing out the old outbuilding for them. It is not ideal, but it is a much better option than the alternative. We return to Apple Tree as the afternoon draws late. The day is dismal and it will be dark early.

It turns out to be very easy to catch the first half of the chickens. Those cowering in the coop, we simply lift out and put in boxes; similarly, the ones in mid-lay, much to their indignation. A peck from a chicken does not hurt, but avian outrage is loud with protesting squawks.

A few chortling noises and a handful of grain thrown to the ground, and some of the others out in the field come running. We either catch them by hand or net them, put them into boxes and load them into the car.

The remainder of the chucks are not nearly so simple to catch and it is easy to see why they have thus far survived the fox. Wily, cunning and fast moving, they refuse to be drawn in and are disinclined to enter the coop.

After an exhausting half hour of chasing, attempted entrapment and failed attempts at netting, we are both exhausted, and the light is failing. We will return tomorrow. In fact, takes me three days to catch the last of them.

Returning to Wayside with our refugees, John has hastily made our dilapidated pre-fab ready for them, at least as much as he was able to, on the short notice of our rescue mission.

Thinking that the chickens would appreciate hidey holes, nest boxes and places of concealment, he has found cardboard boxes and crates, lined them out with a bed of straw and placed them in quiet corners of the building. Some old kitchen units and cupboards have been brought back into service by opening the doors to create tucked-away corners where a frightened bird can rest quietly until her nerves have calmed.

The general chaos and clutter of an unused building is scattered around, garden tools, jar of screws and nails, broken vacuum cleaners, a wheelbarrow; but we think that the chickens should be safe and comfortable enough until the new coop arrives which I plan to order off the internet. I scatter the floor with grain, stale bread, and dried fruit, whatever I have to hand which might make suitable fare for a chicken. If they have plenty to eat, they should settle quickly.

The Four are deeply interested in the smells and squawks coming from the car, and so I close them into the house.

Then, lifting the crates and boxes carefully out of the car, so as not to frighten our new Girls, we place them on the floor of their new temporary home, open the lids and stand back.

There is a moment or two of wing rustling and feather fluffing, then one of the hens, a large white individual, jumps up onto the edge of her crate, pins me and John with a beady eye, then spies the corn on the floor. She hops down and starts gobbling it down as though food has gone out of fashion.

As the other hens see her eating, they all move at once and we have a sort of chicken tornado ascending from the boxes, then settling down to eat, each hen grabbing as much as she can while she can.

The shallow water bowl I have put down is almost immediately up-ended, so I go in search of another container, one less easily moved. I find a heavyweight but shallow, earthenware casserole dish, fill it with water and put it down on the edge of the seething activity around the corn. This time it stays put.

The food disposed of, the Girls set about exploring their new home. They do not seem even remotely nervous. Every nook and cranny at floor level is explored and every hen takes her turn to poke a scrawny chicken neck into cupboards and holes. Straw is scratched up and the concrete underneath is inspected. Shelves, furniture, ladders, stepladders and a small scaffolding tower are scaled. John and I decide to go and have a meal while they settle in. When we return an hour later to check up on them, the boxes, crates and cupboards are abandoned.

The chickens have all settled in to roost on the metal roof supports, crossbeams eight feet from the ground, and are involved in a clucking, pecking dispute over possession of prime perches. It is fast falling dark and the temperature, already frigid, is tumbling again. I worry that the Girls may be cold, but there is little I can do about it now. They seem contented enough; feathers are bustled large, and as we close them in for the night, there are contented chuckles and clucks from above.

The following morning, it is spectacularly cold. The weather forecast is for snow, snow, more snow and record low temperatures. A slight breeze leaves my face wind-raw and the keen frost bites fingers and toes alike.

I am a 'chicken-virgin' and so, consulting the internet, I give myself a crash course in poultry care, reading as much as I can on the diet of chickens. They are omnivores and I conclude that they will eat more or less anything they can get hold of, so I decide to give priority to getting calories and water inside them.

The water bowl has frozen solid overnight. I replace it with another which I fill with hot water, bringing the original into the house to thaw out. The Girls seem to enjoy the hot, though rapidly cooling water

Within an hour, there is ice beginning to glaze the surface again. I find myself replacing the water bowl every couple of hours to keep the Girls in access to liquid water.

Their corn, I stew up into a hot mash. I reason that the 'porridge' I am giving them should provide calories, water and warm insides.

Certainly the chickens are enthusiastic about eating it, each guzzling it down as fast as she can. Quickly I learn to put the hot mash into several bowls scattered widely across the floor. If it is only in one container, then only the senior hens eat, the subordinates pushed to the side-lines.

The temperatures are nose-diving to unbelievable levels. Seldom have I experienced a British winter where the mercury fell below minus four or five. Now, is crashing to minus ten. I read up on the susceptibility of chickens to cold and learn that in fact, they are fairly resilient to chill. Their feathers keep them so well insulated that, so long as they are fit and healthy, low temperatures are seldom a problem for them. Rather, it is the heat of summer that is likely to make them uncomfortable.

On this basis, I decide that so long as I ensure that their insides are powered with plenty of calories, the Girls should manage. I bake potatoes in their skins. The chicken love 'em. I boil up Jerusalem artichokes, which the garden has in abundance. The Girls are not so keen on these, always leaving them until last if there is a choice of food. I buy a hotel sized bag of rice, boil it up fluffy and shovel it out to them, still warm. The Girls fall on this like ambrosia from heaven.

I acquire cabbage leaves and old vegetables from a local greengrocer and the chickens seem equally delighted with these, needing only a little help in matter of grating carrots.

When first thrown in, the chickens can peck a carrot down to nothing in a few hours, but once the vegetables freeze, they are too hard for beaks to break up, so I process them into chicken-beak-sized morsels. One day the greengrocer gives me a large sack of cauliflowers that have gone brown. They are perfectly edible, but unsaleable. I give half the caulis to the Girls as they are, whole and raw, and the rest I microwave one at a time and serve them up warm. This delicacy causes chicken warfare to break out, so I serve them up several at a time, placing them in around on different parts of the floor, so that everyone gets a fair share.

The winter is hard, very hard. Temperatures crash to minus nineteen.

The snow comes down, blanketing the Common, the garden and the cottage in a two-foot thick carpet. The dogs love it, gambolling in the snow and playing snowballs, but we are very isolated here. The track across the Common, our lifeline to the outside world, is slightly raised above the general level, a causeway from our gate. Each day we make a point of driving out at least once, to open the track and to ensure that we can drive out. In the house, I fill our large chest freezer with all manner of food, meat, vegetables, bread and an array of soups, stews and casseroles. I am preparing food which, should we lose our electricity, I can prepare on one the lounge stoves.

All the water pipes freeze. Bathrooms, kitchen, garage and every tap, outside or in, is solid. I cook Christmas dinner using melt water from snow, gathered into my large jam pans and left by the fires to thaw.

Fortunately, Wayside Cottage has a superb central heating system, with stoves in the lounges as well. The house itself is wonderfully warm and comfortable. We do not have a repeat of the early Apple Tree Farm experience, with its freezing interiors.

However, the outbuilding, the chickens' temporary home, has no heating and is full of holes and cracks. It provides shelter from the biting winds, but nothing will warm the interior.

The chickens are entirely unmoved by this. During the day I find them contentedly scratching around on the floor. At night they continue to roost in the 'rafters'. They show every sign of being in the peak of health. Eyes are bright. Feathers are glossy. There are none of the coughs or wheezes I read about in my gruesome research into the ailments of chickens. Regardless of the Siberian conditions, all is well.

The coop arrives, flat-packed for home assembly. Assembly on arrival is impossible. The large cardboard crate sits out in the garden under a blanket of snow for several weeks. I do not worry unduly; it is basically a small wooden shed. What harm can come to it?

By the time the weather has improved enough for me to attempt assembly, the outer cardboard casing simply peels off, damp, slimy and rather revolting.

However, the contents are in good condition and the instruction leaflet is inside a zip-up plastic envelope, untouched by the damp.

I have researched quite extensively on the internet for a good quality housing for the Girls, which I could yet afford to buy.

Somewhat horrified at the prices asked for some of the coops and runs on sale, I have bought a coop which is sold as being suitable for 'up to sixteen average sized chickens'. It consists of a central coop with an add on run at either end so the Girls can have outside space. Operation Chicken Rescue resulted in fourteen hens in all, so it sounds ideal.

I am competent at self-assembly. Give me a set of IKEA instructions for a flat-pack kitchen cupboard and an hour later you will have an assembled kitchen cupboard.

Over the course of my several house renovations and furnishings, I have assembled entire kitchens, beds, sofa-beds, wardrobes and garden sheds. I have produced a usable garden shed from the clapped out remains of two that were half rotten, achieving one decent shed and a large pile of firewood at the end of two days' work.

I approach 'Project Chicken Coop' with equanimity. The Gang of Four settle around me on the lawn to assist as required.

Step One - Open assembly instructions and identify English language section. This is separated out from sections in French, Spanish, German, Polish, Russian, several types of Arabic text and two sections in different versions of Chinese.

Step Two - Start to read the assembly instructions, with intention of complete read-through before proceeding. Hesitate after first paragraph and check rest of leaflet to ensure that I am actually reading English section of the instructions.

Note 1: Outer packaging states 'Made in China'. Reflect that original version of instructions was probably written in Chinese. On the evidence, it appears that translation of instructions was performed by native speaker of Swahili into German, thence into Bhojpuri via Urdu.

I decide that for the moment I will pass over the actual instructions and move on to….

Step Three - read list of parts and identify each part with its illustration in the instructions. Lay out said items in an orderly fashion ensuring that small, easily lost items like screws, nails, fixings and handles are contained within, say, a tray or a box.

Note 2: list of screws supplied does not match actual screws in pack. Check box, packing materials and adjacent ground for alternative screws. Diagram in assembly pamphlet shows two inch, brass round-headed #14s.

No such screws enclosed - depart to shed in search of alternative 'home supplied' screws. Place two inch, flat head steel number #12s in tray.

Step Four - Identify 'inside' and 'outside' of wall panels. Also 'up' and 'down' sides of roof panels.

Step Five - Re-read assembly instructions:

Installation Instructions Houses

- Nesting boxes will be installed on the home side. Opening sleeper management side (if any), the panels can be installed anywhere. Switch ports can be placed anywhere.

- Connect the host of wooden windows. It is not on a common base coach, two long sides, air long side, at least one part of the corner connected 2 X + mount bracket hinge pin angle

- Upper and lower support bracket of the corner 5/console streams.

- 2X guarantee basic Panel mount, or if you leave it up, until you easy to used in compliance with trees.

- Nuts + washers are used for the next coach 3X log back wall of pre-holes. Connect same as panels and other substances. After mounting nut washer + 3x coach

- Form back home after dinner

- At this time, while on a pedestal cannot be sure tile and you. Attach the tree to the top. It is given in the same way, as a base. Each coach 2, wooden panels on the safe roof.

- Mining is the best Railway (2X connected together) are used at each end of the rectangular metal.

- That stick installed "T" (in other words, the tree of 1x67 + 1 x 34 1/2 "and 2 x 2 ½ in the" screw) home safe 1-X square panels, each share is divided into two parts, the use of angle bracket. This level is supported by wooden superstructure series

- Using the top panel 4X 2 ½ "screws to fix. Crosses over wavy lines Plate slot. Table mounting screw on each 2-manager side. Each point of the last board will set a long cut.

- Keep the seat of trees on the top panel, and 2 ½ protected "ultimate use Multi-meter to ensure the implementation Parallel - 18" covered wooden house at the bottom, 30 " according to all things house parts, 8X 25MM coast, set according to the plate and hanger.
- Bedded roof ceiling. on the edge shown.
- Cantilevered gutters, 1-2 mm 70" will be the centre of the length of the ceiling compressed hammer nails grow in every two series of nail bottom edge (face up). Now back combination. The first timber (34" blade unit on the edge). use a nail resources are used to fill up all the space.
- Top bar 3 1 ¼ "x screw installation is down. Now home, the door is set. side door to install pop-holes and nest boxes. The second panel is to use the best position, the upper and lower limits.
- Install door lock and key. Now is a different hole in the form of automatic opening statement and meet all the locks and pop together to install the hook inclined to 02:02.
- You will start to be cleared by the door, so hang open. This is not a flat base, because it is. Now screw. 6 holes big plaque mounted outside the door handle.

Step Six - Stare at assembly instructions in complete bafflement then screw up into ball and throw violently away.

Seamus and Minnie leap into action to render immediate assistance. Seamus, being faster and the more nimble of the pair, retrieves balled up instruction pamphlet and consumes with relish.

Step Seven - Apply common sense to assembly of coop panels and completely assemble chicken coop in approx. one hour.

With the coop assembled in front of me, I can see how small it is, not much bigger than a dog kennel. My Girls are supposed to be cramped together in this? I am not happy.

The Girls too, are underwhelmed by their new accommodation. No amount of coaxing, persuasion or outright coercion will get them inside, and I can hardly blame them. They have enjoyed the spacious comforts of the outbuilding so far and this poky little space is just not up to scratch. It might just do for them to sleep in overnight, but it is in no way suitable for during the day. The wire framed 'runs' at either end of the coop will accommodate perhaps three chickens, so long as they don't move around too much. What are they supposed to do? Queue?

I search the internet for a solution, one that is not too expensive, and hit upon 'Heras' fencing. These are the steel mesh panels that you might see outside a building site or road-works, acting as temporary fencing to keep out the general public, vandals and Friday night drinkers. I can buy them second hand quite cheaply and build my Girls a more sensibly sized run very easily.

I order a wagonload of the panels to reduce transport costs. There will doubtless be good uses for any spare panels.

The new run goes up surprisingly quickly. Between us, John and I get the panels upright, lashing them together with cable ties into a rough rectangle.

After that, I can manage on my own, and work at more permanent fixings on the upright panels, and on fitting in chicken wire against the bottom foot or so, overlapping into the turf. Pegged down, the turf will, in time, grow through the chicken wire to produce a fox proof, digging proof, edge to the grass and panels.

Chicken wire over the top, provides a roof that should thwart any attempts to climb in or fly out. Satisfied that the Girls now have safe and suitable accommodation, I wait until dark, when they have gone to roost in the garage, and then, one at a time, pick them off their perches and transfer them into their new home, which I have named Fort Knox.

In fact, over time, the chickens do not stay permanently in Fort Knox. After a day or two, I let them out during the day to wander the garden. They put themselves to bed in the evening and the only issue I have is, occasionally having to pluck one of them from the branches of the apple or plum trees, where she has decided she would like to roost.

Chickens are a lot of fun to have around. They are charming, chatty, entertaining nuisances.

They spend their time gossiping, politicking, sun bathing, dust bathing and exploring. Never mind curiosity killing the cat. Cats are amateurs compared to chickens. Painting a wall? There is a chicken watching you. Up a ladder? Be careful stepping back as there is a chicken on the rungs. Digging a hole? There are several chickens peering in, looking for goodies. Cooking in the kitchen? The Girls have wandered in, checking up for dainties. Since they cannot be house trained and their poop rapidly turns ammoniacal, the kitchen soon reeks and I spend half my life chasing out feathery trespassers.

But, however captivating they are, you must never fool yourself that chickens are nice. Live with them free-ranging for a while and you will realise, and see, that they really are scaled down dinosaurs in feathers. Just as even the smallest terrier is still a wolf in dog's clothing, a chicken is a T-Rex in feathers. They may look cute, but watch them running to chase, say a mouse, and then think of that scene from Jurassic Park with the T Rex pursuing the jeep.

Newly hatched, chicks all look much the same, male or female. Unless they are from one of the breeds where there is some sex-related difference, such as markings on the head, or slightly different colouring, only the very expert can spot the difference between a cock and a hen at this age. Even after several weeks it can be difficult. Vast monies can be made by those who can reliably sort hens from cocks at hatching.

The unfortunate males are almost certainly fated to die at this point.

Over the next few weeks, growing fast, tiny balls of fluff turn into what are recognisably little chickens, but it is still not apparent which are male and which are female. They all grow tiny combs, regardless of gender, so that is no clue. Eventually, depending on breed, the differences in appearance do begin to show, but I have not found them to be reliable and I have made plenty of mistakes in trying to guess the sex of the latest batch of youngsters.

But here is the thing. The chickens themselves know what sex they are, and behave appropriately. This where the trouble starts.

Chickens work on a 'harem' system. It is hard-wired into them. They know how to behave with each other and they get on with it. The Girls have their pecking-order, in which each of them knows exactly where she is in terms of seniority to all the others. Every hen kow-tows to all those above her and queens it over those below her. Infractions are punished swiftly with a sharp peck.

I have read of cases where a subordinate chicken was pecked to death by others, although I have never encountered it myself. My instinct is that this is aberrant behaviour brought on by overcrowding in factory conditions.

In a free-ranging flock, a bird who wants to surrender can run.

It is easy to spot in the flock who is senior and who is less so. At the top of the tree in my own flock is a white hen who, with terrific originality, I have named 'Whitey'.

Just below her are a group of three rather ordinary looking Rhode Island Reds who, at first, I have difficulty telling apart, until I notice subtleties of shading in their neck and plume feathers. I name them 'The Triad'. At the bottom of the pecking order is a rather beautiful Blue Star, who, with her delicately grey, silky plumage, I call 'Bluebell'. Once I have identified the individuals, over time I gain a clear grasp of the hierarchy for the whole flock.

With the boys it is different. With roosters, the fight for seniority can genuinely lead to a fight to the death.

The very first batch of chicks I have is accidental, on my part that is. Once the Girls learn to know me, as I step out into the garden, they come running, following me around and keeping me company, along with the dogs, who concern them not a jot.

This is nice and I enjoy it. I have always liked having a lot of life around me and the Girls are rather good company with their chatty ways and attention to my work. One never knows when digging here might reveal a worm, or clipping that bush could drop a tasty wriggler to the ground.

However, after a few weeks, I notice that as I approach, some of the Girls drop and 'present' to me, an invitation to mating. This I do not like, not because it offends my sensibilities, but because the Girls are treating me as a rooster, head of the flock as it were. For all their freedom to roam and live a 'chickeney' life there is something missing for them. I conclude that my Girls need a man in their life.

I ponder the wisdom of this. Pros: The Girls will be happier. Roosters defend their Girls and look out for them, and are splendid to look at. Cons: It is not my intention to breed chickens. Roosters are noisy. Sometimes roosters can be aggressive to humans. I dismiss the Cons.

I can deal with all of these. I will find my Girls' Mr Darcy.

It is surprisingly easy to obtain a rooster. I have imagined that I may have to spend large amounts of money to buy a good bird. On the contrary, roosters are available everywhere; the free papers, EBay, Craig's List, Preloved; so many offers of 'Free to Good Home'. Hens are expensive; they make eggs and new little chickens. Roosters, no one wants them, not even when they are pedigrees from good bloodlines. Roosters are noisy. They fight. They do not lay eggs.

I choose an amour for my Girls. He is young, about four months old. In chicken terms this means he is a teenager, just learning to be male. But he is handsome, a really beautiful bird. His feathers are golden, silver and lemon with flowing plumes which I suspect will bloom further as he matures.

He seems puzzled but unfazed by the journey to his new home. He watches me through the gaps in his crate, eyeing me as I drive carefully around the bumps and pots in the track to the cottage. I do not want to shake and unsettle him.

My reading on how to introduce new chickens to a flock has been interesting but alarming, as I learn of the dire consequences of getting it wrong; of flock warfare where hens, thrown together as strangers, attack and fight without mercy, or where a lone hen introduced to a flock is slaughtered on the spot by outraged incumbents. So, I unload the crate from the car and put it, closed and complete with occupant, in the middle of the lawn.

The Girls coming running, intrigued by this new development. As I go to make myself a pot of tea, they cluster around, unable quite to get their heads in through the bars, but chortling and crooning at the new kid on the block.

I see no signs of aggression. The Gang of Four have also joined the audience, equally interested in the goings on. They sit, staring in, ears cocked and absorbed.

For half an hour or so, I sit, sipping tea and watching the goings on before deciding that, whatever else happens, the new boy is not going to be murdered on the spot by his would-be wives. Some of the Girls have wandered off. The novelty has gone and they are exploring the possibilities offered by the ashes of the garden bonfire for dust-bathing.

Lifting the drop-down slot door of the crate, I sit back and wait. After a few moments, our boy steps out. The nearby Girls notice and wander back over. Most do not seem very interested, but introduce themselves. It is all very unexciting, almost anti-climactic; in fact, just what is needed for a first meeting.

Bluebell however, behaves quite differently. Spotting the rooster from afar, she shakes off the remains of her dust bath and rushes over to him. As he turns to greet this new arrival, she prostrates herself before him, chest to the floor, wings spread, a clear invitation to mount. The rooster cocks an eye at her, hesitates in apparent puzzlement, and then steps over her, setting off on an exploration of the garden. Plainly he has some maturing to do.

All continues to go well for the rest of the day. I work in the garden to keep an eye on things, but by dusk the rooster seems to be integrated with the flock and is walking with them as a group. He accompanies them into the coop and I close them in for the night.

The following day, as I open up again, the whole flock, man and Girls, come out together and I conclude that initial meetings have gone well.

Overnight John and I have decided on a name for the new boy. In deference to P.G. Wodehouse, he is named 'Bertie Rooster'. Time will tell if he is a drone.

Within a week, Bertie is no longer the newcomer. He is the leader. He chooses where the garden perambulations will lead, and the Girls follow.

It is a relaxed kind of following, with hens wandering off to investigate that molehill, or to check out the possibility of earthworms near that spade, but afterwards, they make their way back again to the loose confederation.

Another week and Bertie's instincts are showing. He now wants his wives to perform their duties.

He is a thug, grabbing them by the neck feathers and wrestling them to the ground until they submit to his attentions. In human terms it is certainly rape, and I begin to worry about my Girls. Have I done the right thing by them? In fact, the senior Girls do not tolerate this behaviour. When he tries to take his 'rights' by them, they peck back until he backs down and goes off in search of an easier target. Bluebell never argues. She adores Bertie and will crouch for him at any time.

Over time however, I see Bertie acquiring good manners and learning how to charm his ladies. If he finds a tasty tit-bit, a worm or a leather-jacket, he chortles to call over whichever girl is nearest and presents her with his love gift.

He learns to dance for them, circling, one wing half stretched towards the object of his affections in a seductive waltz. I see him watching over them, spying for hawks and foxes, shrieking alarm at any hint of danger. He matures into a full rooster, or in human terms, he learns to be a gentleman.

Bertie is living in rooster paradise. With his bevy of maidens, he is master of the roost and lord of all he surveys.

Each night I close up the coop and then the run. Usually, most of the Girls are already inside by the time I arrive. Some refuse to sleep in the coop itself. One or two, the senior hens I notice, sleep with Bertie, on top of the coop. I am unconcerned. I have built the run to be fox-proof.

They are completely safe in there, netted overhead to prevent intruders climbing or flying in, double netted now at ground level to prevent anything biting through the mesh and the turf now grown through chicken wire out to a meter from the run.

I wish that the chucks would sleep in the coop at night, but come fog, rain, hail and snow, they choose to sleep outside. Who am I to stop them? I try each night to count numbers, but it is dark. All I can really see, is that a lot of feathery bodies are snuggled up tight together.

It is June, and a glorious day. Sunshine beams down hot as I carry the 'green bucket' from the kitchen to the new veggie bed I have under construction.

I have a method for making new vegetable beds. Rather than strip top soil from the rest of the garden, I build a framework a foot or so high, from second hand scaffolding boards. Pegged upright using hammered in stakes, I then fill the frame by making 'soil' from whatever is to hand. All prunings and clippings go through my shredder and into the bed, along with litter from the chicken coop.

All waste paper from the office goes through a paper shredder, is recycled as chicken litter and then has a third life as material for the new bed.

And of course, the contents of the kitchen green bin go in there. Potato peelings, fruit rinds, outer leaves from cabbages, caulis and sprouts, apple cores, old bread, meal leftovers, old egg shells (baked in the oven first to prevent the risk of 'mad chicken disease'); in fact, anything other than meat goes in the green bin. The dogs kindly assist in the matter of left-over meat disposal.

The Girls and Bertie, spot me with the bin and come running; they love the green bucket. There could be anything in there.

I throw the lot over the new bed, making a point of ensuring it is well spread. If I let it land in a single heap, only the senior chucks will get any of it; the Girls low in the ranks will not be permitted access to these choice items. For good measure, I grab a handful of old pea-pods and toss them over the lawn, well away from Whitey and the Triad. Bluebell and her friends are also entitled to treats.

I make a head count. Thirteen plus Bertie. Who is missing? It takes me a few moments to identify the missing party, one of the Triad. Where is she? As one of the Seniors, she would never pass up an opportunity for the green bucket. I search the garden, worrying for her, but later see her scratching around in the bed. Who knows where she has been….?

A week later and I am leaning over the stable door from the kitchen with a cup of coffee, revelling in the sun, the snappy breeze and the glorious views over acres of emerald grass and golden buttercups. I freeze at the sight before me, the mug halfway to my lips. One of the Girls, one of the Triad, is standing in front of me with two chicks, tiny balls of yellow fluff, peeping out from under her skirts. For a moment I stand, gobsmacked. How has she done it? She cannot possibly have incubated them in the coop; I would have spotted it. Incubation time for chickens is about twenty-one days. How has she managed to sit on eggs for twenty-one days without my seeing her?

As I stand staring at her, jaw scraping the kitchen floor, another tiny face peeps out from under her feathers and then another, and another.

Trying not to move quickly and upset them, I reach sideways for a slice of bread which had been destined for my morning toast. Breaking it into chicken sized bits, I toss it in her direction.

'Mum' immediately starts clucking and crooning and little heads and bodies break cover from all directions under her feathers. There seem to be hundreds of them. When the scene calms down a bit, I count eight brilliantly yellow little chicks with her.

Mum snatches up the nearest bit of bread and then starts breaking it up into breadcrumbs, into chick-sized bits. She chortles and hums, pecking at the crumbs, but not eating them herself, showing her babies the edible morsels. I am intrigued by the noises she is making, vaguely thinking that I recognise the sound, then I laugh. Mum is making the same call to her babies that Bertie makes to his harem when he something nice for them to eat, one of his love gifts.

I search out what I have to hand that will serve as food for tiny chickens. The standard grain and pellets that the adults eat are far too large for the babes.

Sifting through my kitchen cupboard, very little I have is suitable fare for these tinies, but I find a bag of couscous. I toss it into a bowl with some hot water, then go to check the internet for recommendations and learn that I should buy some specialist 'chick-crumbs'.

Reading on, scouring a variety of sources for information, I learn that I should give the chicks greens, that I should not give them greens, that I should give them kitchen scraps, that I should not give them kitchen scraps, that chicks must not allowed near the rest of the adult flock, that chicks must be integrated as soon as possible......

I give up on the mass of conflicting 'knowledge' and go to check up on Mum and her brood. She has taken her.... one, two, three.... yes, still eight babies.... out into the garden and is giving sheer Hell to anyone who dares approach. This includes all the other hens, Bertie and The Four.

Leading her downy offspring like Moses to the Promised Land, she takes command of the new veg bed and its green-bucket contents, scratching up titbits and dropping them down for her babies. I conclude; Blow the Internet! Mum has managed to get her chicks this far without my even spotting them. She obviously knows more than I do, so I'll let her handle it.

Will she let me near her? The couscous has swelled and cooled by now, so I give it a quick stir to loosen the grains and then take it outside. As an afterthought, I grab a bag of raisins and toss it over the lawn in another direction completely, to occupy the rest of the chickens for a few minutes.

I approach Mum warily, and she eyes me equally warily, but without the fluffed up feathers and outraged clucks that would be warning me off. I toss down a scattering of the couscous and she immediately goes into her cluck-cluck 'Eat this Babes.' routine and I decide that I am welcome, at least while I have suitable offerings for her and her offspring.

It cannot be easy to bring up so many babies by yourself.

Over the next day or so I find, first of all, where Mum has been hiding. The ground immediately outside the cottage is lowered by a couple of feet, for drainage and damp purposes. From the kitchen door to the drive is a tiny footbridge, only about four feet long, just enough to span the drop in the ground level, but Mum has made herself a spot underneath with only perhaps six inches' clearance, and has been incubating right under my feet for the past three weeks, without my suspecting a thing. I bow to her ingenuity. However, when I reach in to feel her nest, I find two more eggs with fully formed chicks inside and one chick, hatched but dead. Hatching, it seems, is a hazardous process, and not all chicks succeed at or survive it.

The second thing I find is even sadder. A drain cover, only a few feet away from the nest, has been missing and in need of replacing for some time. It was no danger to anyone, human, dog or adult chicken, but in there I find, floating in greasy kitchen water, a newly hatched, but very dead, chick.

With a lump in my throat, I fish out the tiny body and place a slate over the hole.

Putting a new drain cover on my shopping list, I go in search of a really shallow dish to fill with water for the other babies.

John is convinced that the sudden appearance of the chicks is a put up job on my part; that I could not possibly have not known that Mum was brooding.

In response, I give him my egg collecting basket and invite him to go find the current day's eggs. He is confused by this, so I explain to him firstly that, roughly speaking, from fourteen hens (minus Mum), since all the Girls are laying, and a chicken in full lay, depending on breed, produces approximately one egg per twenty-six hours, we should be getting ten to thirteen eggs per day. After half an hour he returns with three eggs, all from the coop.

There is an Easter game of 'Hunt the Eggs', chocolate eggs these days of course.

However, I think that whoever invented the game had an agenda, that it was a cheap ploy to get all the local kids trying to find the hideaways that his chickens had for their eggs.

We keep chickens to lay, and in these times, most chickens have little choice about what happens next as, imprisoned in battery farms, eggs are laid, roll off down a chute and are carried away. That is the end of the matter for the hen.

No so for free rangers. I have made a point of giving my Girls as much freedom as is possible, while also being safe at night. In the morning, as I open up, they charge out of the coop, running to investigate the garden, the Common, the house, any recently dug holes or other ongoing project, my shoelaces, the freshly dried laundry I have just taken down off the line....

The Girls are provided with a warm, well ventilated and safe coop, a fox proof run, an acre of garden to roam, eighty acres of Common to further roam, manufactured 'official' chicken pellets, windfalls from plum and apple trees, fruit they can actually pick themselves from currants, gooseberries, vines, raspberries, blackberries; any number of grubs, caterpillars, crickets, grasshoppers, flies and butterflies. This is chicken Paradise. All I ask in return is that they give me, roughly speaking, an egg a day. Not even an egg a day; every couple of days will do. There is only me and John. How many eggs can we eat?

But do they do that? Nope.

The Girls lay an egg a day, but said egg is not to be revealed. It is to be carefully hidden. No matter that the hen has no intention of brooding the egg to hatching. It is sacrosanct and is not destined to be, for example, boiled and served with toast soldiers.

I spend a good half hour a day, every day, looking for eggs. Some will be laid in the nesting boxes provided for the purpose; a few only, two or three perhaps. The rest of the eggs? It is a game we play. Where is the nest?

I acquire an 'eye' for likely spots. The chosen spot, the nest, will be somewhere slightly out of sight to onlookers, but from where the hen herself can see out. It could be under the shade of some nettles, leaning over to create a covered spot, or perhaps under that stack of plywood that I moved from the garage intending to take to the dump, but which, instead, I simply leaned against the wall.

A nook in a thicket of hawthorn or other shrubs is ideal. The plastic dog-basket that I put outside a couple of weeks ago because it reeked and I wanted to let the wind and rain clean it up a bit - the wind blew it over in a winter storm and, upside down, it makes a perfect hidey-hole...

There is the big wooden shed I have erected, intending to line it out with polystyrene sheeting for insulation. The stack of sheets, waiting to be used, has been scratched out into a rough hollow and one of the Girls is there, sitting on, after investigation, eight eggs. From this unlikely spot she produces two chicks. So far as I can tell, neither of the hatchlings is hers. Certainly they look nothing like her.

Hens are not possessive about a nest. If one finds a likely spot to lay, then others will join her and lay their own eggs too. I find the nests, perhaps after only a few days, with a couple of dozen eggs, but only one hen, who has 'gone broody', incubating them. This is a difficult case as I do not have the heart to take her off the eggs. The first time I try to do this, the girl is so obviously distressed, that I put her back to finish the job.

But even when the eggs are in mid-incubation, with a hen firmly sat brooding them, other hens will continue to lay in that same nest. Chicken eggs mature to hatching in twenty-one days. Any eggs added after the start of incubation will either be late, if the hen has the patience to keep sitting, or the semi formed chicks will die inside the shells. The hen will, at some point, become tired of waiting and leave the nest with the chicks already hatched. It is a distressing thing to find, a fully formed chick in the shell, that never had that last chance to make it out into the world.

I acquire the habit of, when finding eggs abandoned by a hen, popping them into the incubator for a few more days, just to give them that final opportunity to hatch. Most never do, but a few crack their shells and then spend their first weeks living in a cardboard box under a heat lamp.

However they hatch, the new chicks are gorgeous. In an astonishingly short time Mum's chicks grow from tiny balls of fluff to big balls of fluff, to sprouting real feathers, to unmistakably small chickens. And as they grow, their behaviour changes.

I cannot tell by looking, which is a hen and which is a cock, but they know, and from their behaviour, I learn. Over the weeks, I see pairs of half-grown chickens squaring up for the fight.

Heads held low, level with the body and neck outstretched, eyeballing the opponent, the boys measure up the opposition. At this stage it is not serious, all posturing with no real physical aggression, but that changes quickly.

The very first clutch, Mum's eight hidden babies, statistically speaking, should have produced four hens and four cocks. What I find I have is two hens and six cocks. The two little girls sail happily through their maturation and grow into really beautiful birds, with their mother's solid build and reliable personality, and their father's good looks. Bertie is stunning and he passes this on to all his offspring, male and female alike. However, his boys, wow, his boys….

In the early weeks I find them pairing up, 'Bring it On', as they learn to be Boys. A month later it is bloody warfare. As youngsters they are no real threat to each other; but maturing, as they develop their spurs and their mastery of fighting, the situation turns bitter and frightening.

I go out to the garden, to find blond and golden feathers, blood bespattered, scattered over the lawn. One of the young boys will be limping, a damaged wing and wounds around his face, blood on his plumage. And as he waits in the wings to recover, there is another battle a-midfield between his brothers.

I try to interrupt these fights; separate the pair and carry one of the combatants off to the far side of the garden.

It is useless. As I snatch up one, his opponent follows, jumping up, tearing and scratching at his disabled enemy.

Eventually I adopt a policy. When I see two of the boys fighting, I establish who is the more aggressive, snatch him out of the fight, and it is casserole time. I do this four times, whittling down my initial six proto roosters to two.

Now there is peace. Neither of the two remaining boys seems inclined to attack the other and so I let them be. Both of Bertie's remaining sons are growing to resemble him, but neither, at the moment, is inclined to challenge him. One of these boys is in fact, rather charming. He is quite friendly towards me and when I come out into the garden, will walk over to say 'Hello' and to ask not just for food, but for attention. He clucks and is really quite affectionate, a bit of a sweetie in fact. I name him 'Lemon' for his gorgeous golden-yellow colouring. His brother is more distant and stand-offish and never acquires a name. I simply call him 'Second Rooster'.

Lemon, for all his lovely personality, and perhaps because of it, never attracts the interest of the Girls. They want a 'fighting man' and Lemon, as a 'man of peace', does not cut the mustard.

I never see him treading any of the Girls. He gets along fine with his dad; Bertie does not apparently see him as a threat. However, his one remaining brother, while not attacking Lemon, treats him coolly and will not allow him to mingle with the flock. I feel sorry for Lemon. He spends more time alone than he should, for an animal belonging to a social species.

Bertie does however, keep an eye on Second Rooster. Over time, as the youngster gains his full plumage, he becomes, chip off the old block, a handsome bird, and the Girls respond, accepting his company, but they follow Bertie. Bertie is tough and manly, but not warlike and I think that, confident in his own status, he does not see the need to press his authority.

Bertie does not like it though, when he sees Second Rooster try to tread any of his harem. The Girls do not co-operate, but their squawking and cries of protest bring Bertie speeding over the garden to oust the usurper.

Over time, as Second Rooster becomes tougher and harder, the Girls become more responsive to him, and I sometimes see them allowing Second Rooster to have his way, when Bertie is out of sight.

This gives me pause for thought. It is in the way of things with animals who live in this type of social group, that an older male will, over time, be superseded by a younger one. However, I am balancing the way of nature against the fact that I like Bertie. He is a fine bird who takes care of his Girls and does everything within his abilities to 'do right' by them. He has an agenda of course, when he presents them with his little presents, but the Girls seem to enjoy his attentions, so that's fine. I am also concerned about possible inbreeding. When I see Second Rooster trying to tread his own mother - he does not succeed, she repels the uninvited boarder with a sharp peck and then dashes off to stand by Bertie - I start to consider that I should perhaps bring in some fresh blood to my little troop. I have already considered expanding the flock, as I am receiving requests for free range eggs, and so I examine the options.

Reading about different chicken breeds, I research their habits, likes and dislikes, preferred climate, utility - eggs, meat or both - temperament, affability towards humans, inclination to go broody and much else.

I want as broad a mix of breeds as possible. This will be decorative in the garden; some of the breeds are really lovely, with feathers in gold, silver, black and chestnut, it will give me a nice range of differently coloured eggs, the individuals will be more robust against disease and parasites, and the flock will remain as genetically diverse as I can make it, which will give the new chicks the best chance of hatching healthily.

I visit a local chicken breeder and buy a dozen hatching eggs, a mix of breeds; Light Sussex and Wyandotte. Carefully transported home, I pop the eggs into the incubator along with water for humidity control and a thermometer, and I wait. The incubator is not ideal, a cheap model I bought off the internet. But I follow my carefully read instructions as closely as I can, maintaining humidity levels and temperature as nearly as I can to the ideal, turning the eggs twice a day so that the chicks inside do not stick to the inside of the shell, and occasionally 'candling' the eggs to check the progress of their occupants.

This last means holding up the egg, in a darkened room, and shining a torch or bright light through the egg. With practice you can see, through the shell, the developing chick. Get it right and it is possible to spot a surprising amount of detail, even blood vessels in the embryo.

Three of the eggs never develop at all, their contents remaining an undifferentiated murk through the shell. Of the remaining nine, I can see something happening inside, and I count the days until hatching is due.

On day nineteen, I hear chirps coming from inside the shells. I cluck and croon back, making my best attempt at the sounds I have heard Mum making to her chicks.

On day twenty-one, right on schedule, tiny cracks appear in some of the shells as the chicks inside chip away at their prison. Enraptured by the sight, I constantly return to peer through the small window of the incubator, quite unable to get on with any other work.

The micro-spectacle is bewitching. The hatching process starts with the chick chipping at a spot on top of the egg, using a small spike on its beak. It is important in the last couple of days of incubation, that the egg not be turned. At this stage the chicks are positioning themselves for hatching. Somewhat like a human baby in the womb, it is important that the chicks be positioned correctly if they are to make their successful way into the world. A chick ready to hatch lies facing upwards and with its long legs tucked up under its belly, head at the blunt end of the shell, with access to the air sac.

The tiny chip at the top of the shell is the chick's starting point. From there it works its way in a band around the mid-line of the shell, gradually breaking the shell into two halves. It is an exhausting process and can take several hours. When the crack is long enough, and the shell more or less in two halves, the chick heaves, head one way, legs and feet pushing the other way, to split the shell and escape. Sometimes the shell breaks cleanly. Sometimes it takes several attempts.

At the end, the chick tumbles from the shell and then lies prone, utterly spent.

In the normal way, at this point, the chick would be under the plumage of its mother, warm and protected. In the case of my incubator babies, as soon as each one is free of its shell, I scoop it out of the incubator as quickly as possible, replacing the lid immediately to keep the heat and humidity in.

The new babe then goes into a large cardboard box I have set up in my office. The bottom is lined with a thick newspaper and wood shavings and the heat lamp has been switched on for some hours, preheating the box. Newly hatched chicks have no internal temperature control and must be kept very warm for several days.

To my disappointment, not all the chicks hatch successfully. Of the nine developed eggs, six hatch. When, after two more days, the remaining three still do not hatch, I open them up, carefully, just in case the occupants are alive inside. Instead I find a stinking mess of half-developed embryo, and conclude that my cheap incubator is not up to the job. I order a much better model from a reputable supplier.

Newly hatched, the six chicks look quite pathetic. Their down is plastered wet against tiny bodies and they lie limp, drained of all energy, but within an hour or so, under the heat of the lamp, magic happens and the little bodies fluff up, the chicks become alert and responsive and they stand, gathering in a group under the warmest part of the lamp.

They do not eat at this stage, living on the remains of the yolk inside them for a day or two, but they already have the instinct to peck.

I put down a small bowl of chick crumbs and a specially designed chick drinker for them; a water bowl designed to be very shallow and into which they cannot fall. I have learned my lesson from the dead chick in the drain.

The chicks are utterly charming and I am bewitched by them. They run to my hand when I reach into their cardboard nursery. Chickens are a species which 'imprint' on the first thing they see, so I guess that they think my hand is their mother. Having read all the conflicting advice on the do's and don'ts of what to feed to chicks, I ignore the lot and treat them as I saw Mum treating her brood. Out in the garden I collect small amounts of cabbage leaves, nettles, beetroot tops and grass trimmings. These I dice into tiny, chick sized pieces and put them in the boxes. The chicks are keen to 'eat their greens' and thrive on the diet.

I go in search of a fresh batch of eggs for the incubator. This time I buy local breeds, the 'Burford Brown', noted for its large, very dark brown eggs, and the 'Cotswolds Legbar' which has the Araucana breed in its ancestry and lays beautiful blue eggs. As local breeds, they should be resilient, happy birds and ideal for my garden conditions.

In their new incubator, with thermostatic temperature control and an automatic 'rocker' to turn the eggs regularly, I am confident that in twenty-one days, I will have a good outcome.

Meanwhile I make preparations for my rapidly growing brood to move to larger accommodation. Visiting local suppliers and scouring the internet, I find, as I did when I bought the first coop, that buying new, purpose made chicken runs and coops is very expensive.

However, there is a lot of equipment out there that, sold second-hand and perhaps advertised as 'rabbit run' rather than 'chicken run' can be acquired much more cheaply.

I am also looking for some suitable accommodation for broody hens. I have two Girls desperate to brood and I am constantly picking them up from nests under the hedgerow where they are trying to sit on eggs. I do not want them sitting for three weeks, in a spot where they will be naught but a snack should a fox come calling.

I find a small ark, with a nice private chamber and a small run, enough for a sitting hen to be able to stretch her legs and answer nature's call, and a rabbit hutch with a built in run underneath. Again, ideal for a hen who wants a bit of peace and quiet while she incubates her eggs. I buy them second hand off the internet and get them for a tenner apiece.

So as not to have the new babes in the main run with the rest of the adult chickens, I build an addition to the current run from some of the leftover Heras fencing panels; an extra 'cell' with a shared wall to the main run so that two sets of chickens can see each other through the mesh, and get used to the idea of each other before they actually meet. This way I hope that half-grown chicks, introduced to the adults, will already be known and accepted by the flock.

The two new broody hutches I put in the new run extension, popping in my two would-be Mums, one to each hutch, along with half a dozen of the eggs she has been sitting on.

I do not close up the run at this stage, allowing them free access in and out of the garden, in case they are unhappy with their accommodation, but they seem quite content with the new arrangements.

Soon though, I find that I have to close the run anyway, as the rest of the Girls come calling by to lay their own eggs in the new hutches.

The new chicks in their cardboard box develop at speed, losing fluff and growing into proper little chickens. Over several days I lower the temperature in their quarters until they are living at room temperature, then choosing a fine day,

I take them to their new run with the broodies. By the time the broodies have hatched their own babes and want to be out of their nests, these guys should be properly independent and able to cope.

Over time, the presence of the chickens, changes some of the character of the garden. When John and I first move into the house, the lawn is rather thin and straggly, the grass looking as if life is a bit of a struggle, being thin and patchy, or yellowing in places.

When the chickens arrive, with their free-ranging life style, they are free to scratch, dig, pull, uproot, and of course, poop, anywhere they wish. Consequently, the turf is constantly but gently scarified, aerated and fertilised by an army of keen volunteers. In the area of the run itself, the soil is bare. The turf cannot survive the attentions of so many chickens in such a confined area.

However, outside the run, the lawns thicken, green and flourish. John, who loves mowing grass, starts to complain about the frequency with which he must mow. After only a couple of seasons, the lawns are lush and verdant.

The other major effect of the chickens on the garden is in pest control. Chickens are omnivores. They will eat almost anything they can catch, subdue and get down their necks. In consequence, I have no garden pests. No caterpillars roam the veggie beds. No maggots infest the apples or plums. The roses are aphid free. But there is a price to pay for this avian vigilance.

Chickens love fruits and veggies. The fruit around the garden is no problem. Apart from the trees already in place when I arrive; apples and plums, I plant many more fruit trees and shrubs; raspberries, blackberries, blackcurrants, damsons, elderberries, grapes, passion fruit and more. I pick, eat, freeze, bottle and jam as much as we need, more in truth; I enjoy jam-making and John loves his jam. The rest is either picked by the chickens directly from the bush, vine or tree, or as the fruit ripens, they enjoy the windfalls. I am growing free chicken feed and ensuring that everyone, human or avian, gets a good mixed diet.

The veggie beds are a different matter. The Girls strut around the cabbages, cock a head, focus one eye on a target and then, peck, one caterpillar is no more. Wonderful. However, chickens love cabbage itself and most of the other leafy greens. Between them they will peck a cabbage down to a stub in a day, and they are utter death to seedlings.

The scratching habit of chickens will uproot anything newly planted in a matter of minutes and a carefully laid out bed of young plantlings can be destroyed by chickens in less than an hour.

So, I spend several weeks making cages for the veggie beds to keep the chickens out. The Girls respond to this as some sort of Pavlovian intelligence test and devote hours to breaking in. I have a running battle to keep my vegetables growing, constantly fishing both hens and roosters out from under the netting. At times I consider coq au vin as an answer to the problem, but then one of the Girls will jump up to sit on my knee and accept a bit of toast crust from me. My will crumbles and I just shoo the chucks away from the beds.

More Guests

Having moved into Wayside Cottage, there is still a mortgage to pay, and, having ceased the holiday lets there, John and I are now receiving no income for the property. Our eyes turn to the scruffy outbuilding to the side. Over Winter, it has homed the chickens, but now we start to consider other uses.

Originally a double garage, it is a long time since it has been used that way. The building contains an office, a workroom and a bedroom, laundry facilities and a toilet. It is fully plumbed and wired for electricity, properly built on a large concrete pad, and the views from the window over the Common are panoramic. However, it is damp, cold and the roof is leaking. No one would want to sleep in the bedroom with its mouldy walls, and the wiring is very suspect.

We start by clearing out the detritus left by the chickens. The Girls have been thoroughly at home during their winter occupation and very much made it their own. Sweeping out old straw, shavings and guano, I dump the lot in the veg beds. Giant cobwebs festoon the building, but their owners have long since been dealt with by the chickens; no spiders here.

John draws plans to turn around the room design to give two bedrooms, a kitchen, a bathroom and a decent sized lounge.

We build the bathroom and kitchen around the plumbing, drains and sewers already in place but bring in an electrician to strip out the wiring and replace to a modern standard.

I consider how to floor our renewed building; bare concrete is no good for anyone.

Insulating throughout, we make all walls and ceilings as snug and warm as possible.

The roof is replaced and the roof space insulated; no more chickens roosting in the rafters. The damp and stinking plasterboard of the walls is stripped and replaced, again backed with insulation. For the concrete floor, I buy a plastic membrane to cut out the damp, lay insulation over the top and above that....

Working in the garden on my raised vegetable plots, I bought a job lot of second hand scaffolding planks from a supplier I found on the internet. The planks are well past being safe for construction site use, but can be used a thousand and one other ways. For economy's sake, I bought a truckload, so we have plenty to choose from. The timbers have cost about three pounds each.

John and I work our way through the planks one by one, selecting this one for good wood grain, under the cement splashes and the building site muck; rejecting that one for a long split down the middle. This plank has a nice straight edge. That one is warped and will not lie level. We need enough planks to floor our new 'Summer House'.

The Gang of Four all assist in their various ways. Shannon sits to one side and nods sagely in agreement with our selections. Seamus widdles on the stack, and Minnie and Duncan lie on top of the planks as we try to move them into their respective piles. Bertie and the Girls help out too, the Girls by dashing in to check what is under each plank as we move it, woodlice, centipedes and beetles, all snatched away in triumph. Bertie's contribution is to sit as close as possible to my right ear, crowing loudly.

Our stack of selected planks at the ready, we set to, removing the end straps; metal bindings, stapled into place to protect the end of the plank from splitting. Although early in the year, the weather is hot and sticky and the work takes all day, but at the end of it, we are ready for the next phase; knocking off bits of cement, brushing down with a stiff brush and painting with woodworm and anti-rot treatment. It takes three days of work to complete all this but at the end of it, our planks are ready to be installed.

And now comes the fun part. Inside the Summer House, the plastic membrane is laid over the floor, followed by the insulation, a tough and relatively hard wearing foam sheet. The planks are laid carefully atop the insulation and knocked hard against the walls and each other with a mallet. The Gang and the Girls have to be firmly ejected from proceedings; we want no trapped paws and feet as the planks are banged into place. The chickens are particularly difficult to keep out.

They are afire with curiosity as to what we are doing in their old home.

The work is a joy to do; talk about an instant result, better even than fitting carpet. The work gets finicky towards the end, either finding planks that are a good fit, or cutting them to fit, but in a day, we have the floor down.

Just now, our wooden floor is not beautiful, stained with muck and cement, but that is going to change. I hire an industrial floor sander and spend a day working, wearing ear-muffs and face mask as I slowly walk the sander up and down, over the floor. It is difficult work, because within five minutes, the air is so full of dust that it is almost impossible to see even to the windows, let alone judge the quality of the surface below me. The noise is ear-splitting. Within seconds of first starting up the machine, neither dogs or chickens are anywhere to be seen.

The sander does a great job of the initial coarse sanding, removing muck and detritus from the surfaces and levelling off the planks, but it is far too unwieldy for the more delicate work to follow. Dispensing with the large machine, I get down on my hands and knees with a hand sander. It takes three days of crawling up and down at floor level, dragging a cushion along as I go, to avoid housemaid's knee, sanding the timbers to the point of displaying their lovely grain. Vacuum cleaner out, dust sucked up and a wipe down of surfaces with a damp cloth. Our wooden floor is ready to be stained.

Opening a large tin of wood-stain in a shade of dark oak, a test on a bit of plank offcut shows it to be too dark, too intense.

I dilute it a little, noting my proportions, so that my application can be consistent. When I have the shade I want, it is back down on my hands and knees to stain the timbers, being careful not to paint myself into a corner. I paint each timber, one at a time, to avoid 'tide marks' in my staining, and break off at regular intervals to take some fresh air; the fumes from the stain are quite powerful. Staining the timbers is another full day's work.

The following day, the stain has dried and the floor is really beginning to look good. Another day's work, this time, a final light sanding and then I am ready for the final run; oiling the floor. This will bring out the true beauty of the wood. The first couple of coats of oil are instantly absorbed by the timber, sinking almost without trace, but the timber comes up to a lovely dark sheen with honeyed amber highlights glowing out from the whorls and swirls of the grain. I keep 'feeding' the wood with oil, then polishing. The floor is a thing of true beauty now, and I am immensely pleased and proud of it.

Later on, I do my sums and calculate that our polished wooden floor has cost less than £450; about £300 for the scaffolding planks, perhaps £70 to £80 in wood stain and oil and the cost of hiring the industrial sander. Oh and sore knees for me. I estimate that this is perhaps 20% of what it would have cost to buy the floor and have it installed by a commercial company.

Work continues apace and in only a few weeks we have a small but perfect holiday cottage, complete with its own fenced off garden area and views to die for. For anyone who wants peace and quiet and a country holiday, it is matchless.

I plant daffodils by the fences, and clematis and climbing roses to scramble up the slightly bleak looking, outside areas of the Summer House. It will not take long for the plants to soften the edges of the freshly painted walls.

We have targeted Easter for our first holiday guests. I have been working on a website and other advertising to target local shows and fairs, music festivals and campers, country lovers, dog owners and anyone wanting to be truly 'away from it all'. I follow my usual tactics of 'keep it cheap' and 'keep it filled', and again the holiday rental is a success.

Our guests are a really mixed bag. One group of regulars is a family of cockneys who normally never see a growing thing from one week to the next. They travel up at weekends to cram themselves, ten at a time, into accommodation intended for four to six. Another lady stays regularly with her rescue dog, Ben, an enormous Rottweiler with personality problems. She swears that Ben benefits from the tranquillity of the spot. Moreover, she can let him run loose on the Common without worrying that anyone might get hurt.

Over their regular visits, I see Ben's transformation from terrifying Death Hound to slightly problematic big dog.

The phone rings. "Hello. Is that the Summer House? Yes? You allow pets; is that right? Yes? Oh, no, it's not a dog. It's my budgie." The enquirer explains that he is a little nervous about staying in such a quiet spot, but makes a provisional booking for a week. When he arrives, he walks briefly around the Summer House and its garden and, on the spot, extends his booking to a fortnight.

He is a monk, looking for a retreat holiday for a few days; somewhere he can use as a base to tour the area and photograph the local churches. He is a fascinating man, and John and I have a number of interesting discussions sitting out in the garden, sharing a pot of tea.

One couple who visit, check very carefully beforehand that dogs are permitted and that the Summer House garden is fenced off properly. They arrive with eight assorted terriers and spaniels, all hell-bent on having a great time dashing around the garden.

The dogs are hilarious and very lovable, dashing round, barking like mad at everything in sight. A couple of the dogs regularly break out, to come and play with The Gang. The couple apologise for the chaos and the barking, but, as I always explain to all visiting dog owners, with four of our own, barking is the last thing that will upset us.

And - I wave my hand in the vague direction of the Common - there is no one else to upset. There is no one else nearby at all.

I make it clear to the guests, particularly the dog owners, that the fence to the Summer House garden is only there for their privacy. It is not a barrier. If their dogs want to play with our dogs, they are welcome to do so. It is good for the dogs to play together, particularly for Minnie, who benefits enormously from being exposed to so many new experiences. I explain that there is only one 'sin' that dogs can commit here; chasing chickens. So long as the visitors behave themselves and leave the chickens be, they are free to roam.

I am in the Wayside kitchen one day when a large fat Labrador toddles in. She has an egg in her mouth. Her flushed and embarrassed owner dashes up from behind. "Oh, I'm so sorry." she says. "I couldn't stop her. Marley loves eggs and she found a next under the hedge over there." I laugh. Marley has found a nest that I missed. I go to collect the eggs, and then give one of them to Marley in a saucer.

The Final Journey

Someone needs to go back up North for a few days. The Pendon Edge house is up for sale, but it needs work doing. The tenants renting the house have been less than ideal and the house needs some TLC to get it into saleable condition.

John has his hands full with his business and so we agree that I will travel North, taking the Gang of Four with me, so that John has some peace and quiet to work. The dogs can occupy their old premises of the garden floor of the big georgian house. This gives them lots of space, and with access to the back garden, they will be fine, leaving me free to work on the house. It will make a nice change for them and I can get something useful done.

So with the dogs in the car, their mobile kennel, we take the couple of hours' drive northwards to Lancashire and our old home.

Parking up in the car park to the rear as I always did, the dogs are less than enthusiastic as I let them into the garden. In the ground floor flat, with their assorted favourite baskets, cushions and blankets, no one seems impressed. Not even putting down some special bowls of fried liver strips, prepared for the occasion, raises more than a perfunctory wag.

Things improve a bit when I take them along their old walk down the side track, under the railway bridge and out onto the hills behind.

Shannon and Seamus take their usual lead position with Minnie behind, and Duncan potters along at his own pace with me. Back here now after a few years, I notice the difference in Duncan's speed, so much slower. He is older now. They all are. When we return to the house, there is a marked gloom with the canine contingent. None of them want to be here.

I must stay for the week. There is so much to do. I have a four storey house to paint almost from top to bottom, so like it or not, the Gang of Four must make the best of their situation.

There is some sniffing around the garden and a couple of holes are dug with an air of 'for the form of the thing', but if I show signs of heading for the car, they are all around my feet, jumping up and asking to come with me. They all want to go to 'proper home' at Wayside Cottage, not remain in this pale imitation.

The end of the week arrives. I have completed my planned work, and gratefully, I lock up the, now redecorated, house. I lead the dogs past the mown lawn and tidied borders, and opening the back of the car, the dogs almost as one, leap inside, only Minnie slightly bringing up the rear, as she now needs a hand under her bottom to help her in.

Within minutes, the dogs know we were going home; as soon as I turn onto the motorway. Shannon spots me indicating for the filter lane and barks excitedly. The others take the hint from her, and I have four bouncing maniacs in the car for the next fifteen minutes or so until they settle down a bit.

A couple of hours later, as I come off the motorway again, they become more and more restless until, as I pull onto the track onto the Common, they are in full swing again, leaping around the back of the car, barking, baying and creating mayhem. I dream of the moment I can let them out and stop the ringing in my ears.

Oddly, when I pull up onto the drive and open the back of the car. Shannon, Minnie and Duncan all become very civilised and relaxed about their arrival back home. This is how it is supposed to be. They can take it in their stride. Stepping quietly out of the car, they set off to check out the garden, the chickens and any new visitors in the Summer House. Nonetheless, they are obviously pleased to be home. They move as a group together around the hedges and lawns, reassuring themselves that all is well with their home.

Seamus is a different matter; he launches from the car like a rocket and runs in hysterical circles around the garden, around and around, barking and yipping excitedly.

Stiff at the joints and his back unbending, he moves like a rocking horse, but his old limbs seem to bother him not a jot as he shoots around the lawn like a young dog again. He is a joy to behold.

This is where my Gang of Four belong, their home. I make the decision now, that I will never take them from here again.

Friends and Loyalties

I am in Wayside Cottage amid a whirl of activity. One of the pretty little sitting rooms needs a fresh coat of paint, and so furniture, TV, cushions and books are piled up willy-nilly in the hall, while old sheets, step-ladders and paint buckets have taken up residence in the lounge.

The Four are of course helping, each in their own way; Shannon by watching closely and pointing out where I have missed patches of paint. Seamus and Duncan are milling around the bottom of the stepladders, collecting white emulsioned stripes on their fur from the walls. Minnie is lying out in the hall, keeping up the rear in a patch of sunshine and showing her teeth to a couple of the chickens who have wandered in and would also like to bask in the sunny spot.

Surveying my handiwork, I lean back from the stepladder trying to get a decent view. Painting cream on top of white, the light is not good in the small room and it is difficult to see where I have painted. Stepping backwards off the ladder, my shoe comes down on Seamus' paw. Seamus, never one to suffer in silence, yelps loudly, and Duncan, interpreting this as an attack on Mum, launches himself at Seamus, biting onto the side of his face.

Duncan is a terrier. The motto imprinted on his genes is 'Never Let Go.' Of The Four, although the smallest dog by far, he has the largest teeth, much larger even than Shannon's. He has not just bitten into Seamus. He is hanging on. I am shouting at Duncan to stop, but he is deaf to my calls. Seamus, innocent victim in all this, oddly, has frozen and gone silent; perhaps he knows that Mum must sort this out. In response to Seamus' yelp, Minnie has shot in, and is dancing around the room, yapping wildly. This is not helping.

I finally disengage my feet from the tangle of dogs around me, drop to my knees and, using both hands, force Duncan's jaws apart. Released, Seamus beats a hasty retreat and I follow to check his condition. He is not seriously hurt, just some tooth marks and bloodspots. Fortunately, Duncan was not actually trying to tear Seamus' face off, which I think he might easily have done, had he really been trying. Seamus is a gentle soul at heart and Duncan was acting in, misguided, defence of his Mum. Seamus has come away with some punctures and bruises, but once I have cleaned his face down and cuddled him for a bit, he is essentially unhurt.

Nonetheless, it is some months before Seamus and Duncan are really friends again.

Era's End

My Boys and Girls are slowing down. I adopted The Gang of Four all within a year or so of each other, and I know that they are aging together.

Duncan, as the baby of the family, is still full of life, not old, but middle aged. Only perhaps eight months old when I adopted him, at twelve years old, he still has a spring in his three-legged step. Terriers tend to be long lived and I am far more concerned about the continuing health of the joints of his single front leg, than about his age as such. He is full of vim and vigour and my little tripod still enjoys a romp around the garden.

Minnie is old and obviously failing. I know that I am counting down the time to when I fulfil my last duty to her, and ensure that she passes peacefully.

Seamus, my beloved Seamus, is showing his age. He still loves life, but he does not have the energy he had once had. His limbs are no longer supple, and while he does not seem to be in any pain, he runs slowly now, his back and knees straight as he romps. What really concerns me though is that I begin to see the signs of his rear legs muscles weakening.

Seamus is a long legged dog, tall and gangly when he was younger, although he has filled out with advancing years.

Inside Wayside Cottage, the floors are tiled and slippery; Seamus has lost his footing occasionally and fallen, though he has never seriously hurt himself. Beyond his loud cries of torment and despair (Seamus was never one to hide behind dignity if he was hurting; always, he has called to 'Mum' for help), there has been no real damage, but the thought that my Lovely Boy is growing old brings a lump to my throat.

I am beginning to wonder about how I should handle things with Shannon.

Several years younger than Seamus, and always such a beautiful dog, there is a real bond between her and Seamus. Shannon is certainly going to outlive him. Should I think about finding her another companion as Seamus slows down? No, that is not fair to Seamus. I put it from my mind.

※

Taking The Four for a walk over The Common one day, I notice that Shannon does not seem to be herself. It is hard to put a finger on the problem, but she does not have her usual joie de vivre. Her eyes are dull and she has lost some weight. Minnie and Seamus are pottering along with us too, but I think that Duncan and I are the only ones who are enjoying the walk.

A day or so later I am really worrying about Shannon. She is obviously poorly, and is losing weight almost as I watch. After years of being sleek, beautiful and athletic, she suddenly is looking thin. I make an appointment with the vet.

It is not good. The vet probes under her belly. "I can feel something there." he says "We need to x-ray. Can you bring her back tomorrow?"

Oh God! This is Shannon, the young and beautiful one. The one who is supposed to outlive all the others and who will be with me for years. Supposed to….

I return to the clinic the following day and Shannon has her x-ray. She is almost falling apart in front of me. In the space of a few days she has transformed from canine beauty into a bag of bones. I do not need to see the x-ray to know what I am going to be told. The surgery calls. "Can you bring her in again?" the nurse says. "I'm sorry but it's not good."

The following day, I make ready to take Shannon back to the vet. John is sitting on the floor with her, hugging and stroking her. She leans into him and licks his hand. Shannon has always been far and away the most intelligent dog I have ever known, spookily so sometimes.

I well up inside and then pull myself together. I have to drive and I cannot do that with swollen eyes.

As I pull away in the car, Shannon gazes out of the back window at John, who watches us drive away. In the mirror I can see him standing there until we are out of sight.

At the clinic they show me the x-ray. It is appalling, one of the most horrible things I have ever seen. Shannon's entire abdomen is infested with cancer. There is barely any normal tissue left.

How can this have been happening and I not have known?

There are no choices. Her condition is so bad that I do not even feel that I can take my preferred option and take her home, to ask the vet come out to her. The condition has progressed so fast that it can only be a very, very short time before my girl is in agony.

I hug her to me as they slip in the needle, then feel her slump into my arms. "Goodbye Girlie." I whisper. The vet and other staff leave the room to give me a few moments with her. My tears drip onto Shannon's still face.

John is waiting for me as I drive back up the track, Shannon's body by me on the passenger seat. I collapse into tears and he just holds me. "She knew you know." he says. "She said goodbye to me. I swear she knew as she looked out of that back window, that she wasn't coming back.".

We bury Shannon in the back garden. It is Autumn and so I place daffodil bulbs in her grave with her. The following Spring, they are very beautiful as they bloom.

Minnie has astonished me. I adopted her believing that I was giving an elderly dog a short 'retirement' of a couple of years. Quite the opposite: when she first came to live with me and the rest of the Gang, despite all her personality defects and her aggression, she visibly de-aged.

It has been similar to watching Fudge when Seamus had arrived. Minnie did not at first, like the other dogs, but by golly, they were good for her. Over time she has settled into her role as part of the Gang of Four, accepting her role as 'maiden aunt', never a bride, always a bridesmaid, always there on the shelf and in the background; but her life has been a happy one and I am proud of her.

But age is telling. I have no clear idea of how old Minnie is. All I can say for certain is that she has been with me for ten years and I believed her to be old when she came to me.

Over time she has become blind and starts to lose her hearing. She is safe enough pottering around in the garden; being short legged and barrel shaped, she is in little danger of falling and hurting herself. She enjoys a hug, a tummy rub and a scratchy ear. This in itself, is a thousand miles from the Minnie who first come to live with me. I can tell myself she has had the happy retirement I promised her.

Her little world becomes gradually smaller and smaller. She does less every day and starts to suffer from incontinence. This does upset Minnie. For all her other faults, she has always been spotlessly clean and has never, ever been dirty in the house. If for some reason I was late and she was locked in, Minnie would suffer agonies rather than relieve herself in the house. As the door opened, she would dash past, pushing me out of the way in her haste to get outside the house before urinating.

So to suffer incontinence is hard for her. I can see her struggling to get up to go outside and of course I help her, carrying her out to the lawn and the clean fresh grass. This is already happening when I lose Shannon, but whereas Shannon's death has been a horrible shock, I know that Minnie has lived her full due. She has had a good life in the end and I feel that I have done right by her.

When find Minnie's fur damp a few days later, and see the start of urine burns inside my little girl's thighs, I know it is time to call in the vet.

I give her a special breakfast of fried liver, something she loves, and as she dozes on the tiles, the vet slides in the needle. I do not think the Minnie even notices. She drifts into unconsciousness and as I rub her ears, she stops breathing. The vet checks for a heartbeat. Minnie is gone.

So for the second time in a month, I dig a grave in the garden and plant a rambling rose over Minnie.

I always feel this is the best way to bury a beloved pet. There is something beautiful to remember them by afterwards, and always a place to point and say 'Yes, that's where she is.' Goodbye little girl.

※

A couple of weeks after Minnie's death, my mother is staying with us. She has always loved Wayside and I think also, that she has come down because she knows I am still very upset about Shannon.

She has always been very fond of Seamus and he in his turn is always delighted to see 'Ginger Biscuit Grandma'. They make a big fuss of each other and Seamus will always find a way to sleep on her bed, with or without her agreement. I think in the last year or so, he has always been given more help with that than Mum admits to.

In the night he is free to get up and go out because, as ever, I ensure the dogs always have outside access to the garden.

I am shocked awake in the darkness by crying and yelping from downstairs. Leaping out of bed, I rush downstairs just in time to meet my mother in the hall. Turning on the light, we find Seamus. He has slipped on the smooth tiles and is now spread-eagled, all four of his long legs in different directions, and quite unable to rise out of his situation.

Yelping for help, he calms down as we lift him into a standing position, and then guide him to a rug where his feet have a firmer purchase. He teeters for a moment, so we bring over his big cushion - he is too stiff now to curl into a basket - and help him to lie down.

We cover him with some blankets and then doze on the settee for a while until Seamus has properly dropped off to sleep.

Seamus' hindquarters have become weaker and weaker over the last few months. As he becomes very old, he is suffering a common fate of the very elderly and is losing muscle mass. This is only going to get worse not better. I imagine my nightmare scenario.

What if Seamus has a fall like that while there is no one around to help him? If I am out for the day and he is trapped like that for hours? It does not bear thinking about.

But this is Seamus. My 'Best Boy'. I feel sick at the thought of what is coming. My Seamus.

I have already lost two dogs only a few weeks apart. How can I lose another? Three dogs out of my Gang of Four. I want to weep. And so I hold on, hoping against the inevitable.

I can see Seamus failing, his body gradually closing down. He is so old, seventeen years old. He cannot climb stairs anymore. Tottering around the garden, his legs look longer than ever against his now thin, old body.

But he is happy enough. When I sit down next to him to give him a hug and a scratch, he leans against me and licks my hand. My oldest boy still knows me. I put rugs down wherever I can on the smooth floors so he can walk around the house, and I hope for the best.

A day arrives, all too soon, and I know the end is close. Seamus meanders around the lawn, enjoying a little heat from the sun, but apart from that he does not seem to take much in. I call and he does not really hear me, or if he hears me, it does not register. The end is close. I just want him to lie on his cushion, go to sleep and not wake up. But Seamus wants to walk. So I walk beside him, making sure that he comes to no harm.

He could stray into a ditch without knowing it, or fall and not be able to get up. I stay by him. As I type these words I am crying. This feels as fresh as the day it happened.

The crisis point comes. Despite my best attempts to prevent it, as I leave Seamus for a moment to get something from another room, he slips and falls, his legs splaying. He shrieks and John and I both dash to his side, helping him upright. I pick him up; he seems to weigh nothing, and then lay him on his side on a blanket by the fire.

He lies there panting and staring into space. I cannot control my crying. I know the end has come. My Lovely Boy has no quality of life any more. I must do my duty by him.

To call the vet out as I would prefer, needs at least a day's notice, and I do not think we have a day. John drives us to the vet's while I sit the back of the car with Seamus. I have him wrapped up warm in a blanket and I ring ahead to the practice telling them we were coming. I say that I do not want Seamus to go into the surgery. He has always been frightened of going to the vet and I do not want him to die frightened.

When we arrive, the vet is waiting in the car park. Seamus' last moments are in the back of the car, as I cradle him in my arms, talking to him as he goes limp.

Seamus is gone, my Beautiful Boy.

I have no children, but I feel as though I have lost my First Born.

Aftermath

After having my Gang of Four for so many years, I have lost three dogs in the space of six weeks and I am bereft. Losing Seamus has been by far the hardest. He has been my friend, ally and champion for so long that I have forgotten what it feels like not to have him around. He has been an integral part of my life and not having him there is unbearable.

I still have Duncan of course, the last of the Gang of Four and I wonder how he will cope. Duncan after all, has been part of the Gang of Four, albeit the most junior member, almost all his life. I wonder if he even remembers his time before.

Dogs do not always understand death. I know that some do, and so, as I bury Seamus, I make sure that Duncan is inside the house. I do not want him to see the burial.

I remember Seamus' odd reaction when Sophie died, his puzzlement at her body, that his friend would not wake up. But Duncan is sharper than Seamus was and I think that he will understand and be frightened. Duncan is the last of The Four and it is hard to imagine what a dog might think in that situation. It is easy to anthropomorphise, but I do not want Duncan to add everything up and then start wondering 'What about me?'

Perhaps this would not happen, but I do not want to risk it. So as I plant an apple tree over Seamus' grave, Duncan is safely inside, snoozing by the fire.

Oddly, at first Duncan does not seem to realise that there is anything amiss. For a few days we carry on with life much as we always have. Duncan is not young himself now, but he still enjoys his walks, hoppitting along beside me as we stroll along the track.

The first time John and I have to go out together for an extended period, things are fine. We leave Duncan in his basket, with his door open to the garden and he is happy enough. When we return about three hours later, he is definitely pleased to see us and I cuddle him on my knee for a while, to calm him down.

Whenever I can, if I have to go out, I take Duncan with me. With his basket beside me on the passenger seat, he is perfectly happy and waits patiently for me if I have to leave him in the car for a few minutes. However, it is not always possible to take a dog with you. If the weather is hot, leaving a dog in a car is out of the question, and at times Duncan must stay in the house by himself.

The bottom drops out of Duncan's world about a fortnight after Seamus' death. Suddenly, he seems to realise that he is the only one left and he panics. I go from one room to another and he follows. If I walk down the garden, he is there, determined not to let me out of his sight.

Of course he has always followed me; all the dogs did so, but it was a casual thing, part of the 'We're all in it together.' camaraderie. Now, for Duncan, it is a frantic necessity that he be with me, all the time. If I have to go out without him, then he transfers his attention to John. While John tries to work quietly in his study, Duncan is crying and whimpering outside the door to be let in.

We have already decided that there will be 'another dog', a friend for Duncan. It is simply not fair to keep him by himself, but it is the depths of Winter. It seems better to wait the few weeks until Spring comes, when a new dog will be able to settle into his new home playing out in the garden, or with long walks over the Common. Being trapped inside a strange house by bad weather seems like a poor idea. So the plan is, to wait until April before looking for Duncan's new friend.

All this makes no allowance for Duncan's state of mind. He goes from bad to worse, his confidence visibly eroding day by day. And then comes the Crunch.

John and I must go out. We must both go out, and it is going to be a long day. Duncan cannot come with us. He must stay at home by himself. In the days of The Gang of Four, this was never a problem. We would go out. The dogs had their own access to get in and out of the house as they wished, and they were left in charge of the house, garden and security. No one was foolish enough to try to invade a house with four dogs looking after things. The Gang of Four worked as a harmonious whole, entertaining each other and informing anyone who came by that this property was defended.

But now it is different. Duncan knows we are going out and he hops around behind me as we make ready to leave, crying and whining.

I tuck him up warm in his basket and make a big fuss of him, giving him a scratchy tummy and telling him what a good boy he is. He licks my hand frantically, but seems to settle. With plenty of food and water nearby, and cosy in his blankets I hope he will sleep for some hours. When he does need to go out, he can use the flap.

We have to go. Driving down the track, I notice members of the local shoot setting up around the Common. They are no problem; careful where they aim their guns and a couple of times a year, turning up at the gate with a brace of pheasants as a gift. I do not give them a second thought.

It is February and the nights are coming in early. When we arrive back home, it has been dark for some while. Pulling up to the gate, I miss the canine chaos of having four dogs issuing their wild greetings as arrive. Now, coming home, there is only silence.

At first, I do not worry. Duncan's hearing is not so good these days. He is probably asleep in his basket and has not heard us.

But Duncan is not in his basket. I check the next room, then all the ground floor rooms, in case he has somehow locked himself in; it happens sometimes. There is no sign of him.

Now I go upstairs, checking all the bedrooms and the bathroom. Still no Duncan.

I grab a torch and run out into the garden, pitch black with a moonless, misty night. Raising the alarm with John, who is still unloading the car, I work my way around the garden, calling for Duncan, trying to penetrate the dark with the torch, the thin fog swallowing the dim beam. Perhaps he has fallen in a ditch and, three-leggedly, cannot get out. But if that had happened, by now he should be yelping for help.

I walk right round the garden, John searching too. We both keep calling Duncan's name, but there is no response.

We gaze out into the Common, eighty acres of it, pitch black, and calf deep in mud with the winter rains. Snatching a jacket from the hall and donning my wellingtons I walk out, calling for Duncan. John takes the car down the track, flashing the headlamps and sounding the horn. If Duncan is lost in the dark, it will give him something to follow.

Hours later and approaching midnight, we admit defeat and come back to the house. I pick up the phone and ring every number I can think of to report a lost dog; police, RSPCA, local vets....

Of course, so late at night, all I get are answer phones, but I leave my name and number with Duncan's description and hope that someone gets back to me. The one comfort is that a three legged dog does not need too much description.

I do not sleep much. The thought of Duncan, who has always been an overgrown puppy, lost in the dark, perhaps fallen in a ditch or trapped by mud and unable to escape is unbearable. The following morning, I am up with the light, not that early in February, perhaps eight o'clock. Checking the garden again and the immediate area of the Common again, I find nothing.

Just before nine, I receive a phone call. "Christine Brooks? Yes, we got your message. I don't have your dog, but I know where he is."

Ten minutes later I am driving to Malvern, a half hour drive

The previous day, as we left in the car, Duncan followed us down the track, a long journey for him. Where the track curves out of sight of the cottage, he spotted one of the stands for the shoot and hopped over to join them. Perhaps he decided that any company is better than no company. He spent the morning with six assorted retrievers, spaniels and Labradors and their owner. At the end of the morning, the owner, not knowing where Duncan had come from, not realising there is a cottage at the far end of the Common, and not liking to leave a three-legged and slightly geriatric dog alone, had taken him home.

I arrive at their house to find Duncan reposed in splendour, in the centre of a gigantic heap of cushions, thoroughly enjoying himself and playing with a couple of springer spaniels. Another springer is looking very put out, and I am told that Duncan has appropriated her cushion.

The couple who own the springers and who have taken Duncan in, are quite charming and tell me that they had already decided that they would have kept him, had he not been claimed. I thank them profusely, and drive back home with Duncan on the passenger seat, totally unconcerned about the havoc he has caused.

So Duncan is safely back home, but the episode has rung alarm bells. We cannot wait to get him a companion. Duncan needs a friend, and he needs a friend sooner not later. We cannot wait until Spring.

Oliver

There is no difficulty about looking for another dog. There are always plenty of them out there in need of rehoming and it goes without saying that the new dog is going to be a rescue. However, all of the Gang of Four were 'mine'. John came into their lives relatively late, and though he has loved them, and they him, it is only fair that the next dog should be 'John's Dog'.

Left to myself, I will always pick the dog that, for some reason, is going to have rehoming problems. I like mongrels and actively seek them out. I like the cock-eyed smiles, outsized ears and coffee-table-sweeping tails that go with them. Whatever else you might think of mongrels, you always have an interesting animal. However, I know that John wants an elegant dog, preferably a pedigree. He wants a dog that will lie gracefully by his feet, one that would look not out of place on the pages of a glossy magazine.

The pedigree part is no problem. Should the right dog turn up with, shall we say, doubtful parentage, I can blag it and tell John that it is an Argentinian water hound or an Iranian hunting spaniel or some-such. But it is important that it be a beautiful dog. I'll admit to being wary about this after my experience with Sophie. I do not want to make the mistake of again choosing a dog just for good looks.

I work my way around the local shelters. This is fine by John. He is very busy with his work and the plan is that I assemble a shortlist of likely candidates and he can make the final choice.

It is heart-breaking, as it always is in the shelters. I must pass by any number of lovely dogs that I would willingly take home with me.

Scruffy little terriers, collies whirling like spinning tops, far too many staffies. The Long, the Short and the Tall, all trapped in their pens until someone takes them home and calls them Family.

In one particular shelter there are two unusually good looking collies. They can go on the short list. Glossy coated, bright eyed and full of zest for life. A rather lovely spaniel joins the list too. She is a little older, but has a sweet face and holds herself well. Then I see him, and I know that whatever other dog I add to the list, this is the dog that will be coming home with us.

He is an English setter, not large for the breed, but a 'looker', and he is frolicking around in a pen with his companion, a collie cross. They look like good pals. I walk right up to the mesh and hunker down, holding out my hand to sniff. "C'mon lad." I call. The collie trots over to say 'Hello.' but the setter ignores me completely, trying instead to pull his companion back for play. Checking the notes on the mesh, I read that the setter is called 'Floyd', a good name. I like it. "Hi there Floyd. How are you doing?" Still he pays me no attention. After several minutes of trying, I have still been unable to get him even to acknowledge my existence. I am disconcerted; this is new territory for me.

At the reception desk they can tell me very little about Floyd. He has only been in the shelter for a few days, shipped in from Ireland with a job-lot of other rescues. He likes the girls at the centre but is very wary of men. And that is about as much as they know. I take him for a walk and have the same odd experience of Floyd looking right through me. He cringes at a word and holds himself low, timid beyond belief, and will not, on any account, look me in the face.

I do not at this stage put my name down for Floyd. I simply take my shortlist to John and, on a return visit to the shelter, guide him around the dogs I feel may appeal to him. As I expected, he immediately homes in on Floyd.

We take him on a walk together. Floyd wants nothing to do with us, so instead we find a quiet spot to sit and spend a few minutes stroking and talking to him, letting him get used to us, our smell, our voices. He does not respond to any of this, except to make himself as small as possible.

I have my doubts as to the wisdom of adopting Floyd, but John is taken with him. He signs up for adoption and renames him 'Oliver'. A week later, Oliver comes home to Wayside Cottage.

Oliver is haunted by his past. I am pleased that he has come to us as I am not sure how he would have managed in almost any other home. Someone has terrorised him, and he deals with it by running.

All dogs love to run, but Oliver is different. There is eighty acres of Common out there, a vast open space edged by hedges and ditches. Oliver simply runs, and runs, and runs. There is no joy in his running, no exuberant smile as his ears flap and his tail ripples in the wind. He is running from demons, running from nightmares. I can see the desolation in his face and his body language. He runs miles in a day. He will answer no call, no tapped thigh to invite him for a love and a scratchy ear. He returns home only after hours of running and then, when called, hugs up desperately, burying his head in my chest. "Please don't hurt me."

Perhaps when he has run enough, he will feel that he has left the monsters behind and that he is safe.

It is March. Oliver has lived here now for several weeks and, although settling in, is not becoming the contented dog that I want him to be. His obvious unhappiness tugs at me. How can I help him to leave his past behind?

It is the season for hares, the 'Mad March Hare' of legend and song. There are perhaps a dozen of them out on the Common, leaping and boxing, madly gyrating, very visible against the brightly sprouting Spring grass. Oliver can see them from the garden and for the first time I see real enthusiasm in him. He launches himself out to them, eyes bright and tail up, bee-lining the hares. Of course they flee, and he gives chase.

No amount of calling or yelling will stop him, and in truth, my calls are half hearted. For the first time, Oliver looks happy.

He does not catch the hares of course. It is a very, very good dog that can outrun a hare; typically, it would be a lurcher or greyhound, bred for speed and stamina. Oliver comes from a line bred for waiting, watching and retrieval. Still, he gives the hares a good run for their money. They duck, twist and swerve, Oliver following every move, before the hares dive under the hedges, out, and beyond to far fields.

Oliver returns, panting, waggy and smiling. He has actually enjoyed himself. He does not arrive grovelling and frightened, asking to be forgiven. Instead, he trots in with spring in his step and confidence in his gait. Is this his turn-around, the real start of the New Oliver?

I have watched Oliver very carefully with regards to the chickens. He is after all a gun dog breed. It would be the most natural thing in the world for him to regard chickens as prizes to be brought home to Mum and Dad. Retrieval has been bred into him; this is how to be a 'Good Boy'.

But he shows no sign of wanting to hurt the chickens, or chase them. I have introduced Oliver to the flock by walking him, on a lead, around the garden and through groups of the Girls, dust-bathing, pecking and scratching, preening. The hens are unalarmed by Oliver. They have survived foxes and they know a killer when they see one. Oliver is not a killer. The Girls free range over the garden and out onto the Common, two dozen sets of eyes taking turns to watch what is out there.

At times I see every avian head stretched up, raised to the horizon and the alarm cluck raises among them. As I follow their gaze, I see the vixen out on the grass, seeking food for the cubs she has back home. There is plenty for her to eat out there; rabbits infest the Common. I feel sorry for the rabbits, but everyone must eat, foxes included. I however, must look after the charges in my care.

Over the weeks I notice, that when the weather is good, Oliver sits out on the lawns in the sunshine, choosing to place himself among the chickens. The roosters accept him and the Girls are happy enough to have him around. Oliver himself is a picture of contentment. Perhaps this quiet life of scratching birds and sunshine is what he needs and wants?

Dark. It is dark and I am woken by a noise, a clamour out in the garden. The chickens are going mad. Screeching and squawking echoes across the darkness in frantic pandemonium. Oliver is barking out there; not just barking, but almost baying. I check the time. Three a.m.

Dashing on slippers and dressing gown, I sprint downstairs and out. At the far end of the garden, I can hear shrieks and cries from the hens and roosters.

Checking Fort Knox, as I believed, the chucks are closed into their coops, so they are safe enough, but there is no sign of Oliver. I wave my torch out into the darkness of the Common, but the beam is simply swallowed into lightlessness, lost in the vast empty night.

Back in the kitchen, I make myself a hot drink and wait for Oliver to return. 'Just in case', I turn on all the outside lights so he has something to follow back, but I need not have worried. Five minutes later he comes into the house panting, shoves his nose into my hand with a 'Well that's that!' air and then downs most of his bowl of water.

The following day, I find the scratch marks of attempted digging outside the run and I know that the fox has paid a call. She could not have dug through anyway; Fort Knox is proof against any vulpine depredations.

But Oliver has taken on the mantle of 'Guardian of the Chickens'. This has been entirely voluntary and his own idea. Perhaps this is his answer? We all are better for knowing our place in the scheme of things. Maybe, just maybe, this will be Oliver's saving.

※

Oliver never attempts to hurt the chickens. His self-assumed mantle of Chicken Guardian fits him well. He seems to understand clearly the difference between chickens and pheasants. Chickens are part of the Team and are to be nurtured and protected. Pheasants are wild birds and are fair game for a bit of fun.

Oliver spends endless hours patrolling the brambles, hedgerows and thickets of the Common, trying to find pheasants, rabbits and hares. Never does he catch a hare, but he does occasionally return with a rabbit or a pheasant. On one occasion I catch him in the act of burying a pheasant. The poor beast is still alive, just, and is fluttering and quivering as Oliver noses mud over it. I retrieve the bird and put it out of its misery before I take it to hang in the shed for a few days.

※

The only time Oliver has difficulty with the chickens is when he does not recognise them as chickens. He has trouble making the connection between chicks and the adult birds. Each time there is a fresh influx of chicks from the incubator, I have to carefully introduce them to Oliver in an enclosed run, explaining to him that these are more of 'his' chickens and that it is his task to look after them.

The chicks raised by the hens do not need this careful introduction. The hens themselves give the dog a royal seeing off if he approaches too closely. Always he backs down meekly.

On one occasion, I have two hens who have jointly incubated a batch of eggs. There are five lucky chicks who have two 'Mums' to raise them and care for them. No one dares to come close to these chicks.

Oliver is given a feathery battering. The roosters back away from them and even John receives a surprise assault when he makes an incautious step too close.

Oliver is fond of burying his treasures, and not just pheasants.

I am preparing the Sunday dinner, roast leg of pork. I check that the meat is properly defrosted and place the joint on the work surface to wait while I prepare the vegetables. It is still in its plastic wrap from the butchers so I am not worrying about flies or other insects near it. Popping out to fetch potatoes and carrots from the shed, I get distracted by two of the semi-mature roosters squabbling, and make a note of which is the more aggressive. If he a determined trouble-maker, it will be chicken casserole for the next Sunday dinner. I peel potatoes, peel and slice carrots and parsnips, chop onions and make the batter for the Yorkshire pudding. Next task, score the pork and rub in salt for the crackling.

I turn to pick up the joint and - there is no pork joint. Confused, I turn to the other work surface. Clearly I have made a mistake as to where I put the meat. Still it is not there. Like an idiot, I stand on the spot, spinning, hands splaying, trying to conjure up my missing joint.

A perplexed John comes into the kitchen holding a strange object. "What's this?" he asks. "I just found it down the back of the settee." It is of course, the missing joint, slightly chewed, but still in its plastic. Oliver has 'buried' it, for safekeeping until a time of starvation.

I remove the wrapping, and continue making our, slightly delayed, Sunday dinner.

Leaving

~~~

Wayside Cottage is wonderful. The house is gorgeous, the setting is amazing and the views are to die for. I have a lovely home, a loving, and loved, partner, my dogs, my chickens, a huge garden; everything I could want. So what is wrong?

The first winter at Wayside is astonishingly cold, dropping to minus nineteen for days at a time. Frozen pipes aside though, the cold does not bother me, it never has. I have spent time in Finland and Sweden in their sparkling Artic Winters. Alaska, with its glaciers, was amazing, if frigid. Walking on the fells, the Yorkshire moors, Pendle Hill and the Lake District in mid-Winter, it is only necessary to be sensible and wear extra layers of clothing, the right boots, gloves, socks. You can always keep the cold at bay with a modicum of forethought. John and I have mornings in January at Wayside when, despite the sub-zero reading on the thermometer, we sit outside in a snowy garden, lit brilliantly by sunshine, having breakfast of spiced porridge and coffee laced with brandy.

The second winter at Wayside is just as cold. Snowy mornings, iced mists and frost crystals on the grass only add to the almost ethereal beauty of the Common. Because the land of the Common is very flat, any rain that falls is held there, trapped in the turf.

Cold mornings raise eerily ghostlike mists, wreathing through the dawn. Frost crystals, once started, grow and keep on growing, forming intricately branched diamonds which envelop every blade of grass, twig and spiders web in a scintillating mosaic of fractured light. It is exquisite.

The following winter, the weather changes. It starts raining in October and continues right through to March. Everything turns to mud. It is impossible to go outdoors without full wet weather kit; oiled jackets, boots, rain-hat. The dogs are constantly plastered in mud.

Duncan in particular finds it difficult as, with increasing age, his three-legged hop-along walking style becomes more and more laboured in the mire and the muck. I resort to old methods, acquire a second-hand pushchair and take him for walks as a passenger. He still does not like it much. None of us do.

The Winter following, is just as bad. Five solid months of nonstop rain. I am an outdoor type. I want to be able to walk, to be out in my garden, to enjoy my dogs and chickens. The dogs sit huddled to the fire, stinking of wet fur, and the chickens sit under the eaves, sulking in bedraggled feathers.

John finally speaks up. "I know you don't want to move again, but how would you react if I suggest moving to another country; somewhere with Winter sun?" John has always hankered to live in the Mediterranean, but he knows that I love England and, while he enticed me away from my Northern homelands, I have always resisted any suggestion of leaving the country.

He is astonished when I say that I might consider it, but I have conditions. We must find a place which is to be Home, not just the next project; and it must be a place where we both have the things we want to be happy. In his case, this means sun and access to the sea, and for me it means mountains, wild areas and a large garden.

He agrees, and I start a search for our new Forever Home in the sun.

It is two weeks before the expected leaving date, three years since we first discussed leaving the UK. Most things are prepared. I am busying myself finishing off as much paperwork as I can before we leave; anything that might be needed by accountants, service suppliers, banks and anyone else who might need to know that I am no longer in the country. The more I finish now, the less I must either, take with me, or deal with once I reach Spain.

John is also very busy with paperwork, and he is tense. I see it building up over several days and am beginning to wonder if he is having second thoughts. If he is, we have a problem. Wayside Cottage and Apple Tree have tenants now. We have nowhere to live, and are 'camping' in a caravan in the grounds of Apple Tree until we leave. From my point of view, this cannot be too soon. The caravan is small, and is not a long term option for two adults and two dogs.

"What's wrong?" I ask.

It is plain that John is worried. "I've got so much to do. I don't think I can get it all finished in time. And we can't stay here."

I relax. There is an obvious answer to this. "So I'll go in the car with the dogs, and you follow by air when you've done what you need to. End of problem."

I see the weight of the world fall from his shoulders. "Would you mind? I mean, it's a heck of a journey by yourself."

I shrug this off. "It's a long drive that's all. To be honest Love, it's easier if it is just me. There will be more room in the car without you, and I'm better at roughing it when it comes to sleeping in cars and camping."

My alarm goes off. Five thirty a.m. It is November, pitch black outside, and, having slept on the settee bed of a caravan, I am cold. The bed is not inviting and does not hold me. The air is chilly and smells damp.

Kettle on.

Wake Oliver and Duncan. They protest at this uncivilised arousing, but heartlessly, I put them out into the cold, dark yard. I need them to 'conduct their business' before we set off. Duncan informs me that his blankets had better be kept warm for his return.

Clean teeth. Splash freezing water over face. Brush hair. Clothes on: laid out the night before.

Coffee is very inviting and I enjoy the steamy scent warming my sinuses as I wrap stiff fingers around the mug, encouraging the blood to flow. I have never enjoyed getting up in the dark. It feels completely unnatural, and a five thirty start on a wintery morning is just beyond the pale. Still it is my choice. I have booked a ticket for the nine thirty train through the Channel Tunnel and I need to be moving.

The car is already packed. My worldly wealth, or at least as much of it as can travel with me in a Peugeot 107, is in there. The car has been chosen for economy, reliability and a left hand drive, not for size. It is nippy and cheap to run, but small. My worldly wealth therefore consists of the clothes I stand up in, a couple of changes of jeans, tee-shirts, warm pullovers and underwear, two enormous boxes containing the files that must go with me (for the benefit of banks, inland revenue officers and similar annoying officials), my laptop and associated kit, one rather aristocratic English setter and a geriatric canine tripod with associated baskets, blankets, bowls, food and their official paperwork. I have spent the last couple of weeks agonising over the paperwork that allows me to legally take the dogs out of the UK, through France and into Spain, checking the regulations, time and again to be sure that I have Pet Passports, vaccination certificates and any other bureaucratic detritus that might get me stopped at a border with my dogs.

Everything else must follow in a van, later, when cash and circumstances allow. I am really, really hoping that when I arrive at our new Spanish home, it will, as described, come complete with everything that was in there when we viewed.

My travel food is also packed. I need only make up my coffee flask. As the kettle boils for a second time, John stirs and I make an extra cup.

"Don't get up." I say. "Stay where it's warm." When I touch him to kiss him goodbye, he does not feel very warm, so as an afterthought, I fill a hot water bottle and slide it under his covers.

John and I say our goodbyes for the week, but I want him to stay in bed.

Nothing is gained by his getting up into the cold and losing his sleep. I give him a final hug and kiss. "See you in a few days."

"Take care." He says. "Drive carefully. You've checked your insurance, and your passport and…."

"Yes, it's all done. Go back to sleep. I'll call you later when I've reached France."

Outside, I lift Duncan into his basket on the passenger seat and cover him with warm blankets. Almost immediately he goes to sleep. I lift Oliver into his space at the rear of the car, and again, under warm blankets, he drops his head to snooze position.

The engine "Brruummms" into life and, driving as quietly as I can down the dark lane, I set off for Spain.

The story will continue in

'Scrumping for Lemons'

Important Points to Remember When Keeping Dogs

- The best place for a canine lavatory is right under the washing line.

- Dogs have no sense of 'personal space'. They want to be as close to you as possible. Preferably on you. Ideally surgically implanted.

- Dogs are amazed by cats.

- Regardless of what anxious owners may tell you, there are no 'picky eaters' among dogs. We are discussing a species that considers horse dung to be a delicacy.

- It's always the white ones that roll.

- Dogs sniffing at trees and lampposts is their equivalent of reading a newspaper. They learn of all the other dogs who have passed by, the state of their health, what they are eating. And of course, like all newspaper readers it's nice to be the last one to add to the comments column.

- From a dog's point of view, the postman is an invader. The postman arrives, dumps stuff through your letterbox and your dog goes into war mode. When the postman leaves, it is obvious to your dog that he has driven off the intruder.

- A dustman is also an invader. He even steals your stuff. Of course he must be barked at.

- Dogs, even when complete strangers, know from a hundred yards away whether or not they like each other.

- Chihuahua is a hard word to spell, and harder to stop spelling.
- Perplexity: The expression on dog's face as it watches the microwave while you make popcorn.
- You will never have a truer friend than your dog.

A Dog Came Home With Me Today

I wrote the poem below a year or so back, with the express intention of using it to raise awareness, and ideally funds, for animal rescue services. Anyone wishing to use it this way, is free to do. I am happy, and give permission, for any use of this poem relating to animal welfare. I ask only that you attribute the text to me.

Copyright remains with me, Christine Brooks, at all times. If you have any queries, please do not hesitate to contact me. I will be happy to help. Contact details are on the final page of this book.

A DOG CAME HOME WITH ME TODAY

Fudge came home with me today.
Was it that she was too old?
Did her grizzled face mean that she deserved,
To be thrown out to the cold?

Lisa came home with me today,
Cigarette burns in her fur.
I had to explain to the vet,
It wasn't me that had hurt her.

Seamus came home with me today.
He'd been tied to a hedge and left,
Did you think that because he's 'just a dog',
He'd be any less bereft?

Minnie came home with me today.
They had her on death row,
Too vicious to be allowed to live.
Unhomable? Not so.

Shannon came home with me today,
She'd been used a lure,
By a paedophile out hunting kids.
What had she endured?

Duncan came home with me today.
Someone threw him out to beg,
Just past the cute stage, eight months old,
And it's cost him a leg.
It was in the news, 'Pup hit by car.
Donations needed here.'
I rang them up to do my bit.
It's not enough to shed a tear.
'Many offers of a home?' I asked.
I assumed that there would be,
Lots of them, but there were none.
So he came home with me.

I found Bracken dumped in the woods today.
He was angry. He was scared.
He really got me frightened.
Was I quite prepared,
For another dog? Already four,
Could I take another in?
A kindly friend then volunteered,
And Bracken went home with him

Oliver came home with me today,
So nervous and so scared
A gun-dog who's outlived his worth?
So no one really cared.
If you look at him he shakes with fear.
A word, he hits the floor.

But desperately he asks to be hugged.
"Please don't hurt me anymore."

Blanca came to my gate today
And she's trying hard to fit.
A feral dog? How very odd,
That she knows how to 'Sit'.
Somebody got bored with her,
To their eternal shame,
But Blanca is okay now,
As she gazes into the flames.

My dogs are all alright now,
Despite what was done.
They're all healthy and well fed.
Happy, having fun.
But I can't bring them all home with me,
However much I care.
For the dogs abandoned and betrayed,
Who will help them? Who's out there?

Written by Chris Brooks - The Word Smith

www.the-word-smith.net

Want to Read More About The Gang Of Four?

FREE BOOK

Two Legs, Three Legs, Four Legs

More Rescue Dog Stories
With Duncan the Canine Tripod and his Friends

You met the 'Gang of Four' in "The Long, The Short and The Tall. Life with Rescue Dogs" Seamus, Shannon, Minnie and Duncan, the canine tripod. Now the Gang of Four rides again!

More stories and adventures with Duncan and his friends. Take a walk over Pendle Hill with the Gang of Four. Learn how Duncan almost lost another leg!

TO CLAIM YOUR FREE BOOK, VISIT

http://www.the-word-smith.net/two-legs-three-legs-four-legs/

Want To Read More About What Happens Next?

FREE BOOK

Scrumping For Lemons
The Sneak Preview!!

'**Scrumping for Lemons**' picks up where 'The Long, The Short and the Tall' left off.

The author sets off for a new life in Spain, dreaming of sunshine, blue skies and her new home in her Spanish finca. As she starts her journey, driving through gales and storms, she takes only the bare essentials of life: her car, a couple of changes of clothes, two giant boxes of official paperwork (for banks, Inland Revenue and other annoying officials who might want to know what she is doing) and her dogs, the handsome English setter Oliver and Duncan, the geriatric three-legged terrier.

With a run-down 'villa', two acres of dilapidated orange groves, and another dog turning up at the gate within days of arrival, learn what happens next in a dream life of mountain living, dog rescue, writing and her relentless pursuit of the perfect marmalade

Scrumping for Lemons is scheduled for release September 2016, but you can read the SNEAK PREVIEW.

With excerpts and samples chapters from the book, get an early taste of lemons.

**To Claim Your FREE copy of
'Scrumping for Lemons. The Sneak Preview'
Visit**

http://www.the-word-smith.net/scrumping-for-lemons-coming-soon/

And Finally

I hope you have enjoyed reading this book. If you have, please help others to enjoy it too by making it more visible to interested readers. Please rate it on Amazon, or even better, write a review.

You can find contact details for me below. Do get in touch with me if you would like to. I'll be happy to hear from you.

All the Best,

Chris Brooks

Contact Me:
christine@the-word-smith.net

The Word Smith Website:
http://www.the-word-smith.net

For my Amazon Author Page:

http://www.amazon.co.uk/Christine-Brooks/e/B00R4NEKHU
or
http://www.amazon.com/Christine-Brooks/e/B00R4NEKHU

Follow Me on Facebook:

My Personal Page
https://www.facebook.com/christine.brooks.568089

The Word Smith Page
https://www.facebook.com/ChristineBrooksWriter

Printed in Great Britain
by Amazon